A NEW AGENDA FOR HIGHER EDUCATION
EDUCATION

A NEW AGENDA FOR HIGHER EDUCATION

Shaping a Life of the Mind for Practice

William M. Sullivan and Matthew S. Rosin

o

Foreword by

Lee S. Shulman and Gary D. Fenstermacher

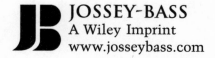

JOSSEY-BASS
A Wiley Imprint
www.josseybass.com

Published by Jossey-Bass
A Wiley Imprint
989 Market Street, San Francisco, CA 94103-1741—www.josseybass.com

Readers should be aware that Internet Web sites offered as citations and/or sources for further information may have changed or disappeared between the time this was written and when it is read.

Limit of Liability/Disclaimer of Warranty: While the publisher and author have used their best efforts in preparing this book, they make no representations or warranties with respect to the accuracy or completeness of the contents of this book and specifically disclaim any implied warranties of merchantability or fitness for a particular purpose. No warranty may be created or extended by sales representatives or written sales materials. The advice and strategies contained herein may not be suitable for your situation. You should consult with a professional where appropriate. Neither the publisher nor author shall be liable for any loss of profit or any other commercial damages, including but not limited to special, incidental, consequential, or other damages.

Jossey-Bass books and products are available through most bookstores. To contact Jossey-Bass directly call our Customer Care Department within the U.S. at 800-956-7739, outside the U.S. at 317-572-3986, or fax 317-572-4002.

Jossey-Bass also publishes its books in a variety of electronic formats. Some content that appears in print may not be available in electronic books.

Library of Congress Cataloging-in-Publication Data

Sullivan, William M.
 A new agenda for higher education : shaping a life of the mind for practice / William M. Sullivan and Matthew S. Rosin ; foreword by Lee S. Shulman and Gary D. Fenstermacher.—1st ed.
  p. cm.—(The Jossey-Bass higher and adult education series)
 "A research seminar, Life of the Mind for Practice, convened over two years by The Carnegie Foundation for the Advancement of Teaching"—Introduction.
  Includes bibliographical references and index.
  ISBN 978-0-470-25757-9 (cloth)
 1. Education, Higher—Philosophy. 2. College teaching . I. Rosin, Matthew S. II. Carnegie Foundation for the Advancement of Teaching. III. Title.
  LB2322.2.S85 2008
  378.1'2—dc22
                                                              2007049558

Printed in the United States of America
FIRST EDITION
HB Printing   10 9 8 7 6 5 4 3 2 1

CONTENTS

Hessel Bouma III, "Human Biology," Calvin College
Elliot N. Dorff, "Issues in Jewish Ethics," American Jewish University
Gary Lee Downey and Juan Lucena, "Engineering Cultures," Virginia Tech
   and Colorado School of Mines
Daisy Hurst Floyd, "Advanced Legal Ethics: Finding Joy and Satisfaction
   in Legal Life," Mercer University School of Law
Allen S. Hammond IV, "Contracts," Santa Clara University School of Law
Robert McGinn, "Ethical Issues in Engineering," Stanford University
Timothy Murphy and Michele Oberman, Selected Cases from "Ethics and
   Law," University of Illinois College of Medicine
William C. Spohn, "Scripture and the Moral Life," Santa Clara University
Barbara S. Stengel, "Foundations of Modern Education," Millersville
   University

FOREWORD

Lee S. Shulman and Gary D. Fenstermacher *

"HOW DO YOU GET TO CARNEGIE HALL? Practice! Practice!"

One of the oldest gags in the American canon of humor somehow captures the setting in which this work began. About ten years ago, we at The Carnegie Foundation for the Advancement of Teaching initiated several parallel research programs. The first was a long-term comparative study of education in the professions of law, engineering, the clergy, medicine, nursing, and teaching. Professions are all about practice and performance. Unlike the traditional disciplines, whose goal is understanding, professionals are obligated to act, to perform, to "mess with the world." Nevertheless, at least in the United States, professional preparation in universities must be preceded by or accompanied with more general liberal education in the humanities, social sciences, and sciences. What are these disciplines supposed to contribute to a professional's capacity for practical action? Or are they primarily intended to influence the moral or ethical grounds on which action is undertaken, rather than the skill or technical acumen with which professional performance is enacted?

As we thought carefully about the role of theoretical or disciplinary knowledge in preparation for practice, we also began to consider the question of whether, when those disciplines are taught in the service of future professional practice, they need to be taught in different ways. That is, should teachers of the liberal arts disciplines be expected to orient their teaching in the interests of practice if their students intend to pursue careers of professional practice?

To help think through these difficult questions, I organized a four-person study group: my colleague Bill Sullivan, a philosopher who was also coordinating our multiple studies of education in the professions; Albert Jonsen, a medical ethicist whose book The Abuse of Casuistry *(with Steven Toulmin) dealt with the history of case-based practical reasoning; and*

*Note: Lee Shulman's comments appear in italics and Gary Fenstermacher's in roman type.

Gary Fenstermacher, a philosopher of education whose scholarship had emphasized the role of philosophical and social understanding in the preparation of teachers and the centrality of the concept of "practical reason" for understanding the professional practice of teachers.

Gary Fenstermacher was central to this effort from beginning to end. He recalls his perspective on our work and on the particular efforts that led to the preparation of this volume, as he reviews the evolution of his role in the work and the impact of the work on his own professional practice—teaching philosophy to future teachers:

———————— o ————————

As many of us do, I often fret about my teaching. Are the students getting it? Are they fully engaged? Are the course requirements too easy or too burdensome? These and other questions nag at me with every course, but they seldom produce a crisis of confidence. Such a crisis occurred just twice: When I first began to teach, and now, once again, as I close in on the end of my teaching career. The first crisis can be attributed to the sheer anxiety of doing something one has never done before, in front of scores of critical observers who are only a few years younger than oneself. The second crisis was precipitated by a project at The Carnegie Foundation for the Advancement of Teaching. That project is the subject of this book.

If you had asked me about my teaching just a few years ago, I would have said, "Yes, I'm a fairly good teacher, although modesty prohibits my saying much more than that." If you dug deeper into my past you would find a university distinguished teaching award, as well as course evaluations that almost always placed me in the top tier of my peers. And as retirement nears, such accolades as have been received nearly always mention the impact of my teaching. Yet I sense, quite strongly, that I failed to give my students all that they deserved from me.

Why? Because I thought the greatest gift I could impart as a teacher is to foster an appreciation for my subject matter and deepen the students' grasp of that subject matter. I could not imagine a nobler end for collegiate instruction than developing a profound and thorough understanding of the subjects I taught. But just a few years ago, I was prodded by some very special colleagues at the Carnegie Foundation to wonder what my students would *do* with their newfound understanding. What actions would follow from what they learned from me? How would their conduct differ because they gained a deeper understanding of the material I taught? It was more than mildly discombobulating to realize I had no ready answers to these questions. I could mouth a few rationalizations, but no real answers—at least none that provided any measure of solace.

In hindsight, I should have recognized the signs much sooner. One clue might have come from all those doctoral committees I sat on, where students who received top marks in my courses comported themselves as if they had never heard of the material we studied together. Or when a colleague would ask me if so-and-so was *really* enrolled with me last semester in a course that was supposed to be a prerequisite to the course that colleague was teaching this semester. Or when I observed undergraduates in a field practicum the semester following a course they had taken with me; when asked to give an account of what they were doing and why, their explanations often proceeded without a hint of the material we had previously studied together and which I thought would provide an excellent account for what they were doing.

I passed off most of these experiences as a lack of due diligence on the part of the students. I did not give much consideration to the possibility that the fault might be with me—with my beliefs about what I was seeking as a teacher. The lure of understanding as the *sine qua non* of collegiate instruction was simply too strong to be resisted . . . until joining a small planning team at Carnegie. The team was searching for a way to conceive of the liberal arts and the professions as seamless contributors to the overall education of college and university students. My charge was to bring the work I was doing on practical reason to the consideration of other members of the team. Together we would ascertain whether notions of practical reason might offer a productive way of bridging the liberal arts and the professions, and if so, how. At the time, I thought of my involvement in this work solely as a consultant, lending what scholarly expertise I possessed to the deliberations of the team. I had not a clue that the project would profoundly transform my thinking about the proper ends of my own teaching.

The supposed connection between the liberal arts and the professions has been vexing academics for many decades. Faculty members in arts, humanities, and sciences frequently lament the lack of foundational knowledge on the part of those whose undergraduate education takes place predominantly in the professions. Faculty members in professional schools protest the lack of real-world studies in the liberal arts. On many campuses there is a virtual wall separating the schools. Even in those rare settings where rich, collaborative discussions take place between the liberal arts and the professions, it is a huge challenge to locate key ideas that provide a sense of cohesion and basis for mutual benefit between the two.

This absence of cohesiveness and mutual benefit could be what stirred William Sullivan, Lee Shulman, and several of their Carnegie colleagues to supplement their extensive studies of the professions with one more study: a study of how the liberal arts and the professions might serve one another, in ways that are more symbiotic than oppositional. It was, as I recall, Sullivan's belief that notions of practical reason, particularly as they occur in the work of John Dewey, might serve as an integrating mechanism for the liberal arts and the professions. It was in the formative stage of Sullivan's thinking about using practical reason as a source of rapprochement between the liberal arts and the professions that Albert Jonsen (coauthor of *The Abuse of Casuistry* and distinguished medical ethicist) and I became involved with the Carnegie team. Together we sought to determine whether practical reason might serve as a foundational concept to bridge the liberal arts and the professions.

"Practical reasoning," notes Elijah Millgram, "is reasoning directed towards action: figuring out what to do, as contrasted with figuring out how the facts stand" (2001, p. 1). Practical reasoning is typically contrasted with theoretical reasoning, which, as Millgram notes, is about "figuring out how the facts stand." Propositions, in the form of declarations or claims, are the end state of theoretical reasoning while actions (or, as some would hold, intentions to act) are the end state of practical reason. The editors of this volume explain the concept far better than I, so I shall not belabor it here. I need only say enough to explain how the search to make practical reason pedagogically practical (which turned out to be the *real* task of the project) precipitated the crisis of confidence in my own teaching.

When understanding is the terminus of one's teaching, theoretical reasoning may be sufficient to achieve that end. A knowledge of and appreciation for "how the facts stand" may be both a noble aspiration for the teacher and a worthwhile achievement for the learner. These are the ends I aspired to "pre-Carnegie." What I failed to see then was that knowing how the facts stand does not ensure that one can figure out what to do. That is, proficiency in practical reasoning does not, mysteriously but ineluctably, follow from the development of theoretical reasoning. Like theoretical reasoning, practical reasoning must be cultivated.

It seems so simple when phrased in this way. Indeed some who read these words might be wondering how I could be so naïve to miss such an obvious point. Alas, my own observations of my colleagues over the years, as well as considerable study at Carnegie, suggest that the notion is not nearly as obvious as one might think. One reason is that many collegiate teachers who do grasp the point do so as an instance of theoretical reasoning but do not have a clue how to convert this understanding into pedagogical practice. As it turns out, the pedagogical implications of this insight are not all that obvious nor are good examples easily located. This book remedies both these adverse conditions.

_____o_____

As Gary, Bill, Al, and I continued to meet, we realized how much we needed the company of others who also wrestled with these questions. As the book details, we convened a study group that included representatives of the liberal arts disciplines, as well as educators from the various professions with which we were engaged. As those deliberations developed, our questions became richer and even more complex. Shortly after the first seminar was completed, we were joined by a young philosopher of education who was completing his doctorate at Stanford, Matt Rosin. We began to consider, for example, questions moving in the opposite direction, from the professions to the disciplines themselves. Were there ways in which introducing questions of decision, action, and practice could enrich the quality of disciplinary understanding so often the sole purpose of the liberal arts? Moreover, to the extent that the broad rationale for liberal education is to prepare all citizens—whether future professionals or future parents, politicians, or merchants—to act with integrity and intelligence in a democracy, might those purposes be enhanced by framing classical liberal learning in settings of practical reason? That is, could students become good citizens or good men and women if their liberal learning were solely theoretical?

_____o_____

In my case, I fear that I missed the full implication of remarks made by John Dewey (1916a) in the early pages of what many consider his landmark work, *Democracy and Education*. Late in the first chapter, Dewey remarks, "When the acquiring of information and of technical intellectual skill do not influence the formation of a social disposition, ordinary vital experience fails to gain in meaning, while schooling, in so far, creates only 'sharps' in learning—that is, egotistic specialists" (p. 10). My heavy focus on understanding and on theoretical reasoning was not yielding the social dispositions noted by Dewey. Instead they were creating "sharps." These are people who pass one's own course with high honors but cannot apply what they learned to many of the living situations where such learning can and should be used, hence those students of mine who missed the implications of our work together for their dissertation studies or field practica.

Perhaps I judge myself too harshly here. Yet that is a risk I would choose over the possibility of failing to prepare students to consider what actions follow from such knowledge and understanding as they may gain from my instruction. Understanding is undoubtedly a vital outcome of teaching and learning. But unaccompanied by social disposition, it is heir to all the maladies that Dewey decries in *Democracy and Education.* Had I a better grasp of these tensions earlier in my career, the second crisis of confidence might have been avoided. Or at least diminished in its intensity.

○

As our deliberations moved along, they too became increasingly practical. We asked participants to stop talking abstractly about teaching for practical reason and to bring to the table actual cases of teaching in the form of the syllabi for courses that they or colleagues had been teaching that attempted to bridge between theory and practice, between action and ethical or civic formation. We recognized again how frequently those courses proceeded through the use of cases *and* case *methods, whether in the teaching of ethics or of engineering. Cases are remarkable teaching tools. They sit precariously between the dilemmas of practice and the analytic powers of conceptualization. When faced with a case of practice, students and teachers must be prepared to move in two quite different directions. They must ask: What shall I do—now? And they must also step back and ask: What is this a case of? What larger set of problems does this represent, and how might I profit from considering that larger set as precedent, as conceptual organizer or as moral lesson?*

As the deliberations advanced, Bill Sullivan increasingly took the lead in organizing the work, with the close collaboration of Matt Rosin. Together, Bill and Matt took on the difficult task of transforming our intentions, our deliberations, and all the materials we had brought together into a volume that could profit those who had not been present at the seminar table in the same way it had enriched those of us who had worked together. This book represents the fruits of their labor together.

○

Fortunately, the reader of this book has in hand the means to avoid my fate. Within the fabric of pedagogy of practical reason resides much promise for resolving the traditional, contentious dualisms of the liberal arts and the professions. Indeed, this book offers what may easily be viewed as a compelling justification why the liberal arts and professions need one another and how they can each contribute to the greater success of one another's students.

○

I join my colleague Gary Fenstermacher in expressing gratitude to the many scholar-teachers who brought their ideas, their course designs, and their values to this challenge. We are particularly mindful of the creative ways in which the philosophers Sullivan and Rosin transformed our conversations into this volume and its lessons for liberal and professional learning and its needed integrations. As the Carnegie Foundation's decade of research on professional education, liberal education, the scholarship of teaching and learning, and the role of undergraduate education in the development of civic and political engagement comes to a close, this work traces an exciting portrait of the potential of undergraduate education in the coming century.

Lee S. Shulman
Gary D. Fenstermacher

For Bill Spohn—

teacher, colleague, friend,
exemplar.

PREFACE

WHAT IS HIGHER EDUCATION FOR? As American higher education edges ever closer to becoming a universal requirement, this is a serious question.

The most obvious answer is that higher education is increasingly important as entry to desirable employment. Although true, this answer ignores much of the content of the college experience. More reflective respondents are likely to point to the cognitive tools gained through higher education. Problem-solving capacities, or "critical thinking," become the true purposes of the college experience.

The first answer speaks from a reasonable concern about the economic outcomes of today's often expensive investments in advanced education. The second response emphasizes the effects of enhanced mental capacities on an individual's quality of life, as well as strategic success. In this book, we endorse higher education's utility for enhancing the practical as well as the intellectual dimensions of life. But we do so by developing a third, different conception of educational purpose.

We propose that the academy's educational mission is a formative one. Higher education contributes most to society and is most faithful to its own deepest purposes when it seeks to use its considerable intellectual and cultural resources to prepare students for lives of significance and responsibility. College is, indeed, concerned centrally with developing in students a "life of the mind." Students should become enabled and disposed to join others respectfully to explore, probe, and engage in our increasingly global cultural and intellectual heritage. This is the long-standing ideal of liberal education. We affirm this ideal here, but we assert that students also need to develop a life of the mind *for practice*.

The Promise of Practical Reason

We use the term *practice* in the way that professionals do when they describe their work: a disciplined activity that is informed, skillful, and exercised with care for a profession's purposes and the welfare of those the profession is pledged to serve. So *a life of the mind for practice* means the cultivation of reflection and criticism, such as advocates of critical thinking promote, but not for the sake of reflecting and criticizing alone. Rather, the point of such cultivation is that students must learn to deliberate about their possibilities for a life well lived, including their responsibility to contribute to the life of their times.

The term we have chosen for this educational aim is *practical reason*. This is not a new idea, but it may seem unfamiliar to many within the academy, including those in the liberal arts disciplines. This is because practical reason, once central to the educational tradition that stemmed from the rhetorical and humanistic studies of the European Renaissance, has been all but eclipsed by a focus on utility, on the one side, and on abstract, analytical reasoning, on the other. We intend to recover and rehabilitate the teaching practices long associated with the tradition of practical reason. We do this not by nostalgically attempting to re-create a past moment. Rather, we work to discover anew how practical reasoning can function to enhance and integrate the academy's current practices.

This endeavor will take us deeply into teaching in the arts and sciences but also in the professional schools. The common element in these investigations will be tracing out the contours of teaching for practical reason. The tradition of practical reason shares with the popular agenda around critical-thinking skills the idea that thinking can be cultivated and enhanced through training. However, for practical reason the focus is on thinking that is oriented toward decision and action. Because of this, we will take exception to the way critical thinking is currently understood and promoted.

This book will show that teaching for practical reasoning is concerned with the formation of a particular kind of person—one who is disposed toward questioning and criticizing for the sake of more informed and responsible engagement. Such persons use critique in order to act responsibly, as it is the common search for ways to realize valuable purposes and ideals that guides their reasoning. Practical reason grounds the academy's great achievement—critical rationality—in human purposes that are wider and deeper than criticism. These orienting purposes are partly inherited and partly constructed as responses to emerging relationships and situations. In the end, practical reason values embodied responsibility as the resourceful blending of critical intelligence with moral commitment.

As we will show, pedagogies of practical reason tend to emphasize certain common features of what it means to judge and act responsibly, especially what it means to interpret situations and draw analogies to prior cases, in order to reach a reasonable decision. Such reasoning is neither deduction from general principles nor induction from particulars to a universal concept. Instead, it requires moving back and forth between specific events and the general ideas and common traditions that might illuminate them, in order to interpret and engage the particular situation more fruitfully. In this way, practical reasoning is never wholly complete. It is like the work of skilled professionals such as judges, physicians, or educators. Cases and decisions always open up new possibilities, even as they resolve problems. The promise of practical reason for higher education is not just the development of better judges, doctors, and teachers, though we believe that it does foster such outcomes. It promises to stir and support the development of practical wisdom among students of all fields who prepare for a wide variety of careers and callings.

"A Life of the Mind for Practice" Seminar

We argue for this perspective not by presenting a manifesto; rather, we report and reflect on experience. The Carnegie Foundation for the Advancement of Teaching convened the interdisciplinary seminar titled "A Life of the Mind for Practice" (hereafter in text: Life of the Mind for Practice) in order to inquire into higher education's responsibility to prepare students for lives of engagement and responsibility. The seminar posed a series of fundamental questions:

1. What best teaching practices might be identified across the professions and the disciplines?

2. In what ways could the professions and the liberal arts and sciences employ one another's insights in order to achieve this end?

3. Might teaching for practical responsibility and judgment prove a unifying calling for contemporary higher education?

Carnegie Foundation president Lee S. Shulman and senior scholar William M. Sullivan gathered teachers from the professions and the liberal arts and sciences to explore these questions over the course of three meetings, held between September 2002 and December 2003. We had fourteen partners in the Life of the Mind for Practice project. Their teaching and their collaboration figure prominently in this book. Many of our partners teach in professional schools. Some come from professions that feature a strong humanistic heritage, such as teacher education, law, and the clergy:

- Elliot N. Dorff, rabbinical education, American Jewish University (formerly the University of Judaism)
- Gary D. Fenstermacher, teacher education, University of Michigan
- Daisy Hurst Floyd, law, Mercer University
- Allen S. Hammond IV, law, Santa Clara University
- Barbara S. Stengel, teacher education, Millersville University
- Sam Wineburg, teacher education, Stanford University

Meanwhile, several of our partners train students for professions making heavy use of science, such as medicine and engineering:

- Gary Lee Downey, engineering education, Virginia Tech
- Arthur S. Elstein, medical education, University of Illinois at Chicago
- Robert McGinn, engineering education, Stanford University
- Albert R. Jonsen, philosophy and medical ethics, University of Washington

Finally, several of our partners teach in the traditional liberal arts and science disciplines:

- Hessel Bouma III, human biology, Calvin College
- Janice Lauer, composition and rhetoric, Purdue University
- Elizabeth McKinsey, English, Carleton College
- William C. Spohn, religious studies, Santa Clara University

The seminar was cosponsored by the Carnegie Corporation of New York. The seminar's direction was inspired by work in The Carnegie Foundation's ongoing Preparation for the Professions Program, which conducts research into the challenges that professional schools face to integrate technical expertise, practical know-how, and normative purpose in professional education. So far, Carnegie has looked at law, the clergy, engineering, medicine, and nursing. Through the Life of the Mind for Practice seminar, we hoped to bring together from across the professions and the disciplines teachers whose pedagogies exemplified the challenge of placing formation for lives of reasoned action at the center of their educational mission.

We knew from the outset that such teaching cuts against the grain of mainstream academic aspiration. We knew from our studies of the learned professions that teaching directly toward responsible student practice usually takes place at the margins of a field. But we did not anticipate the extent to which faculty who are committed to these purposes *within* their own particular fields lack a shared discourse for understanding and engaging with one another *across* fields and specialties. Teachers such as our seminar partners feel called—and sometimes haunted—by the formative possibilities of higher education. They enjoy this kind of teaching and have devoted considerable ingenuity to developing it. Yet we discovered that such teachers often feel at the edges of their disciplines. They struggle for legitimacy in the eyes of their peers and their students. They enjoy few opportunities to talk and share their values and practice with sympathetic colleagues, and have little common language through which to do so.

In retrospect, this is not surprising. The professionalization of the academy that took place during the twentieth century produced not merely the triumph of abstract theory and criticism over formation and action; it also produced a deep fragmentation of fields and specialties. Academics achieved legitimacy and control over the conditions of their own work by establishing and solidifying new forms of expertise and distinction in the form of new academic departments, Ph.D. programs, research centers, journals, and professional associations. Ever more specialized aspects of the world were subjected to expert criticism and analysis. This fragmentation produced an explosion of new knowledge across the professions and the disciplines. It produced powerful new techniques and human capacities for manipulating the world. The academy became modern.

But this knowledge and power have exacted a heavy price. Although specialization has been central to academic professionalization and knowledge production, it has also alienated. Faculty who are committed to the formative possibilities of their teaching and the enduring idea of liberal education frequently find themselves dispersed across a proliferating array of specialties. The members of this diaspora enjoy neither an organized discourse nor material opportunities for collaborating with others toward the mindful improvement of their teaching.

With the help of our partners in the Life of the Mind for Practice seminar, we learned that the calling to educate our students for lives of responsible judgment in complex worlds of practice not only raises difficult questions about what counts as meaningful *student* formation; it also raises the question of how we should value and evaluate the formation of *faculty* in the contemporary academy. This problem requires that we discover new ways to engage with one another across professional and disciplinary boundaries. Faculty must have opportunities to discern meaningful analogies of purpose and practice in order to weave together both a common vision of a more responsive academy and a community dedicated to that purpose. We need a new discourse of faculty identity and the purposes of pedagogy. This book addresses that need. It offers a model of faculty formation that cultivates those practices of engagement and dialogue that can help us realize a richer understanding of the academic calling.

Two Narrative Threads of the Book

This book—*A New Agenda for Higher Education: Shaping a Life of the Mind for Practice*—is composed of two interwoven narrative threads. First, we offer a new agenda for American higher education, based on teaching for practical reasoning and responsible judgment. We explore in detail the teaching practices of our partners in the Life of the Mind for Practice seminar. Through their examples, we highlight practices that bring this new agenda to life for students and faculty. This narrative thread begins to reveal what is possible, why it is important, and how far the American academy has to go in order to become more responsive to the practical contexts and challenges that await our students. This narrative thread is concerned with the just formation of students.

Second, we highlight what is required for the agenda of practical reasoning to become a viable topic of faculty formation. Specialization and the marginalization of practice in the American academy place heavy burdens on individual faculty who remain responsive to the promise of formative education. Such faculty can feel isolated as they struggle against the grain of their disciplines and departments; many are engaged in an analogous struggle.

We believe that the Life of the Mind for Practice seminar provides an example that can help faculty discern analogies of purpose and practice across multiple domains, so that they can recognize how the various professions and disciplines depend on and might learn from one another. We also hope to enlist academic leaders among both faculty and administrators to reflect on the seminar's experience in order to bring this broader vision of education for practical responsibility to life on their own campuses.

———————o———————

The Life of the Mind for Practice seminar was valuable because it enabled educators from parts of the academy that rarely collaborate around teaching to become deeply involved in one another's professional development. Most of our partners in the seminar came from professional schools and programs. This was dictated largely by the seminar's roots in The Carnegie Foundation's comparative study of professional education. The Carnegie Corporation's interest, by contrast, stemmed from concern for the liberal arts. This interest ensured that our partners also included educators from several of the arts and sciences.

Out of this collaboration between two sibling organizations came unusual progeny: common language and understanding that built promising bridges between professional and liberal education. The key to these developments was the willingness of educators from both the professions and the disciplines to enter imaginatively into each other's teaching aims and practices. As they did this, the particular strengths of the two areas of higher education became clearer to all.

In the professional fields, faculty are charged with shaping student understanding and skill toward the standards of competence and responsibility that define the profession. Accordingly, the major contribution of the professions to the seminar lay in teaching practices that provide students with access to the practice of their fields. These ranged from intensive use of case studies to guided reflection on actual performance within professional roles. These professional pedagogies engage students' imaginations while they develop the insight, comportment, and commitment that are critical for informed judgment and action.

Most of all, however, our partners from the professional fields emphasized that their students must learn to be responsible for the effects of their action on others, including clients and publics. Professional practice demands that students learn to blend knowledge, skill, and appropriate attitude in response to unique situations that require expert judgment. The practitioner cannot bring knowledge to bear without skillful performance. Nor can the practitioner apply her knowledge and skill responsibly without exercising proper care and judgment. Professional practice at its best is a prime exemplar of practical reasoning.

It is noteworthy, then, that many of our partners from professional schools derive important dimensions of their teaching directly from the liberal arts and sciences. The bodies of knowledge and habits of thought that distinguish the liberal arts and sciences empower persons to interpret the social, cultural, institutional, and natural contexts of their action. This is the traditional goal of liberal education. Our partners became convinced that developing the ability to interpret the relationship between self and situation is not secondary but essential for competence and responsibility in any field.

Compared to professional education, the modern liberal arts and sciences can seem less practical. They do not prepare students for a specific role in society, save perhaps for the disciplines of the professoriate. Rather, the modern disciplines aim to prepare individuals to stand back from the immediate situations of life in order to consider and evaluate them. Students learn to represent and investigate relationships among elements systematically. This critical mode of thinking is central for grasping the complex interdependence of the natural and social processes that shape our lives. Informed judgment and action in almost any area of modern life depend on critical and scientific awareness, as several of our partners illustrate vividly in their courses.

But liberal education is also heir to a long tradition that sees the fulfillment of critical representation and analysis in our ability to *return* to the concrete in new ways, in order to interpret and perhaps transform it. The educational potential of this kind of practical reasoning in the liberal arts and sciences proved quite attractive to many in the seminar. By embracing critical understanding *for the sake of* engagement, our partners were stirred to new ways of thinking about how the disciplines might be woven more artfully into professional preparation.

The liberal arts and sciences must also draw from the wisdom and values of practice. Our partners became convinced that teaching in the disciplines can be strengthened significantly by drawing from the weaving of understanding, skill, and ethos that distinguishes the best professional practice. Our partners explored how the disciplines might better prepare students for understanding their lives and their world by borrowing from professional pedagogies that focus on each student's responsibility for her engagement with others. Ironically, our partners discovered, the arts and sciences can reclaim the formative mission of liberal education through constructive engagement with the professions.

This reciprocal relation between the professions and the disciplines is premised on the seminar's rediscovery of the culture of the traditional humanities, especially rhetoric. This formative legacy is largely silent within the modern university, where critical thinking is celebrated as the highest end of education. But relating critical knowledge and thinking to engagement and responsibility requires a different set of practices. These are rooted in the traditional humanities, which called faculty and students alike to articulate explicitly the meanings and values that ought to guide human living. As it turned out, the humanistic practices that sustain meaning and value—particularly interpretation and narrative—are vital to our partners' teaching, whether in the liberal arts, the sciences, or the professions.

From the perspective of practical reason, the sciences, liberal arts, and professional domains find their human significance as parts of the broader formative project of higher education. This project, we argue, can only be enhanced through the kind of pedagogical self-reflection and scholarship that the seminar represents.

The Plan of This Book

We have organized *A New Agenda for Higher Education* to emphasize new possibilities for what higher education might yet mean in the contemporary world. It begins with case studies of teachers from a wide array of professions and disciplines who work to educate their students for practical responsibility, often (though not always) at the margins of their fields. The book then tells the story of what happened when these teachers gathered together in the Life of the Mind for Practice seminar. We document the process by which we learned to collaborate with one another across fields and, in the end, produced a new discourse of practical reason. In order to clarify and discern the consequences of this new discourse, the book then engages theory directly by rethinking such key educational ideas as critical thinking in light of the seminar experience. Finally, we offer faculty, administrators, and those interested in the promise of higher education practical suggestions on how to put these insights to work in their own academic contexts.

This journey from practice to theory and back to practice requires some basic appreciation of the contexts and terrain through which we will travel. What is at stake? The Introduction explains in more detail the meaning of practical reasoning in relation to the traditions and aims of higher education in America. The Introduction also begins to illuminate what it means to *teach* practical reasoning. We introduce three of our seminar partners. These professors teach in the diverse domains of human biology, engineering, and law. Despite the substantial differences among these fields, the Introduction shows that these teachers share much in common in their efforts to prepare their students for practice.

Chapters One and Two ("Partners in the Field, Part One" and "Partners in the Field, Part Two") explore differences and analogies in the teaching of practical reasoning across fields by introducing six more of our partners. These teachers work in the fields of rabbinical education, medicine, teacher education, engineering, law, and religious studies. By focusing on particular course syllabi, these case studies bring to life the challenges that each teacher faces in teaching for practical responsibility in his or her particular field. The case studies, which include selections from our partners' own written reflections, reveal a diverse group of faculty whose teaching is oriented by their commitment to the future practical lives of their students, as well as the lives of those for whom their students will become responsible. Chapters One and Two illuminate what teaching toward practical judgment means for particular disciplines. They also uncover the goals, teaching practices, and institutional challenges that bind our partners in common purpose, both across professions and across the professional-liberal divide that characterizes modern academic institutions.

Chapter Three ("A Narrative of the Seminar") explains how the seminar developed a new common language for teaching practical reasoning. It identifies the difficulties and revelations that characterized our times together. In the end, our partners gathered around a set of common pedagogical values and were able to discern the shape of a new discourse about the ends of teaching in higher education. They did this by imagining their own practices anew through engagement with the pedagogical challenges of their fellows. Chapter Three is the story of how we built a new community of pedagogical inquiry and, in doing so, new forms of pedagogical conscience. It is also about meaningful faculty formation.

Chapter Four ("Practical Reason as an Educational Agenda") offers practical reasoning as a new agenda for the modern academy. The chapter looks back on the events, failures, and ultimate success of the seminar experience and presents theoretical conclusions regarding the meaning of practical reasoning, the deep structure of its pedagogies, and its enduring importance for the modern academy. This new agenda reveals important limitations and weaknesses in the notion of critical thinking. We then offer a way forward that maintains what is most valuable about the critical-thinking agenda, without falling prey to its disconnection of abstraction from the ground of practice. The placement of this theoretical turn *after* the case studies and narratives that precede it is meant to exemplify the ideas it puts forth. In practical reasoning, theoretical analysis emerges through engagement with situations and aims at the improvement and renewal of practice. Chapter Four is the "theoretical moment" within a practical and institutional argument.

Finally, the Conclusion ("Conclusion: Taking Formative Action") offers practical lessons from the seminar experience. How might our academic institutions become at once more responsive to their constituencies and truer to the ideals of liberal education? We discuss what is required in order for institutions, departments, or campus centers of teaching and learning to offer local faculty the kind of formative experiences that we document in this book. We also suggest how the agenda of practical reasoning can help faculty, administrators, and chief academic officers discover the common, unifying mission that binds the innovative practices already at work on their campuses, such as learning communities, service learning, community-based learning, and other forms of pedagogy that are concerned with the enrichment and renewal of conduct.

"Appendix One: Partner Syllabi" and "Appendix Two: Seminar Assignments" provide illustrations of seminar partners' classroom practices and methods, as well as the practices we adopted during the seminar itself.

Our goal in this book is to help our students meet the practical and professional challenges that await them with learned insight, technical know-how, and discerning moral commitment. We offer what follows in the hope that it will provide inspiration and tools for the renewal of our vocation as teachers and the mission of higher education.

A New Agenda for Higher Education begins as a reflection on teaching. It ends with a call to action. From practice we have come; to practice we must return.

ACKNOWLEDGMENTS

The authors want to acknowledge how much this book is indebted to the generous contributions and insights of their fellow participants in the Carnegie "A Life of the Mind for Practice" seminar. The authors also owe a deep debt of gratitude to the leadership and staff of The Carnegie Foundation for the Advancement of Teaching for their patient interest and constructive suggestions. In addition, they wish to thank Charles Blaich, Thomas Schwandt, Carla Ingrando, and David Buchanan, who provided insight into how these ideas might play out in further contexts beyond those explored in the book.

The authors wish to thank, in particular, Daniel Fallon of Carnegie Corporation of New York—the Foundation's partner in the seminar enterprise—who seeded the project with ideas as well as resources. They are grateful as well to David Brightman, editor at Jossey-Bass Publishers, and his able colleagues.

All these people enriched the final product a great deal. This book has been far more collaborative in its genesis than most. Its virtues are the gift of many. Its faults, however, are entirely the responsibility of the authors.

ABOUT THE AUTHORS

WILLIAM M. SULLIVAN is codirector of the Carnegie Foundation's Preparation for the Professions Program. He is formulating a research design for the comparative aspects of the studies, drawing out common themes and identifying distinct practices in professional education. The author of *Work and Integrity: The Crisis and Promise of Professionalism in America* (2005) and a coauthor of *Habits of the Heart: Individualism and Commitment in American Life* (2007) and *Educating Lawyers* (2007), Sullivan has examined the link between formal training and practical reflection in effective education. Prior to coming to Carnegie, Sullivan was a philosophy professor at La Salle University. He earned a Ph.D. in philosophy at Fordham University.

———————— o ————————

MATTHEW S. ROSIN is an author and philosopher of education living in Mountain View, California. He holds a Ph.D. in education from Stanford University. Rosin is author of *Obsoleting Culture* (Sense Publishers) and was formerly a research scholar at The Carnegie Foundation for the Advancement of Teaching. He currently serves as a senior research associate at EdSource, an independent and impartial educational policy research agency that clarifies issues in K–12 policy in California.

INTRODUCTION

PROFESSIONAL AND LIBERAL EDUCATION PRACTITIONERS need one another's pedagogical insights. This may seem a startling claim, given the traditional separation of the two types of higher education. Although higher education has historically aimed to enhance the possibilities of life for its students, the arts and sciences and the professional schools have used different methods: the liberal arts and sciences have sought to do this through cultivating in students a life of the mind; the professional schools have focused on providing the means whereby students might "make something of themselves" by acquiring specific kinds of expert competence.

Today, this conventional division of educational labor has come under increasing strain. The liberal arts find themselves encouraged to become more practical and relevant. Meanwhile, the professional schools are reproached for confining training to the technical aspects of their fields, when graduates also need ethical awareness and better understanding of the social contexts of their responsibilities. To reclaim its grand aim of enabling students to live an enlarged life, the academy needs to find new, more effective ways to unite vision with engagement and professional competence with the insights and breadth of understanding characteristic of liberal education at its best.

Proposing a New Model for Teaching

This book—*A New Agenda for Higher Education*—proposes a new model of undergraduate teaching, focused on the interdependence of liberal education and professional training. At its most effective, liberal education provides students with orientation, that is, the intellectual capacity to make sense of their environment and to locate themselves

I

reflectively within the complex influences of their time and place. In such education, the arts and sciences function as sources of insight and methods of understanding that faculty make available to students through a set of characteristic ways of teaching and learning, ranging from the lecture to the seminar. The aim of such teaching is often described as developing students' ability to assume responsibility for their purposes and identity.

Professional education, by contrast, must provide the knowledge essential to a particular field of endeavor. It cannot remain entirely in the realm of observation and theory, however. To be effective, educators of professionals must find ways to provide their students with access to the actual practices, as well as the purposes, of the profession. The teaching practices through which professional schools attempt these ambitious aims emphasize engagement and responsibility for clients. They do this in order to shape their students' identities around the standards of competence and commitment that define the field. These pedagogies range from the discussion of cases to supervised clinical work with actual clients.

We believe that the perspective and teaching practices of the liberal arts can make contributions of great worth to the more effective formation of competent and responsible professionals. We are also convinced that those teaching practices in professional education that engage students in practice and reflection on that practice hold great value for enhancing the teaching of judgment in the liberal arts, but this potential remains largely unrealized.

The chapters that follow provide more than a theory of an integrated undergraduate education, however. They also set out a new approach to developing faculty who are enabled to make this interdependence between liberal and professional education come alive in their teaching. This book attempts to describe the experience of a research seminar, Life of the Mind for Practice, convened over two years by The Carnegie Foundation for the Advancement of Teaching. This seminar brought together educators from six professional fields with faculty from liberal arts disciplines to reflect on their efforts to link intellectual insight to professional engagement and responsibility in their respective fields.

The results, as we show, included a common perspective on teaching toward *student formation,* as reflected in a group of *pedagogies of engagement* across the diverse disciplines. This unifying pedagogical aim was not a given at the start of the seminar. It evolved through intensive dialogue among the diverse viewpoints of our seminar partners. In the process, the seminar produced more than just a new vision of how such pedagogies actually work to bridge the liberal-professional education divide. It also yielded critical insight into the process of *faculty formation* that was shared through the seminar experience itself. In the pages that follow, we try to make both these products and this collective experience available for analysis and emulation by other educators concerned with these important issues.

Understanding the Educational Challenge

Knowledge, judgment, and responsibility for action are often woven tightly together in contemporary life. Today's students will be called on to respond to new possibilities and challenges as family members, as professionals, and as citizens. To meet these demands, students must learn to sift and deploy knowledge of many kinds: knowledge about human life as part of the natural world, about how human societies have come into being and function, including their institutions and their technologies, and about how various peoples and groups understand their own lives. In addition to understanding their world, however, students must also be able to make sense of their place in it. Students necessarily find themselves faced with the demand that they make something of their own talents and commitments in the realms of relationships, occupation, culture, religion, and politics. Their success in meeting this challenge will be directly determined by how effectively they have learned to respond to the world in which they live and make informed and responsible judgments about the role they will play within it.

For an increasing proportion of the American population, the most important preparation for career, citizenship, and life in general takes place in institutions of higher education, especially professional and pre-professional schools and programs but also in programs in the liberal arts and sciences. This places a significant responsibility on educators in the professions and the arts and sciences alike. How should higher education respond to this calling? What sorts of education—what subject matters, which forms of teaching and learning, what guiding purposes—are most likely to assist students in the complex task of preparing to take part in and contribute to contemporary life?

In a first effort to approach these questions, we begin with three examples of educators and their courses from the Life of the Mind for Practice seminar. The first case brings together the liberal arts and sciences—specifically, natural science and the humanities—to enable students to engage with the pressing questions of life and death that are thrust upon us by technological advances in the life sciences. By contrast, the second example provides a window into the complexities of connecting training for a technical profession—engineering—with the concrete challenges to professional judgment that students will encounter, especially in an increasingly global field of practice. The third example comes from a very different professional context: the law school. In this case, future professionals are trained to move back and forth between abstract legal principles and the vicissitudes of concrete practice with clients. In each case, we find a modulated response to the common problem: how to use the distinctive intellectual capacities that each field tries to foster in order to enable students to engage the challenges of practice as professionals, as citizens, and as persons.

Informing Judgment with Knowledge

Knowledge of the basic realities of human biology is crucial for a whole range of professionals, from the health care fields and the sciences to engineering, teaching, law, and the ministry. But it is also increasingly important to the ability to act well as a voter and citizen, and even as a member of one's family. Think of the expanding range of decisions that have sprung up in the face of serious or terminal illness and end-of-life care. As advances in biological science and medical technique have extended life, they have also increased the burden of judgment and decision on both professionals and families. How can higher education help students confront these issues, not only in theory but as preparation for the actual experience of caring for their own health and that of others?

Course Example: "Human Biology"

Consider an undergraduate course at Calvin College, a liberal arts college in the Reformed Christian tradition, titled "Human Biology." Professor Hessel Bouma III provides students with opportunities to come to terms not just with biological systems but with the matrix of difficult questions posed by the impact of biological knowledge on life's potentials and limits. The course is directed toward students who are not majoring in science and is genuinely interdisciplinary in that it introduces students to the characteristic ways of thinking of both biology and moral philosophy in a coordinated way.

"Human Biology" provides an exposition of key findings in contemporary biology. But the course gets its significance not from any intellectual discipline, as such, but from questions about the human import of scientific discovery. Should human life, for instance, be treated in the same way, an analogous way, or in a very different way from other animal life?

These questions arise from the students' actual or anticipated practical involvements and commitments as individuals in the world. Bouma's pedagogy encourages students to respond to these situations by asking what is at stake, for whom, and for what reasons. These questions engage students in the interplay of general principles and purposes, in light of particular loyalties and responsibilities.

This goal requires Bouma to perform a difficult but vital balancing act. A substantial portion of the everyday work of the course is akin to a traditional introductory biology course, taught in lecture format and accompanied by concurrent lab work. In this part of the course, Bouma aims to introduce his students to the basic concepts and methods of biological science. But the course goes further than this. Bouma augments his teaching of technical biological knowledge, such as the structure and function of the nervous and endocrine systems, with periodic discussion sections that engage students in serious consideration of some of the difficult intersections between biological science, morality, and social policy. Bouma refined this practice, in part, through his work as a scholar in the Carnegie Academy for the Scholarship of Teaching and Learning, or CASTL (Bouma, 2001). This integrative challenge is a familiar one for Bouma, whose own professional identity is poised between biological science (particularly human genetics) and matters of medical ethics and health policy.

When teaching about the biological processes involved in human suffering, disease, and death, Bouma asks his students to think about the following question:

> When animals are in profound pain and suffering, we put them to sleep. When humans are in profound suffering, we should put them to sleep similarly. To do so is a profound act of love. Is this a legitimate argument in your opinion? Why or why not? (Respond with sensitivity as you would to a dying loved one who seriously makes this argument to you.) How should we respond to such a request? (Bouma, 2005a)

In order to respond, Bouma's students must relate their understanding of biological processes to several basic philosophical issues. They must also involve their empathic sense by conjuring in imagination a conversation with a suffering relative or friend. All this is focused on the task of coming to a reasoned judgment about the difficult and contentious moral issue of euthanasia.

This assignment requires students to consider what they have learned as theoretical knowledge within a wider, more personally involving context. They must consider the substantive differences between humans and nonhuman animals. What moral status ought humans, as opposed to animals, enjoy? What distinguishes human beings as persons, and how might representatives of different religious and secular traditions respond to the issue? How do various sources of moral insight derived from traditions of moral reasoning, some of which students may bring to the course from other dimensions of their lives, such as the Christian scriptures, the Talmud, papal authority, or scientific views like evolutionary biology, provide a reasoned basis for different positions on these questions?

Bouma's students each draft a written response to the question, which they share with their classmates during a discussion session. These sessions are intended to produce more than just individual soul-searching and moral self-expression, however. The assignment provides the following further instruction:

> After discussion, you will need to write a second response consisting of at least two (or more) paragraphs summarizing the ideas of your small group's responses to the question and rearticulating your response in light of your further thinking and reflection based upon the group's and the class's discussion of your question. (Bouma, 2005b, p. 5)

In the follow-up writing exercise, Bouma's students are asked to place their own first response in relationship to the answers of fellow classmates and to articulate the moral justifications for their own and others' perspectives as fairly as they can. The students must do justice to a range of different and sometimes conflicting understandings of the situation. They are invited to enter into these differing arguments as alternative perspectives through which to revisit their own prior views. This process leads the students to understand more clearly their own first responses by seeing them anew in relation to the responses of their fellow students and relative to important moral and religious traditions other than those they may have considered initially.

Bouma's emphasis on dialogue—listening to and reading others' views, having interpersonal give-and-take, and attending to traditions of moral argument—is deliberate. Students are taught and exercised repeatedly throughout the course in the skills of listening, recognizing the relative strength of arguments in favor of alternative perspectives, and seeing the possibility of revising one's own beliefs as a result. For Bouma, this practice is about more than helping students learn to take up a reasoned stance toward difficult issues raised by modern biology, valuable as that is. He sees his teaching as giving students experience in connecting scientific knowledge with its philosophical and moral significance for actual situations. Bouma's students will eventually be responsible for making decisions about serious health matters. His course provides students with valuable practice, including critical feedback, in approaching such complex practical issues. In "Human Biology," students learn to employ the best available scientific knowledge in dialogue with other inquirers in order to reach judgments that are considered and responsible.

"Human Biology" is a genuinely interdisciplinary course. It provides nonscience majors with an understanding of basic biology and the way biologists think. But students also learn modes of argument and discussion drawn from philosophy that provide a method for approaching questions of practical moral judgment. The major lesson is that students need to be able to draw on both disciplines in order to think effectively about many of the most pressing issues they will face, such as decisions about end-of-life care. Bouma's pedagogical challenge arises from the inconvenient fact that these two perspectives do not fit easily together. To accomplish their integration, the basic pedagogical repertoire of "Human Biology" makes important use of writing as a medium for reflective learning. This is typical of much of liberal arts education, especially the humanities, but it is less typical of teaching in the scientific disciplines.

Science courses usually emphasize bringing students into the methods and conventions of the discipline, including its often formidable fund of established knowledge and general procedures for obtaining knowledge through observation and experiment. Training in the sciences shapes students to see the world through general patterns of cause and effect. The use of mathematics to measure and describe phenomena further encourages students to think of events in terms of general rules and procedures. The emphasis is on learning to work within a consistent point of view, employing standard conceptual tools to frame and solve well-defined problems.

In the discussion sessions of his "Human Biology," by contrast, Bouma introduces students to philosophical questioning and dialogue, focused on the biological perspective and its implications. In this context, the question, What is the problem? can no longer be answered with assurance simply through reference to scientific procedure. The assignments do not ask students to assemble evidence to prove a hypothesis, as scientific courses routinely do. Instead, problems turn out to be open to various plausible formulations. These descriptions frequently contain evaluative judgments that are contested from clashing perspectives. Students discover that navigating this contentious context requires wider and more flexible reasoning skills than those typically honed by careful and rigorous scientific analysis.

Although scientific investigators are often represented to students as detached and skeptical observers wielding proven tools of measurement, students in Bouma's course find that they must enter imaginatively into other students' points of view. All the while, they must assess how their own position looks from these other viewpoints. And, critically, they must be clear about the biological processes involved in the issues under consideration. This complex stance, involving both engagement and critical distance, is developed through pedagogies born from the study of communication and rhetoric, especially the modern field of composition. In these assignments, students are asked to explore divergent perspectives about common issues.

The writing assignments lead students to identify key points of difference among value positions and then to attempt to formulate areas of clear agreement or disagreement, along with supporting reasons for each position. This is practice in solving problems, though in a different sense from what is understood in scientific disciplines. Here, the point of questioning is to make "problematic" and self-aware any proposed resolution, because it must be understood in relation to other possible resolutions. In the learning disciplines, this is often called becoming metacognitive, that is, aware of how one is thinking or learning. As a teaching practice, the point is to invite students into an ongoing dialogue rather than to prescribe an a priori method for arriving at once-and-for-all solutions. Students are learning techniques of dialogue and argumentation that relate multiple, contrasting points of view within a common frame of reference.

Value of the Course

Why is Professor Bouma so concerned about teaching biology in this way, given the intrinsic complexity of guiding students between two such different kinds of intellectual activity, each quite intricate and demanding in its own way? He tells us that he considers it a pedagogical responsibility. His students will be called on in their future lives, whether as professionals or as citizens, to make judgments that are both scientifically informed and defensible morally with respect to such issues. Like any introductory biology course, Bouma's "Human Biology" must necessarily focus much of its attention on the theoretical understanding of basic concepts and systems, yet Bouma also recognizes that no amount of scientific (or moral) knowledge can determine right judgment automatically in practice.

There is much more at stake in Bouma's course than scientific literacy alone. The public sphere contains debates involving contrary positions about which reasonable, responsible people continue to disagree. Contemporary citizenship demands not only the recognition of these multiple stances but also the willingness to learn from, and be changed by, the wisdom articulated from perspectives other than the student's own. "Human Biology" is one response to an educational challenge that affects both professional and liberal education, namely, the challenge of helping students learn to engage with others knowledgably, responsibly, and respectfully in response to divisive and difficult issues surrounding the science of human life and to place their own arguments within a wider pluralistic context.

Introducing Judgment into a World of Facts

Consider another teaching situation. Undergraduate engineering students at Stanford University must prepare a final class presentation for Robert McGinn's course, "Ethical Issues in Engineering." The course is cross-referenced between the School of Engineering and Stanford's interdisciplinary program called Science, Technology, and Society, of which McGinn is the director. McGinn is poised between the engineering world of technological production and the normative and sociocultural concerns of the liberal arts. His challenge is to convince engineering students that responsible technological practice involves not only analytical expertise but also artful consideration of the normative, social, and cultural contexts and consequences of one's professional judgments. This is not an introductory course in the arts and sciences. It is part of the professional preparation of young engineers, yet it involves pedagogical issues analogous to those we met in Hessel Bouma's "Human Biology."

Course Example: "Ethical Issues in Engineering"

McGinn's course parallels Hessel Bouma's in that it constructs a bridge across a customary academic divide, this time between professional training and liberal education in the arts and sciences. Students who have already gained a foothold in the demanding world of engineering are helped across a serious conceptual gap between the clear and bounded "problems" and "techniques" of the typical engineering science course, on the one hand, and the divergent "opinions" that mark the dialectical realm of philosophical discourse, on the other. McGinn's pedagogy makes the same point as Bouma's writing and discussion sessions: solving problems in the world depends on judgment, and this involves both command of scientific knowledge and technological skill, on the one hand, and the ability to assess situations from a cultural, historical, and dialogical perspective on the other.

McGinn's students are asked to produce "an original case study of an incident or episode involving an interesting ethical issue or conflict in contemporary engineering practice," usually in small groups of two or three (McGinn, 2001, p. 7). These group presentations are focused on what McGinn calls a sociotechnical situation. By this he means a *case* that exemplifies a particular ethical issue or conflict encountered in the course of engineering practice. Students explore a particular documented event that raises difficult questions about the ethical nature of engineering practice. They must present the case as vividly as they can to the rest of the class in order to enable their fellow students to imagine the predicament faced by the actual engineers in the case. By presenting the arguments made in the case and the decisions that were ultimately made, students are encouraged to distill "noteworthy morals or lessons about ethical issues in engineering extracted from the case presented" (McGinn, 2001, p. 8).

One telling example that McGinn engages in the course and that he has discussed at length in his scholarly work is the disaster that occurred at Union Carbide Corporation's pesticide production plant in Bhopal, India, in 1984. Union Carbide built the pesticide plant in a poor region of central India, which the Indian government hoped would benefit from new development. The plant was originally set apart from the general population. Union Carbide neglected to consider fully enough the social and political conditions of the region when placing and establishing the plant and its production practices, however. The result was that lethal pesticide ingredients, initially thought to be merely steam, leaked from the facility into the surrounding population, killing over 2,300 and injuring over 200,000 people.

This case brings engineering students into direct contact with the often abstract issue of negotiating cultural differences. It highlights in dramatic and unsettling fashion the collisions of social, political, and philosophical understandings that are brought on by the rapid pace of contemporary globalization. As McGinn explains, "the social institution of zoning had not taken deep root in India ... by 1984, Bhopal had more than doubled in population and human habitation had spread right up to the boundary of the plant site" (McGinn, 2002, pp. 7–8). But it was not only the social institution of zoning that Union Carbide engineers took for granted. McGinn writes:

> Locating such a plant in a poor Third World county should have trig gered extraordinary efforts to train plant workers and educate Bhopal residents . . . engineers and engineering managers seem to have taken the concept of preventative maintenance for granted and failed to inculcate it in the new workforce. Similarly, a sense of urgency about all safety problems and attention to worst-case scenarios, routine in industrial countries, seem not to have been ingrained in the culture of [Union Carbide]'s Indian subsidiary. (McGinn, 2002, p. 8)

Value of the Course

Engaging with this case compels students to consider in new and potentially disturbing light what they may have taken for granted about the nature of professional judgment in engineering. What suddenly stands out is the dependence of professional judgment on institutionalized social practices, such as preventive maintenance and land-use planning, as well as the cultural understandings in which these practices are grounded.

The Bhopal disaster reveals failures of social and political judgment that were tied directly to problems with intercultural communication and relationships between American international business and Indian government and society. Judgment depended on skills of dialogue that were obviously in short supply. By requiring students to interrogate the failures and successes of the past judgments of practicing engineers through a full accounting of the social contexts of the cases under analysis, McGinn hopes to provide his students with a new understanding of engineering practice as more than a purely technical occupation. McGinn intends for his students to learn that social and political judgment is inseparable from the technical aspects of engineering decision making by exploring, presenting, and drawing normative lessons from concrete events.

McGinn's pedagogy urges his students to recognize that, although responsible judgment does not guarantee a single, definitive course of action in any particular situation, there are indeed traditions through which to illuminate better and worse responses to sociotechnical situations. Indirectly, the course suggests that the knowledge about human affairs afforded by the humanities and social sciences is valuable for engineers. Students discover that these traditions of thought can help them to locate themselves reflectively, as they struggle to make sense of the complex influences at work in particular engineering cases. By enabling his students to imaginatively experience something of the complexity of real engineering decisions, McGinn hopes to encourage an expansion of their understanding of the domain of engineering practice, including the value of nontechnical learning.

McGinn's students are developing intellectual and personal abilities to engage a wider terrain of professional work. The conclusion that McGinn intends most students to reach is not a second-guessing of the engineers involved in the cases under study but a vivid realization that the practices of engaged dialogue, far from being extraneous to good and effective engineering practice, are actually central to it. Through repeated practice of such analyses, McGinn intends the course to equip students to discern what issues are ethically salient for responsible action in their own future engineering practice. By doing this, his students are expanding their own understanding of professionalism in engineering.

Resolving problems of professional judgment, especially when cross-cultural understanding is crucial, places a premium on learning how to understand others and being willing to reckon with one's own unacknowledged assumptions. Both these tasks require developing competence in dialogue. As McGinn's students try to make sense of professional responsibility in the Bhopal case, their own assumptions about the nature of engineering practice may well appear problematic, as they become aware of them in the new situation. So the realm of philosophical dialogue that McGinn's students encounter makes unexpected demands, asking students accustomed to "one right answer" to tolerate ambiguity and complexity and to see an issue steadily and whole. Like Bouma, McGinn invites students to enter an ongoing and multivocal dialogue. This dialogue, students quickly realize, lacks the appealing sense of ongoing progress that is the glory of the engineering sciences. Instead, dialogue often leads to the realization that some problems can be managed inventively but not solved definitively. This is a realization more typical of the humanities, but it is also essential to effective judgment in the professions and, indeed, in life.

The Key Role of Cases and Their Interpretation

The use of "cases" to teach these complex intellectual skills is central to McGinn's practice. It is also a feature of Bouma's teaching. This is neither idiosyncratic nor coincidental. Cases have long been standard pedagogical devices in a variety of disciplines. Teaching by cases is especially noteworthy in professional fields such as medicine, law, and business. In these fields, case-based teaching is about the formation of judgment.

Reasoning by cases makes it possible to represent publicly how skilled persons think and decide in practical matters—that is, how they arrive at judgment through deliberation.[1]

In cases such as the Bhopal instance, there is almost always ambiguity or uncertainty about how to characterize the situation. It is frequently unclear what theoretical concept or principle might guide understanding of the situation most meaningfully. In other words, the first difficulty students face is to discern what a particular case is a case *of*?[2] As the students in McGinn's class came to realize, this is a different kind of question from the ones typically raised by the problems they encounter in mathematical and scientific courses. Much of the teaching in engineering courses aims to render the world more amenable to human purposes by developing devices to shape the environment. Understanding the universal scientific principles according to which the physical world operates is the key conceptual instrument to this end. Cases, by contrast, are narrative accounts of particular events and situations.

Cases connect particulars with general principles. But they do so in a way that is quite different from scientific problem solving, where particulars are represented in the form of abstract variables, then operated upon in accordance with general formulas or algorithms in order to produce precise results. By contrast, the question of what Bhopal was a case *of* demands neither a correct deduction from formulas nor an induction of a general rule from similar situations. The Bhopal case demands that students *interpret the significance of the situation*. That significance differs, depending on whose perspective is assumed—that of the company or the facility manager, the engineers operating it, the victims, or the various oversight bodies. How, then, does one make an informed judgment about the salience of the case?

Interpretation is the initial step of practical reasoning. Because it is always provisional, the effort to interpret situations properly is a constant feature of engaged inquiry. Interpretation is crucial, because how individuals or communities understand a situation has great influence on how they will respond to it. Like the more formal logical concepts of deduction and induction, interpretation is an intellectual activity that makes sense of particular events by relating them to general concepts and principles. These principles have consequences for further decision making and acting. Deciding that Bhopal was "really" a case of criminal negligence, for example, is likely to set in motion very different responses from those following the conclusion that it was more likely a problem of accidental malfunction. Different "universal" moral and legal principles come into play, depending on which interpretation is accepted.

On what basis should one accept a general interpretation? This is the question that McGinn's students found themselves up against. They had to ask themselves, each other, and any other source they found illuminating how to understand—or frame—the situation. Though the students were beginners, their activity was analogous to what a skilled physician does when developing a diagnosis of a patient's condition. It is also what moral philosophers or theologians do when assessing ethical decisions. As students became aware of the case's complexity and the dimensions of its human tragedy, they discovered the urgency of the question of what really happened at Bhopal. (What was it *really* a case of?) The question became more complex and more serious still when the students were then led to ask who was at fault and what could be done to prevent a recurrence.

The form of reasoning exemplified by interpretation works in a circular, or recursive, manner. Like McGinn's students, interpreters begin by imagining or projecting a plausible general concept—for example, the idea that Bhopal was a case of accidental system failure—in order to make sense of the situation they are trying to understand. This general concept defines the frame within which the interpreters will work as they try to fit the details of the case within the proposed overall view. These details are put together in the form of a narrative or story. In engineering cases, these stories involve both natural processes, described by the laws of chemistry or physics, and human intentions, words, and actions. These interact to produce particular outcomes. Like detectives (or physicians or attorneys), the students confronting the Bhopal case worked to discern a reasonable definition of the situation under investigation—one on which they could base their judgments defensibly.

The challenge of interpretation, as the Bhopal case illustrates, is that as more aspects of the situation are examined and as wider questions are asked, initial characterizations of a situation often become less adequate. As investigation proceeds, this first interpretation may fail to provide a coherent account of the salient details. Things "don't add up." The account must either be modified substantially or replaced by another, more plausible interpretation. What makes this different from scientific problem solving is that interpretation is always a matter of more-or-less—probability in its commonsense meaning—rather than certainty or statistically calculated degrees of reliability. It is more like courtroom argument than laboratory analysis. Like a courtroom case, most situations require a narrative mode of description: this happened; then that happened; this caused that; this person responded to that in this way, and so forth.

The natural affinity between interpretation and the classic humanities disciplines such as literary analysis, moral and political philosophy, and history is obvious. But narrative and interpretation are equally essential and are cultivated in training for professions such as medicine, the health fields, the clergy, and the law. What insights might their pedagogies contribute to developing approaches to teaching reflective and responsible judgment?

Judgment, Interpretation, and Ambiguity: Learning the Life of the Law

Professor Allen S. Hammond IV teaches at the Santa Clara University School of Law in Northern California. Hammond teaches a section of "Contracts" to first-year law students, at the outset of their three-year course of study. Unlike the students taught by Professors Bouma and McGinn, Hammond's students are pursuing a graduate professional degree. His task is to introduce these aspiring professionals to a critical area of law, on which they will later be tested in the state bar examination. Like other law professors, Hammond helps his students develop legal principles and theories by analyzing instances of legal reasoning and judgment in court decisions. This intense focus on learning the underlying doctrines and principles of American law is typical of American legal education.

Course Example: "Contracts"

Hammond's pedagogical task is far from simple, however. Like Robert McGinn's novice engineering students, Hammond's law students enter his classroom with many preconceived notions about how the law operates. Images of lawyers and the legal system are ubiquitous in our culture. Law students' understandings of what it means to work within their chosen profession are formed through their engagement with the narratives presented in film, television, literature, and other mass media. Hammond insists that these dramatic narratives and the lessons that they teach are highly partial in their presentation of the law.

> One of the predilections [first-year] students must overcome is the socially encouraged notion that application of the law leads to consistent results. On many media programs dealing with legal themes primary prohibitions against theft, misrepresentation and murder are enforced against all manner of wrong doers in a straight-forward

decisive manner. The interpretation and application of the law in these morality plays usually adheres to a strict sense of right and wrong. Rarely are the ambiguities and limitations of laws explored. (Hammond, 2006, p. 1)

As a result, incoming law students view legal thinking as a technical matter of knowing the rules and applying them logically to legal situations. These expectations are analogous to the kinds of analytical thinking that undergraduate students are taught in many areas of the arts and sciences. Hammond must distance his students from their "misguided sense of the certainty of the law's application" (Hammond, 2006, p. 1), in order to help them understand that issues of interpretation and, especially, confrontation with ambiguity and uncertainty are prominent and unavoidable in the practice of law. As Hammond observes, this is no small feat in the competitive environment of the law school, which reinforces students' misconceptions:

> Placement on journals, selection for highly valued summer jobs and research positions most often depend on student performance measured by the grades received. Beginning law students still possessed of the socially engendered perception of law and confronted with the high stakes realities of the first year become certain that if they can get the grades, they can reap the rewards high grades bring. (Hammond, 2006, p. 1)

Like Professors Bouma and McGinn, Hammond must lead his students beyond their initial concern for getting the facts or technical procedures right. His students' future professional conduct will hold serious implications for how people's lives are understood legally. Legal thinking must be flexible without becoming arbitrary—that is, both fair and consistent. Hammond hopes to help his students understand that living a life in the law means navigating a fundamental tension between the logical features of legal reasoning and the law's pressing need to extend its concerns to changing patterns of human interaction. These are matters of practical judgment.

In order to model and unpack this fundamental tension in the lives of his students, Hammond highlights how even the best attempts to apply legal precedents to new circumstances can lead to disagreements among skilled judges. Unanimity is not the rule in appellate decisions. Judging what a situation is a "case of" is a much more difficult process than beginning law students realize. In order to help his students understand what legal judgment is all about, Hammond stresses the importance of studying both majority and minority opinions, known as dissents. This strategy helps students come to terms with how legal doctrine evolves in response to new circumstances over time and does so within a broader tradition of legal argument and justification.

The case of *Kirksey* v. *Kirksey* is particularly effective for this purpose. Two concepts are at issue in the case. The first concept is *exchange of consideration*. Two parties entering into a contract must provide the other with some exchange of consideration, or payment, in order to seal the bargain. This is a basic tenet of contract law. It is part of the logical apparatus that courts use to determine whether or not something "counts" as a legal contract.

The second concept is *promissory estoppel*. Imagine that one party makes a promise to another. The second party then relies on that promise. The concept of promissory estoppel entails that a court is justified in preventing the first party from going back on its promise, to the disadvantage of the second party. This concept is concerned with equity between parties.

There was not always such a concept, however. How did it evolve, and what forms of legal judgment were involved? Enter *Kirksey* v. *Kirksey*, which led to later decisions that gradually developed the theory of promissory estoppel. This change in legal doctrine came about because of conflict between the majority and dissenting opinions. The majority sought to apply the doctrine of exchange of consideration strictly in a case where it seems, in retrospect, to produce manifestly unfair outcomes. The dissenting judge responded by attempting to stretch the doctrine in new ways, in order to achieve a more just result. Like other cases, *Kirksey* v. *Kirksey* is well suited to the task of helping students learn how to "brief a case" by presenting a terse outline of its salient legal aspects. But the case also enables Hammond to combine this basic legal training with a broader consideration of the ambiguities and complex judgments involved in the application of legal principle.

Hammond summarizes the facts of the case:

> Antillico, a widow, receives a letter from the brother of her deceased husband. In the letter, the brother-in-law offers to give her and her children a house and land to till as he has more land than he can use. All she need do is leave her current homestead and come see him. In response, she packs up the family, quits her homestead and moves the sixty miles to her brother-in-law's property. He does in fact provide her with a house and land, but after two years, evicts her and her children from his land. She sues him alleging breach of contract. (Hammond, 2006, p. 2)

How should a court respond to Antillico's claim? Hammond's students must face this question though discussion.

Kirksey v. *Kirksey* produces an important tension in the lives of Hammond's students. On the one hand, as the majority of the Alabama Supreme Court ruled, Antillico's situation does not count as a genuine contract, according to a strict logical understanding of doctrine. Antillico cannot claim a breach of contract, for there was no exchange of consideration. On the other hand, Hammond's students often find this result manifestly unfair. So did the dissenting justice on the court, who struggled to claim that the fact that Antillico changed her life on the basis of her brother-in-law's promise ought to count as sufficient consideration. Hammond's students often find this justice's dissent "more appealing from an emotional and an equitable standpoint" (Hammond, 2006, p. 3).

Hammond proposes to his students that comparing the majority and minority arguments about the decision reveals a deeper legal problem. At stake is a fundamental conflict between legal principle and social outcome or between legal consistency and equity. The majority of the Alabama Supreme Court insisted on a strict interpretation of principle because the court was concerned to maintain the reliability and consistency of legal doctrine as a guide for decision making. But, as the dissenting justice insists, the majority's decision also violates the court's proper concern for equity. His proposal that the court should interpret what counts as consideration in a more flexible way is a response to this concern, whatever its pitfalls.

Over time, Hammond recalls, and "several decades of court decisions later, after creative efforts to apply the theory of bargained for exchange of consideration to circumstances like those in *Kirksey,* promissory estoppel was recognized as a separate theory" (Hammond, 2006, p. 3).

This new theory was a major advance. The theory enabled the law to remain responsive to situations like the one faced by Antillico, in a way that was both consistent *and* equitable.

Value of the Course

Hammond's students make a major discovery by navigating this tension between consistency and equity for themselves through discussion. They discover the need to confront the difficult question, *What is this situation a case of?* before they can begin to approach certainty in their application of principles to cases. By arguing their way through the evolution of promissory estoppel, the students have come to recognize that judicial decisions are not only concerned with theoretical coherence. Courts must also weigh two divergent considerations: (1) consistency of application and (2) equity or justice of outcome. By navigating this fundamental tension, Hammond's beginning law students are brought face-to-face with both the extraordinary intellectual challenges and the practical responsibilities that define the legal profession. From this point on, Hammond hopes, his students will understand better the full seriousness and import of their time in law school, making acquisition of legal knowledge and skill a more demanding but also more significant activity than they had understood previously.

The Common Thread: Practical Reason

The three educators discussed here, although working independently of one another through different disciplinary perspectives, are engaged in a common project. Each has devised ways to introduce students into ever more complex forms of participation in the practices of thought, dialogue, and action that distinguish responsible practical judgment in whatever field the students are in. These educators' teaching practices encourage students to move back and forth between the realm of general theory typical of their fields and the demand to make their learning and intentions concrete in particular judgments and decisions. Moreover, their teaching methods provide students with new ways of thinking about their own efforts to make sense of the problems at hand. Their students are learning how to reflect on their learning and consider it proper direction for their lives. In the language of learning theory, they are becoming metacognitive—that is, aware of how they think and the standards that ought to govern their thinking. They are learning how to learn while developing intellectual abilities that are crucial to leading an informed and responsible life in today's world.

These courses represent to students what it means to be a particular kind of person whose action is founded on certain kinds of knowledge and skill, oriented by particular kinds of responsibility. Bouma, McGinn, and Hammond have each developed, within their particular disciplines, teaching practices that faithfully anticipate and model important features of their students' future practical lives. Students are asked to imaginatively enter into, explore, think about, and deliberate about ways of living as engineers, lawyers, family members, and citizens of contemporary society. They are asked to think and act as reflective, responsible persons.

Each of these courses dramatizes for students the practical limits of analytical or theoretical rationality alone for the demands of judgment.

In many of the domains that these teachers explore, analytical thinking is a crucial ingredient of reasoned action, particularly the understanding of scientific findings and procedures. However, as their students discover for themselves, such thinking proves an insufficient guide in the face of uncertain and complex situations that often involve competing human goods. These courses do not leave students to face their responsibilities with only their own intuitions as guides. Each course *models* a fuller understanding of practical reasoning and argumentation within a particular field and provides thereby a guided introduction to the responsibilities of a practice.

The emphasis on ethical thinking in Hessel Bouma's and Robert McGinn's courses allows both professors to introduce students to key ideas from several traditions of ethical reasoning. By proposing moral traditions as ways of orienting and guiding their thinking in context, they encourage their students to interrogate these traditions in light of the problem at hand, and vice versa. Because of their limited duration, these courses can provide only an introduction to this important intellectual activity. But it is very likely that, by encountering moral traditions as conceptual resources rather than systems abstracted from context, their students will be spurred toward fuller responsiveness to the subtleties of the situations they face.

All three courses make clear to students that good citizenship and good work require that technical considerations be brought into proper balance with a sense of the kind of person one desires to be and that doing this successfully depends on achieving a good understanding of the contexts of one's actions. The particularities of any individual situation play a decisive role in deliberation about the rightness of a judgment or action. This is why situations and cases play such a central role in these courses. This mode of reasoning has traditionally been called practical, as opposed to theoretical. Albert R. Jonsen and Stephen Toulmin describe practical reasoning as thinking in which an "argument" entails "a network of considerations, presented so as to resolve a practical quandary" (Jonsen and Toulmin, 1988, p. 34). Unlike theoretical reasoning or scientific problem solving, the "considerations" needed for practical reasoning include the technical and the theoretical but are not limited to them. This is especially clear in Allen Hammond's course, where his students encounter the tension between the requirement that like cases be treated alike or governed by consistent rules consistently employed and the imperative that the principles of the law promote equity.

This tradition of practical reasoning urges that there is much more at stake in the enterprise of higher education than what is usually understood by the term often used in education: *critical thinking*. This contrast will be a major theme in our explication of the concept of practical reason in Chapter Four. Teaching students how to analyze the presuppositions and consequences of multiple moral and technical traditions or stances is valuable and important work. Critical analysis clearly plays an important role in the formation of practical judgment, but it remains insufficient to approach problems of decision and action. Practical judgment and argument are oriented toward not only understanding the world but also toward *acting in the world in order to render it ever more meaningful and better organized*—indeed, *more understandable in practice*.

The courses we have examined here are concerned with providing students a guided introduction to the *performance* of practical judgment. By confronting particular cases or situations and interrogating them together, students are helped to re-embed their analytical skills and theoretical knowledge within a process of lived interaction with others. Bouma, McGinn, and Hammond have produced models of what we might call *pedagogies of engagement*.[3] These pedagogies derive their meaning and formative impact from the act of taking responsibility for one's judgment or action, through performance, in dialogue with and on behalf of others.

Integrating Against the Grain: Forming Faculty Identity and Purpose

Because they weave together theoretical and practical reasoning, these courses stand out in today's academy. They do not represent the typical experience of higher education. Everywhere in the contemporary world— not just in the United States—universities have become central institutions of high prestige, enrolling millions of students, employing hundreds of thousands of highly trained faculty, and being supported by vast budgets. Universities and the other institutions of higher education modeled after them have become the key sites for providing education and credentials that are now deemed essential for an ever-increasing number of careers.

What sort of education is this, and what kind of institution is the modern university? A variety of researchers have shown that universities do not provide training in a career-specific sense. Rather, universities teach respect for, and at least basic understanding of, a mode of thinking that has come to be identified with rationality and modern culture itself. This is analytical thought: the capacity to understand and manipulate symbolic discourses. These discourses are made up of symbols that translate particular objects or events into general concepts plus rules for combining and manipulating such symbols (see Collins, 1998; Reich, 1991; Schofer and Meyer, 2005).

American universities developed about a century ago, in part as a diffusion of the model of education and research pioneered in nineteenth-century Germany. The new university was above all committed to "science," which at the time meant an ideal of knowledge in which reason was identified with procedures for testing—and correcting—claims to truth. University education was about making American youth modern, that is, able to inhabit an emerging world of scientific thought that, even in 1900, was clearly the key to advancing technology and new forms of wealth. Before that time, higher education in the United States had meant "the college," which embodied an alternative ideal of education and knowledge, rooted in the humanistic culture of the Renaissance. In this older institution, higher education was thought of as shaping the self, especially civic, cultural, and (often) religious habits of mind and character suitable for a life of leadership in society.[4]

By contrast, the modern curriculum of the university continues to emphasize objective and quantitative measurement in the service of universal principles and truths. This has put a premium on formal knowledge, abstracted from context and narrative particularity. Such thinking is held to be a superior kind of knowledge, ultimately applicable to practice through formal techniques for deducing results according to general formulas. Over time, that model of knowledge has become an unquestioned canon, according to which intellectual disciplines are defined and criticized. This model has allowed the university to distinguish itself from more "primitive" claims to knowledge, like those derived from mere tradition or experience. Much of higher education is about induction into this culture of criticism and evidence, which is universal in its claims and understands itself as the cutting edge of humanity's forward progress. At its apogee, the university carries on research. Theoretical, or "pure," knowledge is generated through the application of analytical procedures, and the most prestigious faculty positions are understood to be focused particularly on this high-level activity.

Today's academy continues this conflicted heritage. Today's faculty inhabit a world divided between the ideals of the university and those of the college. But one stream of academic aspiration has never abandoned the ideals of the college. It continues to urge that higher education provide formative experiences that enable students to gain orientation in the world, acquire the intellectual skills necessary for engaging their world, and develop reflective and ethical commitments in response. This is the tradition that we believe needs strengthening and, indeed, recasting.

Our purpose in this book is to recover and rethink this tradition. Many American institutions of higher education continue to profess their intent to provide students with the intellectual ability and the moral understanding they need in order to contribute to the life of their times. Indeed, a casual perusal of the catalogues of many institutions of higher education, especially those identified with the liberal arts, reveals claims to cultivate the ability to do just this. For their part, professional schools are usually committed to more than inculcating up-to-date knowledge and technique. They talk as well about the task of preparing competent professionals for the responsibilities of practice.

And yet, the educational practices of today's universities and colleges typically focus overwhelmingly on teaching analytical or critical thinking—that is, mastering procedures for describing particular events and objects in terms of general concepts. The relation of this training to students' struggles for meaning and orientation in the world, let alone ethical judgment, is all too rarely given curricular attention or pedagogical emphasis. That is why the courses we have highlighted stand out. Bouma, McGinn, and Hammond go beyond the purely analytical to provide their students with experience and guidance in using such analytical tools to engage in deliberation about action. They teach the art of practical reasoning—the art of placing analytical concepts into a mutually illuminating relation with sources of meaning and responsibility in the world of practice. In this way, our partners provide a powerful and much-needed answer to the basic question, *What is higher education really for?*

In this larger perspective, the apparent rivalry between liberal and professional education in the academy is ill-conceived and unnecessary. Fortunately, today's academy is stirring with signs, as yet faint but clear, of a new interest in how we prepare students to respond to complex situations, both as professionals and as citizens. This new interest, like our three courses, spans the usual liberal-professional education divide. But surprisingly little sustained attention has been given to how to realize this potential in practice. Judging from the examples that we documented through The Carnegie Foundation's research seminar, Life of the Mind for Practice, we believe that models are emerging in a variety of disciplines and cross-disciplinary areas that can do justice to the demands of both general principles and situational understanding.

The core insight these models share is that significant education is formative. Formative learning shapes persons and lives as students enter into a practice and begin to acquire new capacities and understanding, sharing the larger cultural community shaped by that practice. This is perhaps most evident in education for the professions, but we insist that it is, or should be, true of the liberal arts and sciences as well. The courses and educators we highlight in this chapter and in the rest of the book provide exemplars of the recovery of the formative dimension of higher education. The teaching practices and careers of these educators have enriched the formative, college-like aims of higher education by judiciously drawing on the multiple worlds of knowledge developed in the contemporary university and its disciplines. Their dedication to drawing together and integrating the often disparate strands of learning in the modern academy models for their students an art of thinking and living well within an increasingly complex and interdependent world.

One purpose of this book is to provide a wider audience for such teaching. Part of this purpose is to propose a way of describing this work that can go beyond the idiosyncratic and the ad hoc and begin the development of a common language. We believe that the example set by our partners can reenergize the defining, formative mission of higher education in new and much-needed ways.

In Chapters One and Two, we meet six more of these partners.

ENDNOTES

1. David A. Garvin, who teaches case pedagogy at the Harvard Business School, provides an overview of the development and spread of case pedagogy in professional education, starting with its introduction at the Harvard Law School in the late nineteenth century (Garvin, 2003).

2. Lee S. Shulman, president of The Carnegie Foundation for the Advancement of Teaching, has emphasized this distinctive feature of education for practice, suggesting that it is a pedagogical strategy of value for the liberal arts as well (Shulman, 2004b, p. 20).

3. This term originates from the work of Russ Edgerton (1997) and has been discussed further by Lee S. Shulman (2004a).

4. A considerable secondary literature describes the great historical transition from the values of the college to the values of the research university (Kelsey, 1993; Kimball, 1986; Marsden, 1994; Readings, 1996; Reuben, 1996; Roberts and Turner, 2000; Sloan, 1980; Veysey, 1965).

PARTNERS IN THE FIELD: PART ONE

Elliot N. Dorff, Arthur S. Elstein, and Barbara S. Stengel

IN THIS CHAPTER AND THE ONE THAT FOLLOWS, we begin our discussion of *A New Agenda for Higher Education* with short narrative accounts of the teaching of six of our partners in the Life of the Mind for Practice seminar, each of whom is an expert teacher in her or his field. Each narrative focuses on a single course syllabus. Each teacher responds to institutional challenges and professional imperatives in order to provide educational experiences that faithfully anticipate the nature of the students' future lives. Each of these narratives, which are spread across the first two chapters of this book, offers a window into one teacher's reflective engagement with his or her own pedagogical responsibilities. The narratives reveal that the practice of teaching for practical judgment is a rigorous but rewarding calling, both intellectually and ethically.

Although each case is unique, these six exemplars are not disconnected from one another. The purpose of these first two chapters is to begin to discern both the uniqueness of each teacher's pedagogy *and* the substantive analogies and family resemblances that bind them. Though these exemplars come from multiple fields, they share in common purposes and respond to similar institutional predicaments. The commitment of these courses to teaching practical judgment runs against the grain of the dominant institutional values of the contemporary academy.

We hope that you will recognize something of yourself in these narratives. That is, we hope that you will discern analogies of situation and purpose between your own pedagogical challenges and those of the teachers represented here. The narratives offer exemplars with which you, the reader, also concerned for the fostering of responsible judgment in students' lives, may keep imaginative company in your own pedagogical efforts.

We also hope to provide a language for making sense of these exemplars for your own academic life. Through the exemplars, we hope to discern the beginnings of a shared discourse for envisioning a richer conception of faculty formation. For what and to whom will each teacher's students become responsible? How should each teacher respond pedagogically? To what extent do the institutional constraints of each teacher's department or discipline sustain or limit meaningful engagement with these responsibilities? These broader concerns, which we refine in later chapters, are responsive to the demands of responsible judgment. They also speak to the deepest aspirations of the professions and the liberal arts and sciences alike. The six courses discussed here reveal that, at its best, there is nothing more liberal than a professional education toward service to others, and, indeed, there is nothing more practical than a deep and abiding liberal arts sensibility.[1]

Educating Moral Guides and the Consequences of Theory

"Issues in Jewish Ethics"

Elliot N. Dorff, Professor and Rector, Ziegler School of Rabbinic Studies, American Jewish University (formerly the University of Judaism)

Rabbi Elliot N. Dorff is a longstanding advocate for the ethical life of Conservative Judaism and has been engaged continuously in studied reflection on the normative meaning of practices in the world. As he points out, the literal meaning of the word *rabbi* is "teacher" (Dorff, 2003c, p. 5). Rabbis provide considered arguments and models for reflection, through which the Jewish community might enrich its ethical orientation toward action in the world in ways that are both creative and responsive to historical tradition.

This professional role is expressed in multiple ways in Dorff's life. His publications, for instance, include a series of three books on Jewish ethics that attend to medical considerations, the personal ethics of intimate relationships, and social ethics (Dorff, 1998, 2002, 2003b). These books present Jewish analyses of important ethical issues and place these analyses in conversation with other traditions of ethical inquiry, both religious and secular.

Dorff's role as a rabbi also involves participation in public deliberation on matters of great importance for the Jewish community and for state and federal policy, such as the Ethics Committee of the Clinton Health Care Task Force in 1993 and the California Ethics Advisory Commission on Embryonic Stem Cell Research. These aspects of the rabbinical role demand not merely immersion in the practices and knowledge of Dorff's tradition of faith; they also demand substantial practices of dialogue, both spoken and written. This is challenging work. Teaching rabbinical students how to engage in this work is no less of a challenge.

———————— o ————————

How do future rabbis learn to engage in this interpretive practice, which is at once informed theoretically and oriented practically? Dorff's teaching in his course, "Issues in Jewish Ethics," is oriented toward this matter of professional formation. The course, which takes place within a professional department of rabbinical studies, provides students with a guided introduction to the responsible practice of reasoning on behalf of others as moral guides within the larger Jewish community.

Course Content

Dorff's course takes place relatively late in the rabbinical formation of his students, who are typically in their fourth or fifth year of study. They have devoted much of their previous studies, whether at the American Jewish University or in Israel, to Jewish traditions of textual interpretation and debate. These studies are incredibly demanding. Dorff observes that

> because so much time needs to be devoted to acquiring the skills to decipher and interpret classical texts (Hebrew, Aramaic, legal reasoning skills, etc.), the moral dimensions of life are not the controlling theme of the curriculum during the first three years . . . while I would hardly call moral issues the dominant theme of the curriculum, it is a recurring leitmotif. (Dorff, 2003c, p. 6)

"Issues in Jewish Ethics" brings these moral issues into sharp relief within the context of students' future roles as moral guides in the lives of others. Dorff's syllabus derives from the academic part of the rabbinical curriculum. As such, it maintains a strong orientation toward the engagement of theory. But the syllabus also proceeds in full recognition that contemporary moral situations emerge from a complex social world that is populated by actors and rationales that are both religious and secular in nature.

In order to remain responsive to the practical demands of students' future professional obligations, "Issues in Jewish Ethics" must bring theory into a mutually illuminating relation with social life and action.

Dorff sets out four goals at the beginning of the syllabus. His students should

1. Gain some knowledge of Jewish and general ethical theories.
2. Learn about the problems and methods of deriving moral guidance from the Jewish tradition.
3. Analyze some specific moral issues from the standpoint of the Jewish tradition.
4. Develop the skills to carry out a Jewish analysis of a moral issue on [their] own. (Dorff, 2003a, p. 1)

Dorff notes further that "Issues in Jewish Ethics" should contribute to the formation of students' powers to discern the salient moral dimensions of situations. Students should also develop an analytical appreciation of the way in which different religious and secular traditions offer unique perspectives and enable different, reasoned stances toward issues of moral importance, each with its own strengths and weaknesses.

In order to achieve these ends, Dorff must place the Jewish moral tradition into dialogue with the diverse perspectives that populate practical settings and dramatize the practice of moral reflection and judgment in his students' lives. The syllabus offers "sample ways in which a Jewish perspective can inform attitudes and behavior in a variety of important social and personal areas of ethics" (Dorff, 2003c, p. 5). In other words, the course assumes that analytical insight is engaged *on behalf of* the rabbi's professional responsibilities to others. Dorff reveals that

> rabbis are looked to for, among many other things, moral guidance; they are asked to articulate a thoughtful and wise response to such issues rooted in the Jewish tradition. This course attempts to give them exposure to some of the major issues in today's society in a way that not only teaches them about those issues but, more importantly, teaches them how to deal with any issues in the future from a Jewish perspective. (Dorff, 2003c, pp. 4–5)

Course Methods

How does the syllabus embody these responsibilities in practice? Dorff leads his students through intensive class discussions of assigned readings.

These readings are organized in the syllabus into three broad categories: (1) Matters of Life and Death, (2) Problems of Sex and Family Life, and (3) Issues in Social Ethics. These are the same three frameworks that organize Dorff's trio of publications on Jewish ethical interpretation. These frameworks focus attention on a particular sphere of life, whether at the level of policy or personal engagement, and the practical problems that each sphere poses for moral living. Dorff brings these matters of rabbinical judgment to life by drawing substantially from his own professional work on state, federal, and nongovernmental panels and commissions.

Dorff begins each discussion session by asking a student to state the problem or issue at stake in the day's assigned readings. A different student then summarizes the argument and position of the first reading toward the problem. Other students offer corrections or refinements. The students then inquire into the practical consequences of this position for living by imagining the meaning of the author's argument for concrete cases. These consequences provide a lens through which to identify the strengths and weaknesses of the author's argument, upon which it stands or falls.

Dorff maintains a similar rhythm in the discussion of subsequent assigned readings, but with a twist. As each new reading is introduced, Dorff encourages his students to imagine how the various authors would respond to one another's positions and claims. Each author serves as an insightful foil with respect to the others, through which Dorff's students illuminate the core concerns, strengths, and weaknesses of each position. Dorff also asks his students to categorize these positions analytically:

> Is this a consequentialist view? A deontological view? A moral character (virtue ethic) view? How is it like and unlike the view of the people who articulated the view in the first place? (Dorff, private communication, 2006)

What is going on here? Dorff's students are learning to recognize and navigate complex networks of argument that embody multiple traditions, both religious and secular. Each of these traditions offers important perspectives and insights toward moral problems of practical significance in the lives of persons. Because Dorff's students are committed to the growth of the Jewish tradition *in particular,* these discussions also illuminate the distinctiveness of Jewish tradition and help students discern the ways in which the Jewish tradition is called to respond to alternative perspectives. Moral theories and traditions are not bodies of premises from which to deduce certain conclusions. They are frameworks for orienting practical argument and action as expressions of care and concern, for which one must offer public justifications. Dorff notes:

> I deliberately chose a reader that juxtaposes opposing viewpoints on topics we consider so that students see clearly that smart and morally sensitive people often do take different sides on a given issue. This prepares them for the fact that although sometimes the good or right thing to do may be clear and the problem is to gain the motivation to make it happen or abstain from doing something, in many cases the good or right thing to do is open to question, and people voice varying opinions, each with its reasons that need to be considered and weighed against the justifications of the opposing views. (Dorff, 2006, p. 160)

Classroom discussions are intended to offer rehearsals in the practices of professional reflection and argument that ought to distinguish the students' final papers. These papers are modeled on the form of rabbinical rulings. Dorff observes that "students see first-hand first how I state, apply, and evaluate a theory and then how their classmates do the same thing until they themselves try their hand at these tasks" (Dorff, 2006, p. 160). By drafting a rabbinical ruling of their own, Dorff's students adopt and reckon with these models for their own action, in order to articulate a defensible position on some issue of moral concern to the Jewish community.

The final paper requires students to articulate a distinctively Jewish judgment on the nature of a contemporary moral problem. In doing so, Dorff's students must be mindful of the arguments and positions that others have offered historically. Their assignment directs them to

> choose any moral issue and provide a Jewish analysis of it. Specifically, explain why it is a problem in the first place; then bring to bear any Jewish (classical, medieval, and modern) and general writings that you think are relevant to understanding or resolving the issue, including at least two who would respond to the issue in different ways; and then describe how you would respond to the issue, together with what you see to be the strengths and weaknesses of your approach. (Dorff, 2003a, p. 1)

In this way, Dorff's students must locate, orient, and justify themselves within an ongoing historical tradition of engaged moral judgment.

Dorff assesses his students' final papers according to the thoroughness with which they consider all relevant aspects of an issue. Dorff also judges the extent to which students recognize the fundamental points on which their arguments turn and consider what would happen to their positions if these core premises were to crumble in the face of criticism from alternative perspectives. In other words, his students must judge the worth and responsiveness of their own arguments for a pluralistic world. The rhythm of inquiry that Dorff exemplifies through classroom discussion provides his students with a model for inquiry, or a "methodology," that will help them orient and justify themselves (Dorff, 2006, p. 160). "Issues in Jewish Ethics" positions responsible moral judgment at the intersection between keeping faith with a tradition and responding creatively to the demands of unique cases and situations.

---

       o

Dorff's syllabus is motivated by a keen sense of what rabbinical judgment is *for*. Rabbinical practical reasoning is always oriented toward the rabbi's responsibility to provide guidance in the lives of others. These others will make their own decisions and take their own risks, however. Dorff stresses that the Jewish tradition is committed to lifelong learning for everyone—" men, women, and children," as Deuteronomy 31:12 specifies. So, although guiding others is part of their role, especially in areas where people are unfamiliar with the terrain, as in life-and-death issues, rabbis' primary task is to teach the community how to use the Jewish tradition in their own moral reasoning. It is very much a *teaching* practice. Rabbinical reasoning can never be a matter of deduction from authoritative principle. The tradition of Jewish moral thought must become instantiated anew in particular lives. Rabbis enable others to come to terms with *what one ought to care about as a Jewish agent, and how*.

Dorff's scholarly and pedagogical life is unified through a common expression of professional responsibility, whether directly (through his publications, rabbinical conduct, and service on major public commissions) or pedagogically (through the formation of future rabbis). His goal is to model the practice of engaged judgment on behalf of others. This broad purpose demands that academic knowledge be placed in a mutually illuminating relationship with practices and problems that exist outside the academy's walls.

Case Teaching and the Engagement of Ethical Dilemmas in Medicine

"Ethics and Law"

Arthur S. Elstein, Professor Emeritus, Medical Education, University of Illinois at Chicago

Course designers: Timothy Murphy, Professor of Philosophy in the Biomedical Sciences, University of Illinois College of Medicine; Michelle Oberman, Professor of Law, Santa Clara University School of Law

"Ethics and Law" was team-taught by approximately fifteen instructors at the University of Illinois College of Medicine at Chicago, including seminar partner Arthur S. Elstein, in the early 1990s.

Course Procedures

In a typical episode from the course, second-year medical students were presented with the following situation:

> A university medical center wants to undertake an organ transplant program designed to "harvest" the organs of anencephalic babies so that they can be used as medically appropriate for other children around the country. Death is inevitable in this condition. The protocol entails obtaining parents' permission to place the newborn on life support for up to seven days to maintain the other organs while an appropriate recipient is located. The baby will be checked for brain function every 12 hours, and if none is present, would be declared brain dead and the organs could be donated. To preclude conflicts of interest, the physicians making the final diagnosis of death were unaffiliated with the transplant team. (Murphy and Oberman, 1993)

Should this practice proceed? Students must consider further the following:

> Parents of these children frequently request organ donation so that "some good may come of this tragedy." Yet this program generated considerable conflict in the medical community. It is difficult to diagnose brain death in infants, and traditional criteria of brain death are not readily applicable to anencephalic newborns because they lack higher brain functions. Some opponents fear that human life is cheapened by treating these newborns as "organ containers." Others fear that the policy risks exacerbating public fears about being declared dead "prematurely" and will inhibit willingness to donate organs. Still others see these newborns as severely disabled, not brain dead, and object to using a vulnerable class of persons in this way.
>
> Is the harvesting of organs of anencephalic newborns morally justifiable, if the parents consent? Why or why not? Is widespread social concern about this policy a sufficient reason to suspend the practice? Is this practice ethically problematic in any other way that should control whether or not it is implemented? (Murphy and Oberman, 1993)

These are difficult questions that promise no single answer. No amount of technical knowledge or diagnostic know-how can determine right conduct in this case. "Ethics and Law" was intended to cultivate medical students' nascent powers of professional reasoning in a way that was responsive to the *normative* dimensions of professional conduct. Toward this end, students engaged ethical dilemmas drawn from actual medical practice. The course, which was designed by two of Arthur Elstein's then-colleagues in the Department of Medical Education—Timothy Murphy (a philosopher) and Michelle Oberman (a lawyer)—aspired to form students' practices of ethical deliberation and justification.

As we saw in Elliot Dorff's course, "Issues in Jewish Ethics," normative argumentation occupies a central place in rabbinical practice and education. Dorff's course revealed a model of rabbinical reasoning that is responsive to the demands of the particular case while committed to the growth of a particular normative tradition. By contrast, the field of medical education struggles often to articulate a discourse and set of practices through which future doctors might learn to stake normative claims and justify their professional actions in response to particular situations. The story of "Ethics and Law" is as much a story about the medical profession's continuing struggle with the limitations of its own institutions and discourses as it is a story about the power of case teaching.

The second-year medical students in "Ethics and Law" were just beginning to be introduced to clinical practice, through both case-based seminars and supervised participation, after a year of analytical lecture in the biological sciences. They had not yet taken on the responsibilities or specialization of clerkships or residencies. Elstein notes that these students' professional formation over the next several years would be

> strongly practical, although it has substantial didactic components. Training is rooted in the problems of real patients, especially in the clinical clerkships and afterwards. Practical experience and clinical know-how are valued as much or more than "book knowledge." Yet there is a strong emphasis on the scientific basis of clinical practice which both supports and is sustained by an extensive biomedical research establishment and the intellectual interests of the faculty. (Elstein, 2003, p. 2)

Medical students are often seduced into thinking that ethical issues are only matters of private opinion, particularly as they pass through their first year of heavily scientific instruction.

Making Reasoned Judgments

In recent years, medical educators have realized that medical education must become broader in scope. It is not enough to diagnose and understand the causes of disease. Responsible practice also demands that professionals make reasoned ethical judgments. Like Hessel Bouma, Elstein notes that new medical technologies pose new ethical problems for physicians. "These new capabilities have created choices—and therefore dilemmas—especially at the beginning and end of life" (Elstein, 2003, p. 3). So too must doctors contend with the increasing economic rationalization of their practice. These problems exceed the physiological alone. Physicians must have access to a shared language and standards for forming and communicating difficult medical judgments.

Murphy and Oberman's "Ethics and Law" was one response to this educational problem. The course's team of instructors represented a wide array of medical, social-scientific, and humanistic perspectives. Through this enriched network of perspectives, the course focused on

> conflicts between parties in the medical narrative (between family and physicians, between one physician and another) or between two worthy moral principles (respect for persons and benefiting others). Although many medical and surgical treatments involve tradeoffs of some kind, the conflicts between competing goals or goods are rarely so explicit. The course exhibits both conflict between parties in a case and between principles, within a single actor. It thus aims to broaden the conception of what the practice of medicine is about by engaging students in cases where clinical practice entails much more than [that which] is the subject matter of the other parts of the curriculum. (Elstein, 2003, p. 5)

In order to illuminate the stakes of such conflicts, the course had to provide students with an understanding of the normative structure, or the core commitments, of responsible medical practice. Elstein describes four widely recognized ethical principles that most courses in medical ethics attempt to instill and bring to life and to which "Ethics and Law" subscribed:

1. [R]espect for *autonomy*, including "the right of a patient to decide upon a treatment, to assent to a treatment plan, or even refuse treatment"
2. [B]eneficence, or "the obligation of a physician to do good"
3. [N]on-*maleficence*, or "the principle that a physician, at a minimum, should 'do no harm'"
4. [F]airness *and equity*, or "the role of justice and equity in the distribution of medical resources" (Elstein, 2003, p. 3)

The drama of ethical medical practice is most heightened when these commitments conflict in practice, as in the case of infant organ transplantation described earlier. No deduction from these four ethical principles can guide right action with certainty in any particular case. The proper meaning of these core principles for medical conduct in unique situations *is precisely what is at issue.* Students must develop practices for discerning what is at stake in such situations and learn to appreciate a multiplicity of defensible ethical perspectives toward the same problem. By attending to dilemmas of practice and conflicts within the medical narrative, "Ethics and Law" short-circuited students' drive toward deductive reasoning. It attempted instead to convince students that practical judgment is central to responsible medical practice, not extraneous to it. There are better and worse ethical justifications for medical action. Ethical reasoning is not merely a matter of opinion.

Teaching Ethics Through Writing

Students in "Ethics and Law" came face-to-face with ethical dilemmas through engagement with cases. The students and instructors alike were already familiar with case pedagogy, as case teaching is well established within medical schools. "Ethics and Law" built on this tradition by broadening the scope of student engagement with cases. This expanded case pedagogy highlighted the physician's ethical responsibility for her conduct and revealed the intellectually demanding nature of ethical deliberation, particularly in cases where any course of action involves a substantive ethical trade-off. If a patient refuses treatment, for example, physicians must chart a course of action that is torn between their obligation to respect patient autonomy and their own obligation to "do good." Students were challenged to expand their conception of what is *salient* about their action. As Elstein observes, it was "the selection of cases that makes it a course in 'Ethics and Law'" (Elstein, 2003, p. 6).

What did this look like in practice? Like Elliot Dorff's "Issues in Jewish Ethics," "Ethics and Law" shifted student attention back and forth between the demands of particular situations and consideration of broader bioethical discourse and between small discussion groups and large lectures. The instructors hoped that this rhythm would prove "instructive and transformative" in the lives of students (Elstein, 2003, p. 4). Elstein recalls:

> The materials for each [ethical] topic consist of a weekly lecture to introduce the topic, readings, a case for discussion, the discussion section itself, and a writing assignment. The writing assignments present another case involving the same conflict or principle or dilemma. Each

assignment poses 2–4 specific questions that the student should tackle
in a short paper of no more than 3 double-spaced pages. (Elstein,
2003, p. 4)

One representative case from the syllabus presented students with a
situation in which the family of an elderly, incapacitated, and terminally
ill woman insists on futile treatment. The woman's doctors "advise limiting any further life-sustaining treatment. Her family insists that all forms
of treatment be continued" (Elstein, 2003, p. 7). How should students
proceed in this situation, and on what terms can their actions be justified?
Should they respect the family's wishes? Or should they, as the doctors in
the case do, advocate for a court order in their favor? This case operates
at several levels of ethical concern simultaneously:

> [A]t one level, the case is about a conflict between the health profes-
> sionals and the family about continuing or discontinuing treatment
> near the end of life. At another level, it is about the judgments
> involved in determining whether the patient's condition is indeed irre-
> versible, but the medical students are not expected to be able to make
> their own judgments about this. At still a third level, the case is about
> the allocation of scarce medical resources, since the money spent
> by the public (hospital, government) treating this patient is not avail-
> able for other patients. (Murphy and Oberman, 1993)

This case embodies two difficult conflicts between core ethical principles,
neither of which is resolved by the diagnostic judgment that the patient's
condition is, indeed, irreversible. The students' ethical obligation to "do
no harm" conflicts with the equally important obligation to respect the
autonomy of the patient or, in this case, the patient's legal surrogates.
Students were also faced with a problem of distributive justice regarding
fairness in the distribution of medical resources. Should these resources
be devoted to the sustenance of the terminally ill patient, or should they
be put to more consequential use elsewhere?

Classroom lecture and assigned readings on the topic of refusal of
treatment were followed by smaller discussion sections that engaged a
case like the one described here in detail. The instructor's pedagogical
attention in these discussion sections was oriented toward illuminating
the multiple, reasoned ethical positions that might be taken toward such
dilemmas. Student judgments were not based on private opinion. Students
learned to articulate their ethical judgments through a bioethical discourse
that was authorized by the broader medical community. The instructors
facilitated the students' growing participation in this practice.

The written exercise that followed presented students with a different case involving an analogous conflict. Through engagement with this new set of particulars, students conceivably found themselves making ethical judgments that were *different* from those they had made in the previous case. The written exercises and small group discussions also constituted a rare moment in the medical curriculum when students came to recognize that they might disagree substantively with their peers about an appropriate course of medical action. Multiple judgments can be recognized publicly as rational and defensible responses to unique situations, provided that they are grounded properly in a full bioethical accounting of a student's reasons for action. This was the point: ethical medical action must engage publicly authorized principles, but these ethical principles are only meaningful insofar as they come alive and are understood through the particular.

Challenging Assumptions

"Ethics and Law" cut against the grain of the dominant medical curriculum in several ways on its introduction, and it challenged incoming students' assumptions about what constitutes "real" medical education.[2] The course presented ethical reasoning as an intellectually demanding aspect of professional medical practice, contrary to students' frequent assumption that ethical deliberation is a matter of private opinion. The course enabled medical students to disagree substantively yet reasonably with the judgments of their peers. The syllabus also stood out because of its writing requirement. Writing is rarely required within medical courses, much less as a central medium for formative assessment and discovery.

Given that the professional culture of medicine places a high premium on expert specialization, the instructors of the course also had to combat the effects of their own particular forms of medical expertise. The goals of the course could not be realized if any instructor acquired inappropriate and counterproductive *ethical* authority in the discussion of an ethical dilemma that happened to involve pathologies or treatments about which that instructor was considered an authority in the world of scientific research. The instructors took care not to allow the richness of particular cases to be subsumed by any instructor's particular perspective, as if that instructor offered a privileged "recipe" for ethical action. Put another way, the teachers were at pains to ensure that the academic vocation of medical research, which fits so well with Max Weber's famous articulation of "value-free" science as the fundamental concern of the academic practitioner (Weber, 1977), did not trump the course's wider normative orientation toward reasoned professional action.

For this reason, the instructors always taught *outside* their own areas of specialization during the smaller discussion sections. Indeed, one virtue of the cases that populate "Ethics and Law" was that novice medical students could enter imaginatively into the human drama of professional practice *without* prior formation of the technical expertise that would be required for actual medical action. In Elstein's words: [T]he students are not expected to be technically competent in the problems examined in the cases; that is, they are not expected to be able to perform life-sustaining treatment or an organ transplant" (Elstein, 2003, p. 5).

The instructors of "Ethics and Law" were called to respond to the scientific orientation of medical research and institutional life in yet another way. Like all medical courses, Elstein recalls, "Ethics and Law" was expected to provide students with concrete and testable content knowledge. "Ethics and Law" responded to this imperative by relating widely accepted ethical principles of medical practice to the lived situations through which these principles might be instantiated anew. The course led students through a sustained inquiry into the intimate relation between learning what one ought to care about and participating in an ethical discourse through which one can deliberate publicly with others. As such, the course was an introduction to the demands and art of practical reasoning in action.

Standard bioethical discourse is often ill-equipped to face up to certain institutional and macro-ethical pathologies of the medical industry as a whole, however. Reflecting on the syllabus ten years later, Elstein notes that "Ethics and Law" reveals contemporary medical education's continuing difficulty in coming to grips with the changing social, economic, and political contexts of medical practice. He writes:

> Looking back on the course, I am struck by [the course's] focus on individual physician-family-patient encounters and its relative neglect of the social context of medical care, problems of access to care, ethical dilemmas in caring for the poor and medically uninsured, etc. For many physicians whom I know personally, the ethical problems of the health care system are better exemplified by cases of unequal access, cases that link socio-economic status to health care. (Elstein, 2003, p. 7)

In retrospect, "Ethics and Law" illuminates the need for medical educators to broaden their conception of how practical judgments are *positioned* within a wider array of constraining, macro-ethical relationships. As such, the course points toward a broader conception of faculty formation and responsibility than is the norm in medical education.

Discernment, Responsiveness, and Pedagogical Responsibility

"Foundations of Modern Education"

Barbara S. Stengel, Professor, Educational Foundations, Millersville University

Like medical education, the domain of professional teacher education is challenged to form students' practices for the critical interpretation of the contexts and institutions of their future action. Barbara Stengel's syllabus for the course, "Modern Educational Foundations," attempts to awaken institutional consciousness in the practical reasoning of future teachers. She encourages her students to reckon with how their future professional role is constrained by others and what possibilities might exist for meaningful action.

Stengel encourages us to imagine the predicament of "an eleventh grade English teacher in an under-funded urban school who must prepare her students for state reading and writing assessment tests set for the spring of the year."

> The curriculum says, "American Literature;" the principal says, "Improve test scores." She is unsettled. She feels as though she can't do both. What should she do? She could set aside one day a week for "test prep" and follow her regular curriculum the rest of the time. She could have students read one piece of American literature each week and develop from that a series of reading checks and writing prompts that will develop the skills the testing demands. She could tell the principal that she is working on skills and teach literature as usual. She could reconstruct her curriculum so that it integrates test skills with the regular American literature content. She could teach the first semester as she has in the past and start a full-time test prep program in January. She could collaborate with other English teachers to determine a common plan. She could ask the principal to provide coaching to improve her ability to work with her students on test skills. (Stengel, 2003b, p. 6)

This teacher is in a difficult position. The appropriate course of action is far from clear. There are no ready-made responses to her situation. Much depends on what the teacher values about teaching English and what activities she believes will serve the best interests of her students. She must also consider the institutional demands of her role as an employee of the school, as well as the government mandates that her school must observe politically. How should she manage these conflicting demands?

Stengel goes on:

> This array of actions, singly or in some combination, is open to her.
> There are certainly other possibilities as well. But it is important that
> she do *nothing*, that she make no response, until she has first asked
> herself what is going on here? This is the interpretive question. It is
> a question that expert teachers often ask and answer invisibly,
> leaving outsiders and novices with the mistaken impression that
> the question of what to do is the only critical one. (Stengel, 2003b,
> pp. 6–7)

The teacher must consider the ends that any particular course of action
will serve—many of which are not of her own making, much less a fair
expression of her own values. She must interpret her position within a
complex set of relationships and, through these constraints, determine
a course of action that expresses her own values as a teacher.

This is demanding work. Yet, as Stengel insists, this complicated practical reasoning, which expert teachers engage in constantly, is often
obscured from public view. It goes unrecognized and unappreciated.
Stengel's students in "Foundations of Modern Education" are unaware of
the full intellectual and moral demands of teaching when they enter her
course. She is challenged to make these aspects of how expert teachers
interpret practical situations explicit.

Teaching Through Practical Experience

"Foundations of Modern Education" is a sophomore-level course for
aspiring teachers. It is the only course discussed in this chapter that is
part of a larger unit of educational experiences that connects practice,
theory, and reflection explicitly. The course is one of three educational
experiences in the School of Education at Millersville University. Stengel's
students also take a course titled "Psychological Foundations of Teaching" and participate in an "urban field experience," or introductory
teaching practicum in an actual practice setting. Together, this set of
courses provides aspiring teachers with an opportunity to participate in
the life of the profession as novice practitioners and to reflect on the
salience of their experiences critically and deeply. Stengel notes that these
educational experiences are foundational because they teach students
how to *interpret* professional situations and form responses that are
mindful of the psychological, sociocultural, economic, and political contexts of action. Stengel writes:

These courses make use of theory, research, and contemporary report-
ing to enable students to "see" more clearly and completely the
macroscopic (social foundations) and microscopic (psychological
foundations) dimensions of teaching and learning in the schools in
which they do their practica. (Stengel, 2003b, p. 10)

Stengel's students enter her course with a wide array of culturally
ingrained, unexamined, and erroneous assumptions about the nature of
good teaching. Indeed, her students frequently have a problem "seeing"
past themselves. They have been in school for most of their lives and
believe they know what teaching is all about. For them, teaching is
"a matter of personality" (Stengel, 2003b, p. 1), not a career of practical
judgment in response to multiple layers of institutions, competing interests, and diverse stakeholders. The complicated moral and intellectual
work of teaching remains opaque to these would-be professionals. They
do not understand the real demands of the "educational system whose
rules and mores they have mastered" (Stengel, 2003b, p. 3).

The romantic convictions of Stengel's students are wildly at odds with
the example of the high school American Literature teacher detailed earlier, who must navigate a web of competing interests. In order to respond
to her situation fully, our hypothetical teacher must form judgments that
are mindful of such matters as the history of the school in which she
works and the needs of the diverse persons who act within it. She must
consider the politics and economics of the school, as well as the educational system of which it is a part. She must decide what counts from a
theoretical perspective as meaningful and just learning in her classroom
and within a democratic culture. The teacher's enthusiasm and care—her
personality—make a difference only insofar as they are engaged through
the multiple layers of concern that constitute her situation.

Stengel must unsettle her students' unexamined convictions about the
nature of teaching. She hopes to awaken them to an alternative vision of
responsible teaching that extends beyond the self. This vision values judgment in response to complex situations over the virtue of one's own intentions. It views responsibility

in terms of the ability to respond to such complex contexts in fitting
ways. On this view, responsibility is not about obedience to rules, nor
about blaming those who do not perform. Responsibility becomes a
form of inquiry, an effort to determine the right response in *this* pedagogical relation and situation. (Stengel, 2003b, pp. 4–5)

Stengel calls this "pedagogical responsibility" (see Stengel, 1999a, 1999b,
2000, 2001, 2003a).

Structuring Students' Thinking

Elliot Dorff's "Issues in Jewish Ethics" and Timothy Murphy and Michelle Oberman's "Ethics and Law" featured recurring rhythms of student activity that balanced academic knowledge with opportunities for forming judgments through dialogue with others. This rhythm was practiced over time, in response to multiple areas of professional concern. Stengel proceeds in similar fashion. Her syllabus is organized around a sequence of six themes that gradually enlarge her students' understanding of what is salient for professional action as teachers:

1. Perspective, power and responsibility in teaching and learning, education and schooling
2. Where did our schools come from? Historical perspectives on schooling
3. Equity and diversity: Socio-cultural and socio-economic perspectives on schooling
4. Power and education: Political perspectives on schooling
5. Is this how it ought to be? Philosophical perspectives on schooling
6. Perspectives, power and response-ability revisited (Stengel, 2005, p. 3)

The work associated with each theme is diverse. It includes classroom assignments, readings, discussion, and clinical experiences. These activities, in conjunction with students' teaching practica, *model* the layers and tensions of the teaching situations to which they will be expected to respond as professional teachers. These activities distance Stengel's students from their incoming assumptions about teaching as they begin to appreciate the complexity of their chosen profession. Her students are ushered toward a broader vision of professional responsibility as practical judgment and the expression of one's own pedagogical values through action in response to difficult situations.

How does this work in practice? The fifth theme of the course, which considers the politics of schooling, provides an example of the layered organization of student work. This portion of the syllabus is intended to enable students "to recognize political disputes, institutional structures, and power relations and to locate themselves in that landscape" (Stengel, 2003b, p. 16). Stengel's students explore political theories of power and education, as well as educational policy, legislation, and judicial decisions. They read political histories of the American educational system and inquire into how local school districts have responded to state and federal educational policy. Through an online forum, they reflect together on their practicum experiences, particularly their struggles to remain responsive to the needs of students while also managing the demands of school bureaucracy. They do all this and more.

These diverse educational experiences model the *layeredness*—institutional, political, historical, economic, sociocultural, and philosophical—of the actual teaching practices to which Stengel's students aspire. They exemplify the uncertainty and complexity of teaching situations and bring Stengel's classroom into an illuminating relationship with the ongoing clinical experiences of her students. Her students are challenged to understand that the work of teaching lies in interpreting and responding to the tensions of particular situations in a way that sustains one's own professional values—in other words, pedagogical responsibility. Stengel's goal is to "*structure* students' thinking without *determining* it" (Stengel, 2003b, p. 8)—that is, to reorient her students' conduct in a more responsible direction. Stengel writes:

> [T]he structure of the course *is* the lesson, the point of the journey . . . they *experience* the layeredness, the choice without control, the value conflicts, and the search for evidence. They are invited to pay attention and to name these experiences, thus making professional and personal sense of them. (Stengel, 2003b, p. 20)

The role of philosophical reflection in "Foundations of Modern Education" deserves special consideration. Although Stengel's students worry continuously about the values expressed through their action, explicit attention to the *philosophical* grounds of their work does not take place until the *end* of the course. Stengel and her students "don't usually turn in earnest to philosophical matters until the end of the semester when field experience is completed. My own sense is that the philosophical question requires more rather than less grounding in practice and more time to incubate than any of the others" (Stengel, 2003b, p. 17).

This is an important insight. Stengel's students form meaningful judgments about the normative significance of teaching only through growing participation in the unfolding drama of practice over time. They cannot be predetermined or derived deductively through theoretical reasoning alone.

Using Self-Assessments

Stengel's students explore the quality of their growth over time through two forms of guided self-assessment. First, they are required to write an essay that reflects critically on their own growth as prospective teachers.

This essay contributes only toward students' final grade in "Foundations of Modern Education." Second, the students compile a comprehensive student portfolio that documents their growth throughout the entire Foundations bloc of educational experiences. These portfolios gather and organize their course work and field work as a whole.

Taken together, these self-assessments provide Stengel's students with structured opportunities to learn how to tell a new story about their professional calling. The goal is for her students to tell a broader narrative of self that aspires to pedagogical responsibility rather than merely personality. In order to understand themselves as professionals, Stengel's students must understand their often conflicting roles as teachers, employees, and agents of state policy.

Stengel's teaching, like that of Dorff and Elstein, is closely related to the ideals that have traditionally motivated liberal arts education. Stengel's vision of the responsible teacher can also be understood as a vision of the liberally educated person, situated anew through particular professional commitments. Stengel writes:

> [A] teacher's ability to make sense of recognition, time, evidence, relation, habit, power, perspective, courage and context will determine the power of action in response. The liberal arts educate this as assuredly as my professional course does. (Stengel, 2003b, p. 22)

For Stengel, professional judgment is not only enriched by the perspectives of the liberal arts and sciences. It depends upon it.

———— o ————

In this chapter, we explored the teaching of three of our seminar partners. Across multiple fields, these teachers work to foster and guide their students' developing powers of practical reason and responsible judgment. As we have seen, their efforts share much in common.

Chapter Two presents the teaching of three more of our seminar partners. Their cases continue to uncover common ground and illuminate the analogous barriers that our partners face in their efforts. They also suggest further relationships between the pedagogies of the professions and those of the liberal arts and sciences.

ENDNOTES

1. This sentiment is derived from a set of four "dogmatic assertions" Lee S. Shulman posed during Session Three of the seminar, in December 2003. These assertions included: there is nothing more professional than

liberal education, properly construed; there is nothing more liberal than professional education, properly construed; there is only limited potential for practical learning without engagement in liberal learning; and there is only limited potential for liberal learning without engagement in practical learning.

2. "Ethics and Law" is no longer offered at University of Illinois at Chicago as a single course in the form described here. The ethical and legal concerns that motivated the course are now integrated into a longer sequence of case-based educational experiences. Thus one might argue that education in practices of ethical deliberation no longer runs as strongly against the grain of the university's dominant medical curriculum as it did previously.

PARTNERS IN THE FIELD: PART TWO

Gary Lee Downey, Daisy Hurst Floyd, and William C. Spohn

IN THE PREVIOUS CHAPTER, we explored three syllabi that endeavor, from particular professional perspectives, to enlarge students' vision and responsiveness toward the larger networks of institutions and traditions through which they will act in their future practice. Drawing from the fields of rabbinical education, medicine, and teacher education, the syllabi also modeled practices for the responsible engagement of indeterminate professional situations, in order to enable students to enter into growing participation in reflective modes of professional conduct that connect interpretation and action. In doing so, the courses worked to deepen, or thicken, the salience of these professional situations in their normative, political, sociocultural, and economic complexity.

This chapter provides short accounts of the teaching of three more of our seminar partners. These teachers work within the fields of engineering, law, and religious studies. Their syllabi explore further the connection between interpretation and action as it is expressed through concrete practical judgments. Their syllabi also begin to shed light on the nature and role of exemplars for the formation of professional and personal identity, as well as the centrality of analogical reasoning for the challenge of making sense of unique situations in ways that are creatively responsive to the demands of the situation and that demonstrate fidelity to substantive traditions of interpretation and conduct. Our partners seek to populate students' imaginations with diverse exemplars of reasoned action and help students locate themselves within this landscape. In doing so, their courses reveal still more hints as to the substantive relationships that ought, in principle, to bind the pedagogies of the professions and the pedagogies of the liberal arts and sciences in common cause and vocation where the formation of responsible student judgment is concerned.

The Encounter of Practical with Technical Reasoning

"Engineering Cultures"[1]

Gary Lee Downey, Professor, Science & Technology in Society, Virginia Polytechnic Institute

Juan C. Lucena, Associate Professor, Liberal Arts and International Studies, Colorado School of Mines

The first homework assignment that Gary Downey and Juan Lucena give on the syllabus for their course, "Engineering Cultures," encourages their undergraduate engineering students to ask some unorthodox questions about themselves.

> In 4–5 paragraphs, identify and describe the images that challenged you as you were considering and deciding to pursue a degree in engineering. Wander outside of yourself and identify the source(s) of those images. Then go back inside and figure out how they challenged you. How, for example, did these challenges combine or conflict with other challenges to shape your pathway? What images are challenging you now? . . . [F]ocus on images you carried around in your head—of engineers, yourself as an engineer, yourself at the time, your goals and ambitions, your fears, etc.—as well as the sources of those images—parents, friends, relatives, teachers, television, books, etc. (Downey, 2003, p. 4)

This is not a typical assignment for engineering students. It does not ask the students to deal with technical matters of analysis or design, nor does it offer a lengthy "problem set" that requires them to rehearse particular technical operations repeatedly.

Instead, Downey and Lucena ask their students to consider the place of engineering in their lives as a potential career and to locate themselves within a complex social world of meaningful relationships. Why is this exercise important? What is the connection between questions about identity and the professional competencies required of the practicing engineer? And how do Downey and Lucena establish the legitimacy of these questions in the lives of engineering students and within the larger engineering curriculum?

Course Methods

Seminar partner Gary Downey teaches "Engineering Cultures" as a general education course for engineering students. The course is situated between Virginia Tech's College of Engineering and its interdisciplinary program, Science and Technology Studies. Trained as both an engineer and an anthropologist, Downey occupies a unique position that enables him to approach the engineering profession as both an insider and an outsider. Like the syllabus of Barbara Stengel, as well as the course co-taught by Arthur Elstein, "Engineering Cultures" addresses an important disconnection between incoming students' assumptions about the nature of engineering practice and the contemporary conditions of actual engineering work with diverse coworkers, including both engineers and nonengineers. This disconnection is a consequence of the forms of technical analysis that dominate teaching in the majority of students' engineering courses, across the engineering specialties.

This method posits the engineer as an individualized decision maker of a particular sort. Downey writes:

> Learning engineering problem solving is precisely about making the bulk of one's identity invisible in work. The engineering method typically follows a strict sequence of steps. One common version labels these as Given, Find, Equations, Diagram, Solution. The student begins by pulling Given data in numerical form from a narrative description of the problem and then decides what to Find in order to solve it. This is known as "drawing a boundary" around a problem, always the essential first step. Then invoking established Equations and drawing an idealized visual Diagram of the various forces or other mechanisms theoretically at work in the problem, the student systematically calculates the Solution in mathematical terms . . . [Students] know to keep any feelings they have about the problem out of the process; these are irrelevant and can only get in the way of reliable judgment. (Downey, 2003, p. 6)

Students cannot become good engineers without technical competence of the kind to which this model aspires. But this model has limitations. It presents the professional engineer as a flexible decision maker who is fully responsive to the given demands of industry and employment. Matters of individual perspective are merely articles of "opinion." The model defines from the outset what counts as the real work of engineering.

Downey and Lucena argue that this model of professional action does not anticipate the challenges of contemporary engineering work within complex organizations faithfully. The "givenness" of actual practice is far from clear in any particular situation. Moreover, the practice of immediately drawing technical boundaries around engineering problems bears difficult implications for action in increasingly international and multicultural workplaces. Engagement with different perspectives for *defining what counts* as the problem at hand is an increasingly central aspect of contemporary global practice.

"Engineering Cultures" intervenes in the one-size-fits-all method of problem solving that dominates the bulk of the engineering curriculum, in order to focus students' attentions on the communicative problems associated with defining engineering problems in the first place. Downey and Lucena work toward "populating the classroom" with different perspectives toward engineering situations that are drawn from global practice (Downey, 2003, p. 16). This goal is analogous to the challenge that a literature or other liberal arts course might face in broadening students' perspectives on the social, cultural, and moral complexity of living. Downey and Lucena's course aspires to help students interpret the communicative conditions of their future professional practice in a more completely just way.

Downey and Lucena argue that the standard model of professional action that dominates engineering curricula divides the world between "us" and "them," between "right" and "wrong." Downey writes:

> The practical reasoning involved in the process of drawing a boundary requires the problem solver to "take control" of a problem with a particular problem definition, e.g., it is a "kinematics" problem, a "fluid mechanics" problem, etc. The problem solver thereby takes up residence entirely inside a given definition in order to carry out the mathematical steps to find the correct solution. What does this mean for someone who is working outside the boundary as one has drawn it? . . . [That] person has approached the problem wrongly and will surely solve it incorrectly. (Downey, 2003, pp. 6–7)

This standard practice, which plays a central role in the formation of future engineers, presumes a workplace that is homogenous. It neglects entirely the fact that engineers are challenged by engineering work in different ways. The differences they encounter are not matters of mere opinion. Engineering work means different things in different times and places, and may embody a variety of different human ends. Also, all engineers face the challenge to work effectively with nonengineers who hold a range of different perspectives. Engineers must learn to engage these different perspectives if they hope not only to respond fully to the demands of the global workplace but also to become leaders who listen to others and critically examine the larger contexts of their work.

Any pedagogical attempt to place history, culture, and the imagination of different perspectives at the center of engineering action faces a tremendous problem of legitimacy, however. Such teaching cuts entirely against the grain of typical practice within schools of engineering. Downey and Lucena must meet this challenge. How do they justify their teaching in the eyes of their students as important and worthwhile? From what resources already present in the engineering curriculum do they draw?

Downey and Lucena ensure that the course requirements for "Engineering Cultures" emulate those of more typical "knowledge courses," which emphasize the acquisition of conceptual knowledge over mere opinion. The course resembles students' other educational experiences. "Engineering Cultures" features regular quizzes on class material, as well as several exams that reward students for attending closely to class readings and discussions. Because "Engineering Cultures" is an elective, however, Downey and Lucena must also be mindful not to be *too* demanding, beyond the perceived "value the course occupies on one's transcript" (Downey, 2003, p. 12). So long as the course remains a general education elective, it can never fully occupy "insider" status in the institutional life of engineering education. It might be very important for the professional development of particular students, however.

Course Organization

The syllabus is organized as an engaging "travelogue" that addresses the historical formation of engineering practice in a number of countries, including the United States, Japan, Britain, France, and Germany. Each destination along the travelogue analyzes the place of engineering work in the evolution of a particular country and the challenges that engineers face in their practical lives. What counts as engineering in each country? What ideals do different engineers struggle to live up to?

> [The goal of the travelogue is] to help engineers learn to work with people who define problems differently than they do . . . . Students gradually become "global engineers" by coming to recognize and value that they live and work in a world of diverse perspectives. Minimally, participants gain concrete strategies for understanding the

cultural differences they will encounter on the job and for engaging in shared problem solving in the midst of those differences. When the course works best, it can help students figure out how and where to locate engineering problem solving in their lives while still holding onto their dreams. (Downey and Lucena, 2005, Course Overview)

Downey and Lucena's syllabus sets out a sequence of educational events that re-situate the student within a diverse world of practices for defining engineering problems. Each event is designed to help displace any problematic assumptions students may have about the nature of engineering work and allow thereby for the broadening of their perspectives toward their future practice. This series of events begins with the homework assignment featured at the outset of this summary. Here, Downey and Lucena ask their students to reflect on the images and relationships that gave shape to their respective paths into the engineering profession.

This assignment accomplishes two important ends. First, students are given an opportunity to begin recovering a broader narrative of self and to discern the place of engineering within that story. Second, the assignment encourages students to begin thinking about their engineering lives as a process of *responding* to dominant cultural images and relationships, rather than a sequence of individual decisions. The syllabus reminds students of the following:

> [W]e are introducing here the course's main method of analysis, which we use repeatedly as we travel around the world. It may take you some time to get the hang of it. We'll work with you. Remember, by "images that challenge you" we are not referring to the series of decisions you made in deciding to become an engineer, the difficult courses you took, etc. Instead, focus on images you carried around in your head—of engineers, yourself as an engineer, yourself at the time, your goals and ambitions, your fears, etc.—as well as the sources of those images—parents, friends, relatives, teachers, television, books, etc. (Downey, 2003, p. 4)

As the travelogue proceeds, students gradually attend further beyond the self. They begin to imagine an ever-wider world of diverse others, any of whom might one day be a colleague in the global workplace. In order for this growth to take place, the syllabus provides structured opportunities for students to recognize the existence and complexity of other engineering perspectives around the world, without becoming trapped by stereotyped portrayals of national identity. Downey and Lucena aspire to make clear that, just like the students themselves, engineers from other nations are people who struggle to respond and live up to the practices and ideals of their time and place.

One homework exercise asks students to do the following:

> On one sheet of paper, draw a stick figure representing an engineer trained in Japan. Above the figure, write at least five images that the engineer may confront. Next, draw one representing an engineer trained in the U.S. with at least five images typical of the U.S. experience above this figure.
>
> Now, imagine that the two engineers switch places (like you may if you decide to work in Japan). On another piece of paper and using your diagram as a guide, write two to three paragraphs from each person's perspective, regarding which of the new images would be the most difficult to face (especially given the set of images each have grown accustomed to), and why. Draw on readings, class discussions, and personal reflections. (Downey and Lucena, 2005, Homework[3])

Students draw from course readings and lectures on the place of engineering in Japanese history and culture in order to imagine the complexity of a Japanese engineer's perspective toward engineering work and the unique burdens and possibilities to which he or she must respond. Students must then imagine their own difficulty in managing these same burdens and possibilities. The goal is to flesh out engineering practice as both technical and empathetic in nature.

Later assignments develop this empathetic practice further. One way that Downey and Lucena achieve this is by asking their students to place themselves imaginatively in the position of engineers different from themselves through role-playing. For example, students might write a dialogue between themselves and engineers from several other nations. These dialogues focus on connections and differences between the challenges that each practitioner faces in his or her work. Downey and Lucena's students also contribute to an online discussion forum. They discuss contemporary problems of global engineering practice, such as the cultural problems that emerged when German automaker Daimler acquired American automaker Chrysler. Through these various practices of writing and dialogue, Downey and Lucena's students learn to engage the perspectives of others and the reasons for differences of understanding in a constructive way. Students develop "practical experience in occupying other perspectives" (Downey, 2003, p. 13). Downey and Lucena call this demand of contemporary practice *global competence* (Downey and others, 2006).

The travelogue then returns to the United States. Now Downey and Lucena help their students understand the diverse perspectives that make up engineering and industrial practice in the United States—and, indeed, populate their own classroom. American engineers chart their professional careers through different engineering specialties, industrial contexts, and cultural differences of race and gender. These differences matter. One homework assignment asks students to consider the following:

> In class we have discussed two recent reform movements in engineering education, one working to expand participation from women and underrepresented minorities and another working to change engineering curricula to make engineers more flexible. Based on your experiences as a student, how would you change the way that engineering is taught in the United States? In 1–2 double-spaced, typed pages, develop a proposal for your ideal engineering educational model. Use a memo format for your document (you may address your memo to college administration, faculty, other students, etc.) and try to make a persuasive argument. Explain what changes you are proposing and back up your suggestions with evidence. Convince the reader that your plan is a good one! Also identify at least one perspective that may not agree entirely with your proposal and briefly summarize the concerns that might be expressed about your proposal. (Downey, 2003, p. 14)

Downey explains the purposes of such assignments:

> [Assignments are to] reinforce the conceptual argument that [different perspectives] exist and are significant to engineers. Homework questions, such as the above assignment to formulate and justify a reform movement in engineering education, ask students to take action in ways that acknowledge and take account of the presence of different perspectives. (Downey, 2003, p. 16)

Such assignments bring closer to home the lesson that engineering is not about analysis alone. It is also about charting a worthwhile professional self.

Having led students through numerous practices for situating the self in relation to others, Downey and Lucena can finally raise the key question at the heart of the syllabus: How can global competence in the contemporary workplace be connected with technical competence? Downey and Lucena offer students a powerful concept for expanding their understanding of engineering method: Problem-Solving with People (Downey, 2003, p. 16). Problem-Solving with People looks like this:

1. *Before* attempting to define an engineering problem, "identify each perspective that's around you and involved in the decision you face." How are these perspectives located according to specialty, nationality, and so forth? In Downey and Lucena's words, What do these persons know, and what do they want? Downey and Lucena make a major intervention in engineering pedagogy by placing perspective-engagement *prior* to problem definition.

2. Second, as one moves to formal problem definition, ask, Whose definition is this? Whose interests and knowledge are served, and whose are marginalized? These questions link analytical flexibility with social engagement in a substantive way.

3. Third, "[m]ap what alternative problem definitions mean to different participants. More than likely you will best understand problem definitions that fit your perspective. But ask: does it fit other perspectives as well?" This task draws on students' growing practice in imagining and engaging perspectives on engineering work other than their own.

4. Finally, to "the extent you find that disagreement exists or that the achievement of fit is insufficient, begin asking yourself: How might I adapt my perspective to take account of the other perspectives out there?" (Downey and others, 2006, p. 115)

The concept of Problem-Solving with People provides students with a new model of responsible engineering practice that operates through persons and culture rather than technique alone. It is concerned with both technical solution and the good of self and other. This enriched method can only emerge at the *end* of the course, however. Students can only understand its salience for their future practice *after* they have "populated" the world with ways of valuing engineering work that are different from their own. Ideally, the concept makes a substantive contribution to students' growing professional identities.

At the end of "Engineering Cultures," the students write a self-assessment essay. They reflect on their own growth over the duration of the course and their various assignments. Like Barbara Stengel in the previous chapter, Downey and Lucena provide their students with an opportunity to begin telling a new, more integrated narrative of professional selfhood. Ideally, these narratives place new questions at the center of unfolding professional identities: Who am I? What do I want? What dominant cultural images and ideals do I struggle to live up to? And what about others? What do *they* want, and in what ways do *they* value engineering work?

Course Outcome

Are Downey and Lucena successful in making these questions legitimate in the lives of their students? "Engineering Cultures" challenges many of the dominant notions about the nature of engineering work that students bring to class. The students' self-assessment essays provide Downey and Lucena with a window into how successfully their teaching intervenes in these dominant understandings:

> Over the past few years, roughly 60% have reported the course to be an experience of major significance in their professional training. As many as 30% see themselves as profoundly transformed, viewing themselves as having a much deeper understanding of how to make engineering judgments in the working world. For another 30%, the course was well worth the effort, for it provided new insight into engineering problem solving and the world of engineering work. Of the remaining 40%, perhaps half are moderately positive, feeling they learned some things they can use down the road but don't see themselves or their work as significantly transformed. Perhaps 15% express concerns of the sort, "It was an awful lot of reading . . . and writing . . . , etc., etc." These students resist the challenge to incorporate new practices in their engineering work and appear to look forward to returning to the relative security of engineering courses. For the remaining 5%, Engineering Cultures was one of the worst experiences of their college lives, if not the worst, for it was either deeply threatening or, worse, thoroughly irrelevant. (Downey, 2003, p. 20)[2]

———— o ————

"Engineering Cultures" attempts to establish congruence between the cultural and communicative concerns of the liberal arts and the demands of engineering work by populating the classroom with diverse perspectives toward the meaning of professional practice. The course offers one approach to the increasingly high-profile question of how to imagine engineering education anew for the global workplace. Downey and Lucena's vision is far-reaching. Not only does it break disciplinary boundaries, but it challenges the academic privileging of the engineering sciences that is typical of engineering education, arguing that they provide one set of valuable tools among many. "Engineering Cultures" suggests new ways that the instructors of engineers might understand the value of their pedagogical work and the nature of engineering knowledge.

Fiduciary Responsibility and the Harmonizing of Professional Identities

"Advanced Legal Ethics: Finding Joy and Satisfaction in Legal Life"

Daisy Hurst Floyd, Dean, School of Law, Mercer University

As we have seen, professional schools are often concerned first and foremost with teaching their students analytical forms of thinking. But practical comportment and ethical formation are important aspects of professional practice as well. If the meaning of professional action is limited to the application of expert theory and knowledge, then how can future professionals learn to be fully responsive to the needs of their clients, which may not be met adequately by such a delimited vision? It can be difficult to get professional schools to take full responsibility for the professional identities they form, for good or bad, through their dominant forms of pedagogy. In the case of law schools, it can be especially difficult to bring the demands of the lawyer-client relationship to the forefront of student concern.

Daisy Hurst Floyd's syllabus, "Advanced Legal Ethics: Finding Joy and Satisfaction in Legal Life," asks second- and third-year law students to reflect on the following questions, over the course of two essay assignments:

> What qualities, apart from a solid work ethic and strong case-analysis skills, will you seek to cultivate in yourself that you think would make you a better lawyer? How do these qualities relate to your notion of profession and particular characteristics of the profession, either as it exists or as an ideal? At its best, what do you think being a lawyer can bring to your life?
>
> Think about the times in your life when you have felt or you feel the most yourself—when you feel the most authentic and alive. Do these times occur when you are in a particular place, doing a particular thing, or with a particular person or people? What do these times tell you about who you are and what is important to you? Do you ever experience this feeling when you are doing something related to the law or to being a law student? Do you think you can experience this feeling through being a lawyer? Why or why not? (Floyd, 2003, p. 4)

These essay assignments ask Floyd's law students to reflect on issues that are not typical of their educational experiences in law school. They encourage inquiry into the proper relationship between the personal and the professional, as well as the relationship between legal analysis and the wider communities through which actual legal practice takes place. The assignments provide Floyd's students an opportunity to imagine these relationships anew for their own lives through writing.

Response to Crisis

Floyd's syllabus responds to a growing public recognition that the legal profession is in the grip of a moral and existential crisis. Recent studies reveal an escalation of alcoholism and drug addiction among American lawyers. Why are so many lawyers so unhappy in their work? Why have their professional lives proven to be a burden rather than a source of personal fulfillment through good work? A growing number of articles and books are devoted to these difficult and pressing questions.[3] Floyd's course constitutes one pedagogical response to this crisis of meaning.

"Advanced Legal Ethics" proceeds from the argument that the contemporary pathologies of the legal profession have roots in the structure of American legal education and the adversarial culture of American legal practice. American law schools are incredibly competitive places. They place a high premium on winning and on acquiring status. Law schools emphasize "thinking like a lawyer" in the process—an ideal that usually means setting aside one's own personal values and normative commitments. Students learn how to engage in legal thinking, of course. It is essential. They cannot become lawyers otherwise. Only through a deep understanding of legal reasoning can lawyers discern the legal salience of the situations that their clients face and discern what counts as a legitimate argument on a client's behalf within legal institutions. But this is only one aspect of what is at stake in legal action. The wider normative and social dimensions of professional practice are pushed to the margins of the law school and are never reintegrated pedagogically into a more expansive vision of the nature of professional action.

As a result, Floyd's students are forced to set aside the commitments that brought many of them to the legal profession in the first place, such as a commitment to social justice. These commitments are rarely revisited. Drawing from her previous work as a scholar in the Carnegie Academy for the Scholarship of Teaching and Learning (Floyd, 2002), Floyd argues that the drive toward winning and status that law schools nurture produces in law students a deep fear of failure. It also produces an abiding sense that the persons that they have become over the course of their legal education cannot be reconciled with the commitments that gave meaning to their earlier lives. To borrow Gary Downey's observation about engineering education, learning to "think like a lawyer" in law school is "precisely about making the bulk of one's identity invisible in work" (Downey, 2003, p. 6).[4] Floyd observes that the law school's "emphasis on compartmentalization as the essence of lawyerly analysis can lead lawyers to compartmentalize their own lives in ways that quickly become unhealthy" (Floyd, 2003, p. 7).

Law schools offer neither trustworthy places for the revelation of these problems nor practical experience in reconciling professional technique with the human desire for meaning in life and work. Students are keenly aware that they cannot admit their fears and crises publicly within the adversarial context of the law school. Floyd contends that students leave law school believing that their crises of normative purpose are merely "personal" problems that signify that they aren't doing a good enough job. Having produced disjointed and incoherent professional identities over the course of several years, law schools rarely take responsibility for helping students learn to put back together what was been torn apart. Through "Advanced Legal Ethics," Floyd attempts to offer a place for such work.

Why is this important? It is important not only for the health and sustainability of legal careers. It is also important because lawyers who cannot navigate the complexity of their own lives from a legal perspective and who only learn to value winning do not make good counselors in the lives of clients. Lawyers must be fully responsive to the needs of their clients. Legal education often presents a severely delimited account of what Floyd calls the "fundamental fact of being a lawyer:" the lawyer-client relation and its responsibilities (Floyd, 2003, p. 2).

Floyd's "Advanced Legal Ethics" offers her second- and third-year law students a rare opportunity to reflect collaboratively on the process of legal education itself and its relation, good or bad, to the demands of actual practice. The course attempts to bring her students' broader identities back into the classroom so that they can overcome their mutual, competitive alienation from one another. Floyd writes:

> [T]he syllabus tracks the process of legal education, the effect of that process on the individual, and how that process relates to law practice (the purpose, individual and daily tasks, the attorney-client relationship, etc.) and to the legal profession (ideals, norms, structure, membership, regulation, etc.). (Floyd, 2003, p. 3)

[In this way, the syllabus asks] students to think about what it means to be a professional, in several senses: what are the characteristics of a professional that distinguish the work that he or she does from the work done by nonprofessionals? What does it mean to be a part of the community of legal professionals? How do the larger social community within which lawyers operate and the particular context of the American legal system inform the lawyer's work and identity? (Floyd, 2003, p. 2)

In order to meet these challenges, the syllabus must set out practices through which law students can engage more reflectively with their chosen profession, toward the interests and needs of clients. It must provide exemplary experiences that approach legal practice as the furthering of life purposes through judgment—the lawyer's *and* the client's. Floyd must help her students approach their professional lives in a way that is mindful of the fullness of both self and other—in Floyd's words, "the practice of law as a calling" (Floyd, 2003, p. 4). She must establish that these considerations are central to the calling and everyday practical reasoning of the responsible lawyer and constitute a legitimate concern for legal education.

The first problem that Floyd faces, however, is her students' competitive alienation from one another. Relations of trust must be built so that a community of future professionals might take shape in the classroom. The two essay assignments discussed earlier provide examples of how Floyd fashions the learned alienation of her students into a topic of classroom discussion and analysis. Floyd employs reflective writing in order to help her students understand legal practice anew as a primary locus for the living out of valued life purposes. Through readings and classroom discussion, Floyd's students recognize the common difficulties that they all face in holding on to the normative purposes that brought them to law school, as well as the common fear of failure that law school has reinforced. They recognize their own hopes and vulnerabilities in one another.

Floyd argues that this willingness to cope with vulnerability publicly through community is crucial for responsible legal practice. Clients come to lawyers primarily in times of personal and legal crisis. Responsible representation of a client entails recognizing the vulnerability and meaning of the client's situation in its fullness and advising the client in a way that best serves his or her needs. Thus the course's engagement of student vulnerability is not intended as a path for individual legal professionals to reclaim their private and selfish ends. Floyd hopes to enable her students to draw meaningful analogies between their own struggles and the vulnerable position of their future clients. This task is both empathetic and analytical. Her students must learn to engage the needs of particular clients. They must also come to grips with the complex interpretive work that is required for meeting those needs.

Design of a Law School

Law school curricula rarely place the fiduciary relationship between lawyer and client at the center of legal pedagogy, however. "Advanced Legal Ethics" encourages students to reflect this omission in their training directly. Floyd's students "collectively design an ideal law school," through writing and discussion:

> We will have the luxury of designing it without regard to budget or accreditation concerns because we will pretend, at least initially, that neither will be obstacles. Please write a short description of your conception of an ideal law school, including answers to the following:
>
> **Who:** Who should be admitted as students? Who should be hired as members of the faculty?
>
> **What:** What should be included in the curriculum, including how much time should be spent in law school (defined in terms of the calendar, or credit hours, or any other appropriate measure)? What teaching methods should be employed? What method of evaluating student performance should be used?
>
> **When:** At what point in a person's life should he or she be in law school, e.g., after certain educational or life experience requirements have been fulfilled?
>
> **Where:** Should our law school be free-standing or part of an educational institution that includes other disciplines; should it be public or private?
>
> **Why:** Be prepared to justify the choices you have made. (Floyd, 2003, pp. 4–5)

Practices such as this are rare in law school. The exercise requires Floyd's students to place the institution of the law school in relation to the outside community and the needs of persons. They must form defensible judgments about what would constitute a "good" or "ideal" law school that is more fully responsive to its wider constituencies. In order to form these judgments, Floyd's students must reflect critically on their own professional formation, identify its limitations, and propose institutional changes that would provide for a more thorough educational experience. In order to imagine an ideal institution, her students must reflect on *who they are becoming*, in light of *who they want or ought to be*. Floyd's students envision an educational institution that is worthy of the challenge of fostering legal practice as a life's calling.

"Advanced Legal Ethics" also helps Floyd's students consider the professional community into which they will enter. Reflection on the development of professional identity requires worthy examples of responsible practice, from which students might draw analogies to their own experience. Floyd provides her students with several opportunities to engage in discussion with practicing professionals—living exemplars.

The Lawyer-Client Relationship

One assignment asks students to conduct interviews with practicing lawyers. Floyd also takes her students on a brief retreat at the end of the course. Six practicing lawyers join them on the retreat, each of whom is sensitive to the challenges of sustaining a career as a calling. The retreat is a powerful pedagogical device and forum for student formation, providing for intense common focus on matters of shared concern.

During the retreat, the group engages in dialogue about the challenges they face in harmonizing their own senses of personhood with the performance of their legal roles. Floyd's students encounter living examples of what it means to live a life in the law. They are introduced to a wider community of professional practice whose ethos provides an alternative to the narrow focus on winning and status that dominates law school curricula. Like the syllabus of Downey and Lucena, the retreat "populates" students' understanding of the professional world with diverse and morally serious perspectives toward legal life. The examples set by their newfound colleagues provide Floyd's students with a powerful basis for reasoning analogically in response to their own particular predicaments.

All of the educational experiences set out by Floyd's syllabus share a common, orienting concern: the relationship between lawyer and client. This "fundamental fact of being a lawyer" orients discussions at the final retreat as surely as it informs students' efforts to imagine the structure of the law school anew (Floyd, 2003, p. 2). "Advanced Legal Ethics" cultivates a model of legal action that is analogous to the model of rabbinical action at the core of Elliott Dorff's syllabus, which we discussed in the previous chapter. The practical reasoning of the lawyer ought to provide a public model, or guide, for the practical reasoning of the client. Although legal analysis is central for understanding the key issues at stake in a client's case, as well as for navigating legal institutions on a client's behalf, legal reasoning requires more than analytical knowledge and technique. The lawyer must also cultivate the lawyer-client relationship with considerable reflective acumen, so that she can respond fully to each client's particular situation and offer counsel accordingly. Floyd writes:

> [In order] to help the client make good judgments, the lawyer must know who the client is; to accomplish that goal, the lawyer has to know who he/she is and what he/she brings to the lawyering tasks. The lawyer who is not reflective cannot form healthy relationships and connections; that failure prevents application of judgment to reach the desired end. Just as the lawyer should seek to answer the questions of who he/she is and what his/her place in the world is, the lawyer ought to help the client answer those questions in the context of the particular problem or need that brought the client to the lawyer: who is the client and what is his/her place in the world? (Floyd, 2003, pp. 2–3)

Only though imaginative social engagement with the needs of another can the lawyer serve as a responsible counselor, or guide, in the life and decisions of the client.

———————— o ————————

Indeed, "Advanced Legal Ethics" advances the striking argument that analytical legal competence contributes to the nurturing of a lawyer's normative commitments and a meaningful career *only* through this kind of social engagement. Like many of the teachers profiled so far, Floyd works hard to illuminate the disconnection between the demands of professional practice and the limited conceptions of professional life that often dominate student formation in professional schools. And, like Gary Downey and Juan Lucena's "Engineering Cultures," Floyd's course helps students chart a more proper relationship between technical and social competence in the life of the practicing professional and the importance of this relationship for students' growing narratives of professional selfhood.

Floyd's "Advanced Legal Ethics" is a powerful example of how the analytical knowledge and fiduciary responsibilities that distinguish the legal profession might be integrated with the concerns for meaning, personhood, and context that distinguish pedagogy in the liberal arts. The syllabus envisions legal practice as a collaborative process of discerning public value in the lives of lawyers and clients alike, through analytical practices and social relationships for which the professional is responsible. As such, the course presents a powerful alternative vision of what legal education is all about.

Reflective Practices of Moral Discernment and Selfhood

"Scripture and the Moral Life"

William C. Spohn, Professor, Religious Studies, Santa Clara University

The courses that we have discussed so far in Chapters One and Two have all explored the nature of pedagogies for practical reasoning and responsible judgment in the various professions. These courses illuminate the challenge of sustaining broader forms of faculty vocation in an academy where such teaching is practiced frequently only at the margins of disciplinary life. Through these examples, we have begun to see how the professions might draw from the pedagogical perspectives and strengths of the liberal arts and sciences in order to contribute more fully to the formation of their students' interpretive capacities as future professionals.

But we also suggested in the Introduction that this need is reciprocal. The liberal arts and sciences also stand in need of the pedagogical insights of the professions if they are to sustain their own traditional and constructive end of person formation in a difficult and fragmentary contemporary world. We now return to this reciprocal relation.

Teaching Through Biblical Narratives

Just as we began Chapter One with questions of religious formation through the example of Elliot Dorff's teaching of future rabbis at the University of Judaism, we now conclude Chapter Two with the teaching of William C. Spohn in the religious studies department at Santa Clara University. This return to religious formation is no mistake. As we noted in our discussion of the teaching of biology professor Hessel Bouma in the Introduction, traditions of religious practice and action in the world offer one source through which faculty might revise constructively the theory-centered conception of academic vocation and the generic conception of "critical thinking" that dominate educational discourse in the liberal arts and sciences. Spohn's teaching in his course, "Scripture and the Moral Life," cuts against the grain of typical academic aspiration, pointing in constructive new directions that have much in common with the pedagogies of the professions.

One key pedagogical moment from "Scripture and the Moral Life" features student engagement with the gospel of Mark, which details particular episodes in the life of Jesus and the quality of Jesus' interactions with others. In conjunction with these readings, Spohn introduces the concept of solidarity, drawn from liberation theology. This concept suggests that participation in the improvement of the situation of the poor and the marginal constitutes a central practice in the moral life of Jesus. By analogy, such solidarity ought to structure the perception and dispositions of Christians who endeavor to lead a life that is responsive to Jesus' example. By situating students' engagements with these biblical narratives through class discussions of contemporary moral issues, the syllabus poses a formative challenge in students' lives. The course suggests the possibility that, in Spohn's words, solidarity constitutes "a central practice that ought to ground practical reasonableness for those who follow Christ" (Spohn, 2003b, p. 7).

This is the crux of Spohn's pedagogy. "Scripture and the Moral Life" is premised on the conviction that serious spiritual engagement with biblical texts provides constructive shape to the formation of students' moral discernment and character. This is not achieved pedagogically through mimicry of biblical examples. The goal is to provide normative and affective shape to the terrain—that is, the *practices*—on which practical reasoning ought to be engaged from a Christian perspective, through the formation of students' powers of *analogical imagination*.

Spohn's course is different from the other courses discussed in Chapters One and Two in important ways. "Scripture and the Moral Life" is an undergraduate course that takes place in Santa Clara University's Religious Studies Department—a humanities department rather than a formal professional school of theology. As such, the course does not attend directly to the particular matters of fiduciary responsibility that distinguish one profession from another. The course is not oriented toward the development of particular professional practices, as such.

Elliot Dorff's professional syllabus, "Issues in Jewish Ethics," provides a useful point of reference in this regard. Although Dorff and Spohn are both concerned with the teaching of religious practices, their courses are necessarily quite different in orientation. Spohn's syllabus is devoted to the formation of student character and the social relationships and causes that grant that character its shape and purposes. Dorff's syllabus is no stranger to these concerns but must be directed more particularly toward the training of professional rabbis who are charged with helping others engage in the kind of moral discernment that is dramatized so powerfully by Spohn's syllabus.

And yet, the syllabi of Spohn and Dorff share a fundamental orientation toward the formation of practical reasonableness, as it is related to the normative commitments that provide shape to the self. "Scripture and the Moral Life" provides a useful frame for considering the connection between the professions and the liberal arts and sciences, where education that aspires toward the formation of responsible practices and discerning judgment is concerned. Indeed, practice and discernment, as well as the relationships and causes that give meaning to one's identity and invest practices with their human importance and dignity, are precisely the central concerns of Spohn's syllabus. Spohn observes that

> the underlying argument of the syllabus addresses an aspect of practical reasoning that is often overlooked when the discussion is confined to decision making in regard to specific moral dilemmas. Practical reasoning intends action, but it also comes out of practice. Regular practices hone specific moral habits and dispositions so that the agent's character takes on a more definite shape. Those habits of the heart equip or hinder the agent from recognizing salient moral issues in experience, framing them adequately, and responding appropriately. In this way habitual emotions play a significant cognitive role in practical reasonableness, whether for good or ill. (Spohn, 2003b, p. 1)

The end of Spohn's pedagogy is not detached critical thinking, though critical practices are necessarily fostered. The end of pedagogy is the integration of students into growing participation in traditions of practice that extend beyond the self.

All undergraduates at Santa Clara University are required to take three courses in religious studies. The third of these should provide a "capstone" or "applications" experience, stimulating "critical engagement of current, open-ended issues in religion." This is in keeping with the university's Jesuit mission, which is oriented toward spiritual practice in the world, with and on behalf of others. Spohn's "Scripture and the Moral Life" fulfills this culminating purpose. As such, the course is charged by the department

> with modeling on-going intellectual engagement with difficult questions and issues involving religion. In terms of cognitive development, this course should be organized around problems, issues, or controversies that require students to explore and assess multiple positions and then make intellectually defensible, integrative, and nuanced decisions. (Spohn, 2003a, p. 1)

Students must learn to respond creatively to problems and discern morally salient aspects of situations by reasoning from religious traditions and texts. "Scripture and the Moral Life" attends to the formation of such reasoning by shaping the spiritual practices of reading and meditation that ought to *ground* moral discernment. The reading of biblical writings and the consideration of contemporary moral issues are embedded with one another in a relation that is mutually illuminating.

How ought biblical texts be engaged toward these ends? Spohn approaches biblical texts from a literary or imaginative perspective:

> [They are] literary forms that appeal to the imagination and through the imagination can have an impact on readers' characters. For some students this literature is also revelatory of transcendent realities, but I operate on the conviction that any religious effect the biblical texts have on the reader follows the same path through the imagination and dispositions as literature does. (Spohn, 2003b, p. 3)

Drawing from the work of Wayne C. Booth (1988) and Martha Nussbaum (1995, 1997), Spohn views biblical texts as opportunities for students to engage worlds and worldviews different from their own. Students learn to place themselves in an imaginative relation to these worlds, through analogy, in order to understand their own moral experiences and actions more deeply. Over time and through regular meditative engagement, biblical images and core episodes give shape to the reader's perception of morally salient characteristics of experience and the reader's disposition to respond emotionally and act virtuously. The syllabus for "Scripture and the Moral Life" is intended to provide students with a structured entry into this kind of sustained engagement.

This approach to the reading of biblical texts presents Spohn with particular pedagogical challenges. Spohn must consider his students' preparedness to engage in the substantive reading and meditation to which his syllabus aspires. Professional courses for the preparation of clergy, such as that taught by Elliot Dorff, can often rely on incoming students' previous experience with religious texts and spiritual practices. Spohn cannot make this assumption in "Scripture and the Moral Life." Although his undergraduate students may have read biblical texts previously, they have not necessarily read them with sustained meditative engagement in mind. Furthermore, because Santa Clara University requires all undergraduates to take three courses in religious studies, Spohn's students need not be religious studies majors. In order for "Scripture and the Moral Life" to contribute to the substantive formation of students' moral stances toward the world, Spohn must work to introduce his students to spiritual practices of meditation and reading. Only through growing participation in such practices can the desired transformation of affect can take place.

Reading in Poetic, Narrative, and Discursive Genres

The first page of the syllabus for "Scripture and the Moral Life" informs students of this:

> Scripture calls for a special way of reading because it is claimed to be divine revelation. For believers, it is not simply a historical text or a source of moral guidance, but a text that is read for meaning, that is, for truth we can live by. This kind of reading requires us to engage imagination, memory, emotions and personal reflection. (Spohn, 2003a, p. 1)

Spohn prescribes several parameters for his students' spiritual practices of reading, in order to give these practices initial form and lay a foundation for this special kind of reading. These parameters are to be observed, regardless of whether a student understands scripture as literature or revelation. His students must devote ten minutes a day throughout the course to meditation on assigned texts. They must keep a daily journal that chronicles their experiences of this meditative practice over time, which is submitted for ongoing feedback and support every two weeks. Each student must also discuss his or her meditative practice with Spohn individually. These prescriptions provide a structured entry into the spiritual practice of reading, while the feedback that Spohn gives in response to his students' journal entries provides an ongoing, formative assessment of their progress. These assessments are augmented further by the class participation, where students must respond to their peers, as well as several examinations.

Spohn's syllabus proceeds through close attention to three literary genres of biblical text, considered in succession: the poetic (for example, the psalms), the narrative, and the discursive, or symbolic. Each genre challenges students' understandings of biblical writing in unique ways. Each pushes them to consider anew the full range of possible relationships that one might take toward experience of the divine. Moreover, each genre exemplifies particular forms for the patterning of moral perception and disposition. Through careful attention to the structure of these genres and their formative effects on character through meditating and reading, "Scripture and the Moral Life" offers not only a wealth of worthy biblical exemplars but *models* the development of spiritual practice.

The syllabus begins with the poetic genre, as exemplified by the psalms. The strong images and emotional content of the psalms provides an accessible entry point for Spohn's students into their respective practices of meditation. But this content also poses unique challenges. Spohn notes that the psalms "exhibit a freedom of speech that students are unaccustomed to in formal religious language" (Spohn, 2003b, p. 5). This expressive range is precisely the condition through which the psalms achieve their formative and pedagogical power.

The psalms offer a structure through which students are enabled to participate in the emotional struggle and resolution of each poem. Each poem's emotional content is reconfigured over time through a succession of images. Spohn explains:

> [T]he psalms move associatively through a series of images that shape and evoke certain emotions. Often the parallel structure of the verses correlates image and emotion, as in the familiar opening verse of Psalm 23, "The Lord is my shepherd, there is nothing I shall want." Usually there is a progression of images that reconfigures the initial emotion toward some sort of resolution: so the fear of abandonment articulated in "though I walk through the valley of darkness" is worked towards some sense that God remains faithful, as in the next words of the psalm, "I will fear no evil for your rod and your staff will comfort me." The final verses' scene of a banquet in the sight of one's foes caps off the sense of trust with vindication. (Spohn, 2003b, p. 5)

Through participation in this reshaping of meaning, with the guidance of classroom discussion of contemporary issues and Spohn's periodic feedback, students' own analogous experiences are illuminated anew through engagement with the psalms, and vice versa.

Spohn's syllabus proceeds next with the narrative genre. The paradigmatic narratives that populate this portion of the syllabus include the stories of exodus and exile in the Hebrew scriptures and the gospels of the New Testament. As with any other narrative, these biblical stories depict protagonists who must make difficult judgments under uncertain conditions and cope with the consequences of their actions. Narratives encourage us to imagine what sort of normative moral or analogy should be drawn between the story and our own practical experiences in the world. These analogies enable the reader to recognize new, morally salient aspects of experience. They provide positive or negative benchmarks toward the reader's formation of virtuous responses to new situations.

In the case of the gospels, particularly the gospel of Mark, students consider the moral examples of Jesus and those with whom he interacts.

As we have already observed, Spohn introduces the liberation theology concept of solidarity at this point in the course. Spohn notes that some students "find this claim that solidarity with the poor is essential to being a Christian quite challenging" (Spohn, 2003b, p. 7).

The pedagogical purpose of this challenge is not to foster mimicry of Jesus' particular actions as if they were prescriptions for living in the present. The virtue of solidarity is not a moral recipe, nor is it a rule to be "applied" to unruly situations. Spohn's syllabus is intended to suggest that solidarity is "a central practice that ought to ground practical reasonableness for those who follow Christ" (Spohn, 2003b, p. 7). The practice of solidarity ought to give particular shape to the moral perception, concerns, and dispositions of the social actor, thus placing the individual student's conception of her own identity in a particular kind of caring relation with the communities and contexts through which she undertakes and undergoes her life.

"Scripture and the Moral Life" then makes a significant turn away from the poetic and the narrative and toward the genre of the discursive and symbolic. Pauline discourse and the parables of the gospel of Luke, such as the Good Samaritan and the Prodigal Son, introduce the practice of normative argumentation to the formative journey of Spohn's students. Some moral stands may indeed be better and more justifiable than others. His students must now wrestle with the proper consequences of core biblical concepts and metaphors for the examination of their own lives. Spohn notes that this argumentative turn poses another significant challenge for his students because "normative considerations are usually absent from the popular understanding of spirituality today" (Spohn, 2003b, p. 8).

This turn is also significant for its timing. Student participation in normative discourse takes place only *after* students have engaged in poetic and narrative practices of reading for spiritual meaning. This sequential organization of the syllabus is tremendously important. It is also precisely the reverse of most academic discourse, which places theory before practice.

Using Moral Imagination

"Scripture and the Moral Life" is not in the business of applying norms to experience in a rationalistic fashion. The syllabus is concerned with the growth of students' capacities to *imagine responsible action and judgment* and their *emergence* from lived practices. This growth is quasi-narrative in form: one's judgment of the normative significance, or moral, of a practice emerges only through growing participation and struggle in the unfolding of that practice over time. Normative argument is grounded on students' growing practices for entering imaginatively into perspectives other than their own, as well as for drawing meaningful analogies between exemplary scriptural episodes and real-life moral situations that require student judgment. Indeed, this latter portion of the course offers biblical arguments regarding the centrality of analogical reasoning by drawing attention to Jesus' mandate at the end of the parable of the Good Samaritan "to act analogously to God's gracious action, to use the imagination to 'do likewise'" (Spohn, 2003b, p. 7).

This quasi-narrative form was also paramount for Barbara Stengel's "Foundations of Modern Education." Stengel introduced explicit philosophical reflection on the normative grounds of teaching only *after* students had been provided with opportunities to engage in novice reflective practice in all its historical, economic, political, and sociocultural complexity. Gary Downey and Juan Lucena's "Engineering Cultures" provides another analogue. Their course introduces a new normative heuristic for the responsible practice of defining engineering problems in social contexts—Problem-Solving with People—only *after* students have developed a fuller imaginative understanding of the diverse engineering perspectives and communicative practices that populate the world.

Each of these courses, whether they hail from the professions or the liberal arts and sciences, shares something very important in common. Each insists that theory, which is absolutely necessary for making sense of the world in both critical and constructive ways, emerges properly *through* the consideration of practice, rather than the other way around. As such, each course poses a common challenge to the contemporary academic vocation, whether in its professional, humanistic, or scientific forms. These courses exemplify a broader notion of faculty formation that is responsive to the challenge of educating students for responsible action in the world.

The fundamental purpose of "Scripture and the Moral Life" is the formation of students' habits of perception, moral disposition, and self-understanding as moral agents in the world. This formation occurs through the development of relationships between Spohn's students and the exemplars or episodes that populate biblical texts. These texts offer "dress rehearsals" for living and an opportunity to explore particular emotions, roles, and values, along with their consequences. Paraphrasing Booth (1988), Spohn observes that his course "intends to populate the students' moral imaginations with exemplars by inviting them to 'keep company' with different models and ideals than those that bombard them in popular culture" (Spohn, 2003b, p. 3). By placing students into a suggestive and complicated relation with biblical exemplars, "Scripture and the Moral Life" also places them into further relation, through analogy, with the community contexts through which they live their lives.

Spohn's goal of populating the moral imagination provides a powerful, more general liberal arts framework for considering the pedagogical work that distinguishes the professional syllabi discussed in Chapters One and Two. This practice is analogous to Daisy Hurst Floyd's attempt to establish student relationships with living exemplars of legal actors who navigate their chosen profession as a vocation. Spohn's pedagogy can also be understood as a more generalized formulation of Gary Downey and Juan Lucena's imperative to populate the classroom with diverse perspectives toward the definition of engineering problems, in order to enhance students' responsiveness to the communicative conditions of good engineering work. Downey and Lucena's goal is to broaden students' recognition of the conditions of their future professional practice, in much the same way that a liberal arts course in literature or religious scripture might endeavor to broaden students' perspectives of the social, cultural, and moral complexity of living. Other analogues can be traced through the syllabi of Barbara Stengel, Ellott Dorff, and Arthur Elstein, particularly insofar as these courses are concerned with the formation of students' practices of perception and discernment.

Spohn's pedagogy shows how literary and other texts might be oriented toward the traditional liberal arts concern for the formation of persons for lives of reflective moral and civic engagement. His teaching is oriented toward the fundamental humanistic recognition that the self cannot develop apart from its formative relationships and commitments:

> This fundamental sense of self is not arrived at by introspection or self-consciousness but by the central relationships that the self has and the causes for which the self lives. (Spohn, 2003b, p. 8)

This compelling conception of the purposes of pedagogy and the faculty vocation is expressed not only through Spohn's teaching but also through his writings (Spohn, 1999) and administrative work as director of Santa Clara University's Bannan Center for Jesuit Education. It is also the perspective of a teacher whose identity is grounded in both the intellectual life of the academy and the lived practice of faith (Spohn, 2001).

Spohn pursues this vision of the purposes of liberal education in a way that places him in common pedagogical cause with professional education at its best. The foundation on which responsible engagement and selfhood are fashioned is not theory or critical thinking in the abstract, to be expertly applied to difficult situations. Responsible engagement and selfhood are founded through appreciative participation in the objective life and growth of practices and traditions of conduct and argument in the world. Indeed, as Spohn notes, proceeding from practices is "the most practically reasonable thing" a teacher can do (Spohn, 2003b, p. 9) if he or she would aspire to teach the art of responsible action:

> Why stress the practice rather than apply biblical norms to these cases? I think that we reason morally from practice: we are more likely to act ourselves into new ways of thinking than think ourselves into new ways of acting. I am not making a case for behavioral conditioning as a substitute for moral reflection. The practices being advocated here are not blind repetitions but the story-shaped habits of disposition and action that enable moral perception and responsiveness. (Spohn, 2003b, p. 13)

ENDNOTES

1. "Engineering Cultures" is a registered trademark of Gary Downey and Juan Lucena. Lucena has developed a follow-up course titled "Engineering Cultures in the Developing World."

2. For a more detailed presentation of course assessment data, see Downey and others (2006).

3. See, for instance, Rhode (2000). A study of recent law graduates by Dinovitzer and colleagues (2004) sheds a particularly interesting light on this crisis as well. The study reveals an inverse relation between satisfaction with the "power track" (or the pursuit of high-status careers) and satisfaction with the legal substance, contexts, and social value of one's work.

4. This aspect of law school pedagogy, particularly with regard to case-dialogue teaching, is profiled in detail by Mertz (2007). See also Sullivan and others (2007).

3

A NARRATIVE OF THE
SEMINAR

SUPPOSE YOU HAD BROUGHT TOGETHER a group of faculty like those profiled so far, in order to undertake a collaborative inquiry into best practices for teaching responsible judgment. What would you do then? How would you foster collaboration across multiple disciplines and professions? How would you enable the faculty to discover new dimensions of their own practices through engagement with one another? Would your partners be able to understand one another at the outset, or would mutual understanding be a hard-won achievement?

Bringing Analogies to Light

Through the Life of the Mind for Practice seminar, we discovered a set of collaborative practices through which such faculty could overcome their academic isolation from one another and locate themselves within a common struggle to prepare their students for lives of responsible judgment. This chapter tells the story of how these practices evolved, as well as our problems and missteps along the way. The seminar experience proved to be much more than a typical research seminar. We hope that the example provided in this chapter, together with the theoretical and practical lessons distilled in subsequent chapters, will provide you with rich resources for imagining analogous work on your own campus.

Each one of the nine professors whom we have introduced represents a different professional or academic discipline. But these professors face analogous pedagogical challenges. Each works to provide his or her students with a guided introduction to responsible engagement in a field of practice. These introductions link distinct bodies of knowledge with understanding of the contexts, relationships, and meaning of action. In the process, each of these professors works against the grain of academic institutions that tend to value generalized argument over practical reasonableness and the integration of knowing and acting. Each works to sustain a broader conception of his or her own responsibilities in the lives of students and the public.

Bringing the analogies that bind our seminar partners to light, much less building on their pedagogical innovations, was no easy task, however. The seminar was convened with precisely these ends in mind, but we found out just how difficult it is to foster such sympathy and solidarity across disciplines. The problem lay not in any absence of goodwill or commitment but in the dominant values of the academy itself. The traditions of argumentation and identity through which those of us who work within academic contexts undergo our professional formation short-circuit sustained engagement with analogies of practice.

A quick note on the narrative form of this chapter is in order. Narratives portray protagonists who encounter and work to resolve problems, in order to bring about a renewed or better condition. This improved destination is the moral of the story. Any attempts to revisit the past through narrative can tend easily toward the rationalistic, as if the goal or moral of the story were always clear from the beginning. It might be tempting to assume—and perhaps even more tempting to claim—that we were always in conscious command of the lessons to be learned from each impasse along the way as we worked to foster a community of educators across the professional and liberal education divide.

This was not the case. In practice, we struggled frequently to make sense of events. We undertook changes in approach that seemed promising and worthwhile but with only educated intuitions about their likely effects, for good or ill. We understood more mindfully what was actually happening, what methods worked, and the ends for which we ought to strive only during our preparations for the final convening of the seminar. Despite our motivating hopes and intuitions, much time and hard work transpired before we truly knew what we were doing in practice.

This chapter is a narrative reconstruction of events, told with the aid of critical hindsight. It illuminates reasons for our failures and successes and unpacks the implications of particular decisions, which were often opaque *in situ*. It describes our *own* learning and practical formation as community organizers. It describes how we learned to see ourselves anew through engagement with one another, across professions and disciplines, and learned to discern and articulate new dimensions of our own practices and values. It is a story about the formation of solidarity, conscience, and vocation.

Opening with Great Expectations

The idea for the seminar began in a spirit of wonder and intellectual excitement. We hoped to build substantive bridges between the professions and the liberal arts through a shared consideration of how best to teach practical reasoning within the modern academy. This purpose remained constant. But our conception of how to *achieve* this value in practice changed radically. This is the story of an inquiry that began with a concept—practical reasoning—and culminated in an exciting exploration of the learning and responsibilities of an interdisciplinary community of expert teacher-scholars.

The core team of seminar organizers included Carnegie Foundation president Lee S. Shulman, senior scholar William M. Sullivan, research scholar Matthew S. Rosin,[1] and two consultants: philosopher of education Gary Fenstermacher and philosopher and medical ethicist Albert R. Jonsen.[2] We proceeded from the working intuition that the best professional preparation is entirely consonant with the purposes of liberal learning. We assumed that there is nothing more liberal than professional education, properly construed, when oriented toward responsibility and good judgment in the world. Likewise, we assumed that practical arguments of the kind that are central to work in the professions ought to be central to pedagogy in the liberal arts, if the formation of responsible citizens is our goal.[3]

The professions enjoy wide discretion in the performance of their work. This discretion is premised on the public's confidence in the value of the specialized knowledge, civic responsibility, and integrity that professionals are presumed to exemplify on behalf of society. These features of good professional work and judgment rest, ultimately, on the arts of practical reasoning. Any thorough professional education requires close attention to practical reasoning on behalf of others, for the welfare of both professionals and their publics.

We assumed that the teaching of practical reasoning is an essential feature of all academic programs of professional education, such as the various forms of clinical and case-based training that distinguish the professional fields. But much of this teaching is scattered among various parts of the curriculum. Knowledge about how to teach practical reasoning is dispersed among a variety of faculty. It is rarely focused and cultivated as a distinct and valuable part of professional preparation. We hoped that the seminar would focus and clarify how practical reasoning is best taught and learned. We also hoped to identify exemplary forms of such teaching.

The cross-field and comparative nature of the seminar, we hoped, would sharpen even further our awareness of what teaching for practical reasoning in the various fields shares in common, in order to make mutual learning between fields more likely and effective. We also included the liberal arts experience in our deliberations, in order to provide a new lens for understanding the institutional structure of higher education more broadly. The overall goals were to examine the virtues and short-comings of educational practice in the various academic fields and to understand better how teachers can live up to their responsibility for the future lives of their students in ever more insightful ways.

Looking back, we now recognize that the success of our efforts must be judged in light of the extent to which we provided conditions for a community of expert teacher-scholars to take shape and in light of our willingness to make substantive changes to our own plans where we were not doing so. Could a diverse group of faculty enter into meaning-ful dialogue about their teaching practices and fashion values of shared concern? Our first attempt to foster such community was humbling. It forced us to reckon immediately with our embeddedness within aca-demic traditions of argument that tend toward excluding or minimizing the practical and the self. We were working against our own professed intentions.

Overcoming the Academic Tradition of Argument

We had much to learn as we tried to bring our intuitions about the impor-tance of practical reasoning to fruition. We were committed in principle to practical reasoning as an organizing concern of pedagogy. But the actual organization of the seminar's first session did not embody this practical concern. We found out very quickly, despite ourselves, how dif-ficult it can be to move beyond the academic tradition of argument.

Academic argumentation decontextualizes knowledge in order to per-mit its widest generalization. As sociologist Randall Collins notes, the academic (or intellectual) mode of knowledge production presupposes that "ideas are meant to be true or significant apart from any locality, and apart from anyone concretely putting them into practice" (Collins, 1998, p. 19). Insights are universalized and applied to unruly contexts. The academic self achieves legitimacy only on these terms.

The practical tradition of argument to which we aspired is oriented differently. Far from supposing a divide between theory and practice, the practical tradition conceives theory and argument as the mapping of human concern—in the words of Jonsen and Toulmin, "a network of considerations" (Jonsen and Toulmin, 1988, p. 34). Theory orients vision and sensibility and offers new public forms for interpreting situations and justifying responses. Whereas the academic mode of argument tends to reduce uncertain and problematic situations in the world to the realm of unreason, the practical mode embraces situations as the enabling occasions for inquiry, dialogue, and action. But subscribing to this broader vision in practice poses significant challenges in the academic setting. Indeed, overcoming this academic mode of argumentation proved difficult at the start of our work, despite our best intentions.

In preparation for the first gathering of the seminar, held in September 2002, William M. Sullivan drafted an introductory essay that we hoped would clarify the concept of practical reasoning and persuade the seminar members of its relevance for their teaching (Sullivan, 2002). The essay describes what humans do when they size up situations and bring knowledge responsibly to bear. Through practical examples from several professions, the essay delineates three key phases of practical reasoning, with a back-and-forth rhythm, from (1) engagement with a problematic, concrete situation through (2) detached interpretation and analysis of what is most salient about the situation for action to (3) more informed and responsible engagement through judgment.

Theoretical thinking of the kind that is valued in the academy, Sullivan argues, occupies a moment within a larger circuit of practical rationality. Theoretical reasoning is central to the challenge of living but does not exhaust it. Sullivan's essay presents practical reasoning as a broader conception that concerns the formation and pursuit of meaning through action. This broader concept struck us as important for how we understand the goals of the academy and for establishing new solidarity between the professions and the liberal arts and sciences. We also assumed (falsely, as it turned out) that we could stir a similarly fascinated community of scholars by arguing for this broader concept academically.

But we did not rely on academic argument alone. We also provided the seminar members with a teaching case for discussion (Anonymous, Ladson-Billings, and Desser, 1993), along with related theoretical readings (Ball, 1993; McDermott, 1974). The case presented our partners with the first-person account of a white high school English teacher's attempt to teach George Bernard Shaw's *Pygmalion*, which focuses on linguistic difference and social inequality, in particular, within a lower-income, urban setting. The teacher struggles with how to present the play in a way that is inoffensive yet relevant to her predominantly African American students, "whose social status is not always equal and whose perceptions of appearances are often jaded" (Anonymous, and others, 1993, p. 13). She decides to draw from her students' own experiences in order to heighten the play's relevance. Along the way, she makes several references to "your" (the students') neighborhood. This does not go unnoticed by her students. One of them challenges the teacher to justify her discussion of "their" neighborhood without also discussing her *own*.

Faced with an awkward occasion for judgment, the teacher does her best to explain herself. One student suggests that the teacher use the neutral term *downtown* instead. The class accepts this suggestion and moves on. The narrative poses a difficult question: Can a teacher legitimately move to "neutral" ground in order to side-step the social vulnerabilities that her teaching exposes, without also sacrificing the full engagement and interest of her students? How the reader interprets the teacher's success or failure in the case is determined by how the reader answers this question—that is, on how the reader understands the significance of the case.

We asked our seminar partners to assess the teacher's practical reasoning in this situation and offer judgments about how such cases might be handled. In other words, we asked them to apply the concept of practical reasoning that was advocated in Sullivan's essay. We asked our partners to analyze the situation, consider the teacher's rationale, offer suggestions for action, and describe the theoretical traditions through which they arrived at these judgments. This assignment is reproduced in Appendix Two. We hoped that this assignment would help our seminar partners picture the drama and structure of practical reasoning in use. We also hoped that they would embrace the concept of practical reasoning as a common language for interpreting their own teaching in subsequent sessions.

In retrospect, we should have recognized that our attempt to apply the concept of practical reasoning and to ask our partners to provide detached, expert commentary on the actions of another would actually violate the vision of practical engagement that we had hoped to embrace! We were trapped by the very academic tradition of argument that we had intended to critique. Not surprisingly, the first session of the seminar did not proceed as we had imagined—nor, we would eventually realize, *could* it have proceeded in such a fashion.

No one in the seminar could agree on what the socially and culturally charged case was *about,* what problems needed to be addressed, or how to address them, much less about the importance and propriety of thinking about these matters in terms of practical reasoning. Nor did the teaching case relate in any clear or substantive fashion to our partners' own disciplines and teaching. Various analogies were attempted, but they could not open up our partners' own values, aspirations, and challenges for searching and trustworthy discussion. We had succeeded only in soliciting their expert advice. The predicaments and challenges of their *own* teaching remained entirely opaque.

Our partners had good reason to withhold such self-revelations from public discussion. Several expressed concern that the concept of practical reasoning described during the first session delimited the full spectrum of human capacities to respond to the world responsibly. William Spohn emphasized the importance of empathy. Gary Downey and Daisy Floyd emphasized the importance of emotion for deliberation and finding purpose, pointing toward a more holistic form of discourse. Meanwhile, English professor Elizabeth McKinsey wondered what a searching feminist analysis of the concept of practical reasoning might mean for the group's efforts. Barbara Stengel also expressed concern that Sullivan's introductory essay did not attend adequately to the early moments of practical reasoning when persons struggle to interpret the situations in which they find themselves.

The concept of practical reasoning proved to be not nearly so uniting and motivating a value as we had thought. The first session was successful in getting the group to begin asking difficult questions about what practical reasoning actually means. But we found ourselves in no better position to imagine and understand one another's pedagogical challenges and practices than before; the group remained trapped by academic modes of argument. As a result, we left the meeting knowing very little about one another. We could not even begin to chart our differences, let alone form common commitments.

The session failed to foster mutual recognition and appreciation between our partners. We, the organizers, came armed with a fully formed concept of practical reasoning and assumed that its relevance would be clear, or at least that our partners' perspectives could be changed accordingly through argument. But we were not open to being changed in turn. We provided no meaningful opportunity for dialogue so that we might work together to discover the full meaning of the concept for our partners' own lives, disciplines, and teaching.

This was a prototypically academic way of approaching the seminar. Without intending to do so, we had reduced the lived practices of our colleagues to mere complications or variations of theory. Intellectual disarray and interpersonal tension resulted—predictably. The concept of practical reasoning alone could not operate as a bridge for forming shared purposes, despite the best efforts and good faith of everyone involved.

We needed to find a new and better way to uncover the *relevance* and *meaning* of the concept for teaching within each seminar member's discipline, so that the concept might be enriched by the motivating concerns of each field. We would then be in a better position to discover both our disciplinary differences *and* our common commitments. We would also be in a better position to recognize and understand *one another*. But how? What practices would best serve this purpose? Although the first session of the seminar had generated hard questions about practical reasoning, the meeting was a chastening experience. We needed to regroup.

Fostering Recognition and Analogy

The first session of the seminar had done little to overcome the pedagogical isolation of our partners from one another. The second session charted a new path.

Our planning for the second meeting was a key turning point, whose significance we would not recognize fully until later. We changed our approach. Instead of continuing to provide case materials, we asked our partners to make cases of their *own* teaching. This had always been the eventual goal of the seminar. We had assumed falsely, however, that the value of practical reasoning could be established separately, independent of such shared self-reflection. We had gotten things backwards.

In charting this change of heart, we followed the lead of our partners themselves. Following the first session, we asked our partners to comment on their experience of the seminar and how it might be improved and advanced. The overriding consensus was that future gatherings should be organized around cases from our partners' own respective fields. Several expressed particular interest in inquiring into the teaching of practical reasoning, as it pertained to their own courses or the courses of their colleagues. One also noted that the first meeting was most productive when seminar members expressed themselves through narrative. She suggested that narrative provided a better basis for recognizing and articulating the richness of one another's pedagogical practices.

These suggestions pointed toward a very different approach. This new path placed the discovery of each seminar member's particularity ahead of the articulation of theory. It recognized that we could produce shared meaning only *through* practical reasoning rather than by applying predefined theory *about* practical reasoning. This new path demanded that we uncover the meaning of practical reasoning by *engaging* in it. Indeed, how else could such learning take place? We followed where our partners led.

The assignment leading up to the second session—reproduced in Appendix Two—encouraged our partners to imagine the lives that their students will live and to reflect on the forms of reasoning required for these challenges. We then asked them to assess their own syllabi, or that of a colleague, in light of how their courses prepare students for these forms of life. They reflected on the opportunities that their syllabi offer students for reasoning through problematic situations that model, in some salient way, the structure of life in a field. We suggested that their syllabi might be understood as narrative artifacts that provide a guided journey into the problems and values of a discipline and that offer an organized series of learning events that model responsible activity in a field.

We reasoned that each syllabus entailed some underlying conception of what is most important for the responsible practice of a discipline or its fundamental *topics*. By using syllabi as cases for reflection, we hoped to foster discussion and insight into the core concerns and values that motivated our partners' respective courses. We hoped that, as these concerns became public, the seminar members would learn to discern and articulate the differences and family resemblances among their disciplines and among the professions and the liberal arts and sciences more broadly. We might then be able to recognize common issues that emerge when attempting to teach practical reasoning.

Our partners, working in pairs, considered these matters prior to our second meeting, which was convened in February 2003. We organized these pairs in a cross-professional fashion: a law professor worked with a professor of teacher education; a medical educator worked with a professor of English, and so forth. These conversations provided an opportunity for each to enter imaginatively into the pedagogical world of another. Our partners helped one another reflect on how their syllabi might contribute to how their students respond to practical situations. We hoped that these pairs would establish a foundation for forming common purposes among teachers from different disciplines, as they helped one another inquire deeply into their own motivations and purposes as partners in a shared inquiry.

The pairs discussed the kinds of situations requiring practical judgment to which their courses respond. They considered the journey that each syllabus organizes in the lives of students, the key events that occur along the way, and how these events anticipate future work or living. The pairs also reflected on what disciplinary concerns would remain fundamental to the course, even if there was substantially less time to teach it. Our partners discussed these questions by telephone or e-mail in preparation for the second meeting, at the beginning of which they met briefly to discuss new insights generated by their conversation.

The pairings proved very successful at fostering empathy and critical understanding of one another's pedagogical challenges. The pairing of teacher educator Barbara Stengel and engineering educator Gary Downey, for instance, revealed a powerful set of analogies. Both of their courses, as we saw in previous chapters, help students locate themselves among the diverse perspectives and stakeholders that populate professional situations. Downey's course, "Engineering Culture," helps students come to terms with multiple forms for defining engineering problems and the meaning of engineering work within the global workplace (Downey and Lucena, 2005). Meanwhile, Stengel's course, "Foundations of Modern Education," helps students learn to respond critically, creatively, and ethically to the conflicting demands placed on teachers by different stakeholders and layers of institutional authority (Stengel, 2005).

Although the professional workplaces that each course presumes are different, Downey and Stengel discovered a deeper analogy through their conversations. The professional teacher is called, possibly against the grain of his or her own discipline, to orient students' growing practices for interpreting professional situations. For them, teaching for practical reason means placing students in a more complex and dialogical relationship with perspectives beyond the self. Only by responding to the demands of these relationships can the student act responsibly.

Several pairings also brought professional educators into conversation with teachers from the liberal arts and sciences, with illuminating results. One pair featured medical educator Arthur Elstein (who was profiled in Chapter One) and Elizabeth McKinsey, a professor of English and American studies and former dean of Carleton College. McKinsey presented a course that had made a tremendous impact on her daughter at Swarthmore College. The course, "Practical Wisdom," is co-taught by political scientist Kenneth Sharpe and psychologist Barry Schwartz. The syllabus distinguishes between practical judgment and decision making based on pre-established rules. In the service of the former, the course engages life issues that are pivotal in the students' present and future lives, including the problems of friendship, education, law, and medicine. "Practical Wisdom" constitutes a fascinating attempt to premise the meaning of liberal education on the importance of practical argument, rather than the primacy of decontextualized theory (McKinsey, 2003).

Elstein and McKinsey discovered interesting points of connection between Elstein's professional teaching and the liberal arts teaching of Sharpe and Schwartz. Their course, "Practical Wisdom," engages the social and political contexts of three different professions: education, law, and medicine. Elstein was struck by the course's engagement of such matters as the commodification of medicine, the market contexts of contemporary doctoring, and the tension between cost containment and the traditional medical virtues—all of which are largely neglected by graduate medical education. Elstein and McKinsey's conversation suggested that a more refined understanding of the mutual dependence of the professions and the arts and sciences might be possible. Whereas professional courses excel in modeling particular forms of everyday institutional life and responsibility, the liberal arts and sciences provide the normative ground for interpreting the contexts and meaning of one's action on behalf of others.

Another particularly fortuitous pairing was that of engineering educator Robert McGinn (profiled in the Introduction) and religious studies educator William Spohn (profiled in Chapter Two). McGinn joked that his "Ethics and Public Policy" syllabus (not the "Ethical Issues in Engineering" syllabus discussed in the Introduction) aspires to "eradicate the weeds" that prevent responsible action, whereas Spohn's "Scripture and the Moral Life" aspires to produce responsible agents by "watering the plants." Out of all the syllabi, Spohn's expresses the most overt concern for the formation of student dispositions and character by "populating" students' imaginations with biblical exemplars of practice (Spohn, 2003b). McGinn's "Ethics and Public Policy," meanwhile, helps students learn to interpret substantive public policy disagreements about scientific and technological advance. McGinn provides heuristic frameworks for engaging policy disputes that are acceptable to his engineering students who desire quasi-technical approaches for analyzing the social and political contexts of their action. One such analytical technique, for instance, encourages students to consider systematically the facts involved in a particular policy argument, the stakeholders whose interests are involved, the concepts and presuppositions that underlie their arguments, and the decision-making processes through which the stakeholders stake their claims (McGinn, 2003).

McGinn was correct about the difference in disposition between the constructive ends of Spohn's syllabus and the critical ends of his own. In other ways, however, McGinn's humorous distinction between eradicating the weeds and watering the plants also obscures as much about the relation between their respective teaching practices as it reveals.

The analytical frameworks that McGinn offers are not merely technical resources. They orient his engineering students toward engaging the ethical stances and traditions of others and toward considering the institutional contexts through which they act. Indeed, as we saw in the Introduction, this critical imagination of situations and others through cases is central to McGinn's teaching. In the end, McGinn's orientation toward professional conduct, though framed in analytical terms that engineering students will accept, is not so profoundly different from Spohn's teaching. Both syllabi dispose the future practices of their students toward the richer interpretation of situations and actors beyond the self—a characteristic also shared by Gary Downey and Barbara Stengel.

What accounts for the tremendous difference in outcome between the first and second gatherings of the seminar? Our initial mistake was to remain trapped, unknowingly, in academic practices of argumentation that were ill-suited to the task of inquiring into the teaching of practical judgment. In order to uncover the full meaning of practical judgment for the teaching of our seminar partners, however, we needed to turn toward a practical mode of engagement ourselves. We had to practice what we preached.

By changing direction, we succeeded in providing a diverse set of faculty with a guided opportunity to inquire imaginatively into each other's teaching challenges in light of their common goal of educating for responsible engagement in a particular field of practice. These occasions were the basis for trust, mutual recognition, analogy, and, we hoped, a new discourse. Inspired by this success, we set out to provide the conditions for a new discourse to emerge through further collaboration. We began to plan the third and final gathering of the seminar.

Finding New Narratives of Faculty Vocation and Purpose

The first session of the seminar produced only a fragmented group of isolated faculty—units of one. The second session brought together a diverse network of pairs—units of two. The third session expanded this collaborative practice. It brought together cross-disciplinary trios who worked together to tell the story of their respective courses and to construct a shared discourse for articulating their growing identities as teachers. These trios would then bring the fruits of their labor to the broader group, in order to forge a sense of group identity. These units of three would contribute, we hoped, to the formation of a new sense of collective solidarity and purpose.

The second session revealed a common concern for practical reasoning as a dramatic process of interpreting the salience of lived situations and responding in ways that produce virtuous consequences in the lives of both self and other. No syllabus illuminated the existential demands of such work better than Daisy Hurst Floyd's "Advanced Legal Ethics." Her course responded to a widely perceived crisis of meaning within the legal profession and its painful consequences in the lives of legal practitioners (Floyd, 2003). Her course reminded us that, in the end, professional and liberal education are both engaged in the formation of lives—clients, professionals, citizens, persons. Educational institutions undertake this role for good or ill, more or less mindful of the moral consequences of their curricula and teaching for practice. In order to help students chart good practical lives in the future, faculty must construct educational experiences with care. They must orient students not only toward disciplinary bodies of knowledge but also toward others, themselves, and the contexts of their conduct in meaningful ways. They must help their students undertake a journey toward a new kind of self in the world.

We hoped to unpack how our seminar partners help their students undertake these journeys by returning to the concept of narrative. We gave our partners a summer writing assignment (included in Appendix Two), in preparation for the final session of the seminar. The assignment asked each teacher to recount the narrative of her syllabus. Courses are like stories. They contain a plot with a beginning, middle, and end. By thinking about courses in narrative terms, we can inquire into what the protagonists—our students—actually do over time. We can inquire into the surprises and problems that occur in their lives along the way, which force them to make judgments with the help of an expert guide. Expert teachers structure these experiences so that they anticipate the salient demands, values, and institutions of students' future lives.

Our partners considered their syllabi as documents that organize a progressive series of problematic episodes that students resolve through practical reasoning and deliberation, stimulating thereby their growth in the techniques and values of a field. This series of events has a point: What is the destination of the journey—the moral of the story? What forms of technical competence are involved? What concerns and values ought to orient and motivate responsible action in each discipline? The concept of narrative offered a helpful framing device for discussing practical reasoning as a purposive and existential enterprise and for reflecting on the quality of the experiences afforded students by each syllabus.

Our partners considered whether or not their syllabi cut against the grain of the dominant pedagogical practices of their disciplines. Because more than one response to any particular problem is possible, the syllabi offered students opportunities to engage in dialogue about how they ought to locate themselves within the life of their discipline. Our partners also considered whether their syllabi shed light on how other disciplines ought to value their work. We hoped that these reflections would set the stage for a productive discussion about how the professions and the liberal arts and sciences might inform one another more broadly in a more engaged academy.

At this point, we finally recognized that the importance of the seminar consisted in its potential power as a process of faculty development and formation. This meant that we needed to reflect explicitly on how our partners grew to understand themselves anew over time through their collaboration with one another. This meant articulating, through analogy, the core concerns that all of us shared in our efforts to teach responsible judgment. If successful, the seminar would produce not just new knowledge. It would produce new forms of solidarity.

In order to get at these issues, we asked our partners to discuss their respective syllabus narratives in groups of three (see Appendix Two). Each trio included two representatives from the professional disciplines and one representative from the liberal arts or sciences. The trio members walked one another through their respective syllabus narratives and helped one another reflect on how their engagement together, across disciplines and the professional-liberal education divide, renewed or transformed their own pedagogical thinking and purposes. We hoped that the trios might teach one another new ways of articulating their pedagogical conscience by inquiring together into the family resemblances and differences between their respective syllabi.

Fashioning a Shared Framework Through Dialogue

The final session of the seminar was convened in December 2003. The session proved even more successful than we had hoped. It produced a new framework for considering the challenges of teaching practical judgment—a framework that posed a strong challenge to the typical educational agendas of contemporary academe. We consider these issues in theoretical terms in the next chapter. For now, this narrative concludes with an account of how the seminar group fashioned this shared framework through dialogue. We focus on a single example: the generalization of the ideas at the center of Daisy Hurst Floyd's course, "Advanced Legal Ethics," through analogy, into a broader framework for considering the teaching of practical reasoning in any field, to which all ascribed.

Floyd's syllabus narrative told the story of her efforts to "broaden" her students' "personal visions of what's necessary to be a good lawyer" (Floyd, 2003, p. 3). As we discussed in Chapter Two, "Advanced Legal Ethics" charts an intimate relation between working toward the good of legal clients and sustaining the happiness and meaning of the professional self. The course helps students reckon with how their legal education neglects the importance of this lawyer-client relationship for their future lives; the course then helps to integrate students into a wider vision of professional practice through discussion and conversations with practicing attorneys. Floyd hopes to rehabilitate technical legal expertise, which preoccupies the bulk of the law school curriculum, through a more fitting and meaningful vision of responsible legal practice in an uncertain social world.

Floyd shared her syllabus narrative with her trio partners, philosopher Albert R. Jonsen and teacher educator Sam Wineburg. Once circulated, Floyd's account of her particular practices and values became a shared source of insight, to be discussed and built upon. When the trio presented its reflections to the larger group at the beginning of the first day, they offered more than Floyd's compelling narrative. Jonsen presented an integrative framework for considering four topics or concerns that are especially central to her teaching. Jonsen argued that Floyd's syllabus proceeds from the implicit presumption that these four topics are central aspects of responsible legal action on behalf of a client and must, therefore, be central to any meaningful effort to educate students for responsible judgment.

Using Floyd's own language, Jonsen presented the following topics: *authenticity, community* (or *connectedness*), *client autonomy,* and legal *bodies of knowledge.* Lawyers ought to bring their legal expertise (*bodies of knowledge*) to bear in a way that takes account of the networks of personal and institutional relationships (*community*) through which the lawyer works, in order to inform and enrich the practical reasoning and *autonomy of their clients.* Only in this way is the work of a legal career sustained as a calling of the self (*authenticity*). These four topics describe the networks of concern that orient legal action and care in the world. Lawyers sustain meaningful careers over time by navigating these concerns.

The seminar group broke into smaller groups again later that afternoon. This time, Floyd's syllabus was discussed by a slightly different and expanded group: Floyd, Jonsen, religious studies educator William Spohn, and biologist Hessel Bouma. The group inquired into the family resemblances that bound their respective syllabi together, as well as the substantive differences that distinguished their respective fields from one another. Again the discussion proved clarifying.

William Spohn presented the results of their discussion to the broader group. He pointed out that Floyd's "Advanced Legal Ethics" course approaches professional legal life using practices and perspectives drawn from both the profession itself and the liberal disciplines more generally. Spohn argued that the four topics at the core of Floyd's syllabus—*authenticity, community, client autonomy,* and *bodies of knowledge*—suggest that the professions and the disciplines are deeply co-implicated in the educational formation of responsible actors in the world. Floyd's course illuminates this possibility by not by focusing on the formal demands of knowledge, as is typical of academic aspiration and the legal curriculum more generally, but by helping students inquire into the reflective and interactive demands of good *practice* in the legal domain.

But even though all agreed with Spohn's characterization, this framework was not yet ready to serve as a unifying set of topics for the seminar group as a whole. The framework had been derived from Floyd's teaching in the legal domain in particular. As such, it was not fully responsive to the various needs of other fields. Different fields operate in many different institutional worlds. They have different kinds of clients or perhaps even broader values, such as civic engagement. The four topics highlighted earlier showed how the diverse concerns of the professions and the disciplines cut across Floyd's teaching in the legal profession but did not yet offer a sufficient framework for considering their relationship more generally.

Floyd's syllabus continued to resonate deeply with the seminar as a whole, however, and our seminar partners were quick to recognize analogies between Floyd's teaching and their own. Education in all the professional fields, as well as in the liberal arts and sciences, understood in the traditional sense of "liberal education," aspires toward the formation of knowledgeable actors in the social and cultural world. These are actors for whom the meaning of their action is tied in some substantive way to the good of others, or a public.

The members of the seminar recognized that the discipline-specific topics at the core of Floyd's syllabus were expressions of more general imperatives of practical action, to which all subscribed. All subscribed immediately to the topics of *community* and *bodies of knowledge* as fundamental concerns of teaching and responsible judgment across fields. All of our partners, in their own domains, aspire to help their students discern what is salient for deliberation and action with others in this place and at this time.

Toward this end, our partners guide their students pedagogically into growing participation in traditions beyond the self for articulating and justifying the meaning of their conduct. They each help their students enter an ongoing dialogue about what constitutes responsible action in a field.

Floyd's concern for *authenticity* and *client autonomy* required some collaborative refashioning, however. These topics captured well the importance of achieving a proper relationship between the good of the self and the good of others through action. As Robert McGinn pointed out, however, these particular formulations were too narrow to make sense beyond the legal domain. What counts as a "client" and its importance for the self in any given situation depends very much on the disciplinary and practical context. Authenticity and autonomy need not be the most salient values at stake for professional or civic action.

McGinn suggested that what was at stake more generally was not the value of authenticity but a concern for *identity*. Floyd's existential concern for authenticity constitutes one important dimension of this broader topic. The other seminar members responded favorably to this suggestion, which captures well the reflective and formative dimension of acting in the world. The self is fashioned through engagement with others, in particular places and times, and through participation in evolving traditions of knowing. The seminar members model this kind of engagement in the lives of their students through pedagogy.

In order to capture the other-directed aspects of responsible action, McGinn suggested that Floyd's worry about client autonomy in legal life expressed a broader notion of "ethical concern." This prospective topic suffered from the same problem as the one it was intended to replace, however. Not all situations demand ethical concern *per se*. As Arthur Elstein pointed out, a surgeon who worries about the equitable distribution of organs while attempting to perform a highly technical transplant endangers his or her patient. The surgeon acts unethically in this moment by spending her energy worrying about ethics rather than acting in a narrowly technical fashion. Responsibility sometimes means discerning when ethical deliberation is called for and when it is not.

Albert Jonsen suggested that the fundamental issue at stake, behind Floyd and McGinn's worries alike, is the nature and demands of one's *responsibility* on behalf of others. The other seminar members agreed. This more expansive topic focused the group's attention on a question of common concern: For *what or whom* do we engage in practice in a field? Only through the trust of those whom one serves does action become legitimate. Keeping faith with this trust through proper care and consideration, whether through ethical reflection, the fostering of client autonomy, or expert technical performance, lies at the heart of responsible deliberation and action in the social world.

Once established, these four topics—*identity, community, responsibility,* and *bodies of knowledge*—enabled collective inquiry into further aspects of teaching for practical reasoning. In particular, they offered a new framework for considering the relationship between the professions and the arts and sciences. What pedagogical strengths does each domain bring to the table? How does each enable the others to realize their own formative ends more fully? How these domains might cohere is a broader vision of what higher education is all about.

A complex picture began to take shape. The pedagogies of the arts and sciences, at their best, are well positioned to help students imagine and interpret the institutions and contexts of their action—social, cultural, political, natural. Toward this end, the disciplines have developed strong analytical traditions and bodies of knowledge that help students locate themselves within broader networks of concern. To do this, the liberal arts cultivate appreciation of uncertainty, whereas the sciences develop particular forms of technical certainty, within recognized limits.

Professional pedagogies, at their best, cultivate the institutional practices that are undertaken and undergone *through* these social, cultural, political, and natural contexts. Professional education orients students' identities toward particular roles and responsibilities and introduces students to the traditions of knowing and acting that distinguish professional forms of life. Professional pedagogies create bridges between the technical certainty of theory and the demands of uncertain situations. Whereas the liberal arts and sciences excel at forming student practices of interpretation and analysis, the professions reveal that these traditions of knowing must become meaningful in the here and now, through judgment and action.

The courses discussed during the seminar drew from both of these sources. Each teacher, whether she represented a professional field or one of the disciplines, recognized that student formation in one domain cannot be realized fully without fruitful and sustained engagement with the meaning of the others. This is one reason why these courses cut against the grain of academic organization, which is oriented primarily toward the production of disciplinary bodies of knowledge in the abstract, rather than the formation of knowing bodies in the world.

As Robert McGinn noted, the careers of many students, beginning with their earliest undergraduate general education experiences, proceeding through more specialized professional training in a discipline, and finally culminating in employment, typically undercut this integrative vision. Many students engage liberal education only through their early general education requirements. These experiences, which ought to provide students with a sophisticated understanding of the contexts and institutions of their future action, occur typically in the moments farthest removed from the everyday work of their eventual careers. Moreover, liberal education is usually pursued in a fashion that is unresponsive to the problems of meaning and the diverse practices that populate society. Neither professional education nor disciplinary specialization, meanwhile, provides students with much opportunity to situate their specialized identities within a broader liberal framework. In the process, we lose valuable opportunities to model how worthwhile forms of identity and responsibility might be sustained through the everyday conflicts and challenges of employment.

Crucially, our seminar partners also realized that the vision of teaching and responsible action that we now shared was much broader than the notion of critical thinking that is celebrated in academe. This issue came to light during the trio discussions of engineering educator Gary Downey, teacher educator Barbara Stengel, and composition-and-rhetoric professor Janice Lauer. They recognized that critical thinking, which values the interrogation of experience and the distillation of underlying structures and causes, captures only a partial aspect of what their teaching is all about. Critical thinking is but an interpretive moment in a broader process that proceeds through dialogue and culminates in responsible action. Downey, Stengel, and Lauer informed the larger group (wisely) that the new framework we had produced—*identity, community, responsibility,* and *bodies of knowledge*—promised a substantial revision of the limited conception of critical thinking that dominates academic aspiration. This broader, formative mission subsumes and, literally, incorporates the meaning of *critical thinking* through lived situations that demand action with and on behalf of others. We expand on this alternative academic agenda in theoretical detail in the next chapter.

The purpose of this chapter has been to tell the story of how the seminar group grew and developed as a dialogical community over time. The moral of the story is that faculty formation for the teaching of responsible action must practice—and must be an experiment in—the engaged reasoning to which it aspires.

Faculty formation of this kind, we learned, must begin with the predicaments and aspirations of faculty *practices*. By offering our partners opportunities to enter imaginatively into each other's pedagogical worlds, they were enabled to serve as exemplars in each other's lives. They stirred each other to consciousness of new dimensions of their own practices through analogy. These analogies, in turn, provided the basis for a new framework of meaning—a new, shared, and public form of pedagogical conscience. Discourse, solidarity, and conscience are three angles of vision toward the same process of collaborative inquiry.

This is not what we typically mean by faculty development, however. Faculty formation of the kind depicted in this chapter entails a broader agenda for what higher education is all about—the agenda of practical reasoning. This agenda offers a powerful alternative to the critical thinking agenda that dominates the academy. Whereas the critical thinking agenda teaches us only to pull the world apart analytically, the practical-reasoning agenda teaches us how to resolve provisionally, through dialogue and action, that which we pull asunder. We turn now to the difference between these two agendas.

ENDNOTES

1. Rosin first began work on the seminar in September 2002 as a doctoral research assistant to William M. Sullivan. He became a research scholar at the Foundation in July 2004, following the completion of his doctorate at the Stanford University School of Education.

2. The pilot stages of the seminar also benefited from the assistance of then-research associate Cheryl Richardson, who worked more recently as a research scholar in the Carnegie Foundation's Knowledge Media Laboratory.

3. Carnegie president Lee S. Shulman first presented this formulation of the relationship between the professions and the arts and sciences during the third convening of the seminar.

4

PRACTICAL REASON AS AN EDUCATIONAL AGENDA

OUR SEMINAR PARTNERS STRUGGLED along a variety of different roads to arrive at educational common ground. As we have seen, the seminar experience revealed this ground to be not general concepts but analogous pedagogical aims and practices. Our partners discovered that they, collectively and across fields, made wide use of cases to foster dialogue between concepts and experience. They emphasized the interpretation of context and tolerance for ambiguity in the application of concepts and principles. They worked to develop student practices of reflective judgment in response to situations of complexity and uncertainty and the responsibilities that go with this judgment. The seminar, through such practical exercises as the syllabus narrative, provided our partners with an exciting opportunity to construct what Lee S. Shulman calls "a literature of shared narratives," through which they might locate and interpret their own practices anew (Shulman, 2004b, p. 20).

These narratives converged on a set of four topics: *identity, community, responsibility,* and *bodies of knowledge.* These topics mark the key issues through which, in the judgment of the seminar, educators concerned with practical reasoning orient their teaching. These topics structure the terrain of responsible practice in any field. Education for practical reasoning teaches students how to navigate the world in light of these four concerns. As we saw in the previous chapter, these topics emerged from vigorous give-and-take. This common perspective did not emerge through the imposition of a single concept but was the product of a dialogical process, through which our partners entered imaginatively into the teaching practices of others and learned to discern new dimensions of their own practice. Through this work of analogy, a new discourse was born.

The academy, of course, is disposed primarily toward *bodies of knowledge* rather than the other three topics. The academy devotes most of its pedagogical effort to disseminating disciplinary frameworks for arguing and knowing. This is important work. For instance, one literally cannot be an engineer unless one has learned to embody particular forms of technical practice and knowledge. But the work of the seminar reveals that concern for practical reasoning expands our pedagogical awareness. We must learn to acknowledge and embody three additional common-places: *identity, community,* and *responsibility.* These additional topics direct and guide how one approaches the subject matter of one's field in response to a practical situation. Knowledge finds meaning through conduct.

The topic of *identity* expresses the reflective and formative dimension of education. It points to the ways in which persons are formed, through institutional and social engagement, as they participate in evolving tradi-tions of knowing. In order to act well, the person must ask herself who she ought to become through her action. This process of formation takes place through *community* with others. Participation with others popu-lates the imagination with models of what it means to engage the natural, social, and cultural contexts of action. These are the contexts through which the person lives up to her *responsibility* for others and for the val-ues of the community. This is especially so for professionals, whose work is premised explicitly on serving broad public purposes. Only by keeping faith with the trust of others does the professional achieve legitimacy and meaning. This fiduciary care, whether it is expressed through ethical reflection, the fostering of client autonomy, or expert technical perfor-mance, lies at the heart of responsible deliberation and action in the social world.

Placing these four topics—*identity, community, responsibility,* and *bodies of knowledge*—at the center of pedagogical concerns casts new light on the relationship between the disciplines of the arts and sciences and the professional fields. The seminar's consensus was that the distinc-tive pedagogies of the arts and sciences, exemplified in many of the courses taught, regardless of location in the division of disciplines, can enable students to imagine and interpret a diverse array of contexts, providing the basis for an expansion of students' imaginative horizons. The humanities provide means of understanding and interpreting the complexities of purpose and meaning, whereas the social sciences help open up for examination the diversity of human possibilities and experience. The natural sciences have developed valuable techniques for establishing relative certainty so as to render the world more amenable to rational understanding and effective action. For their part, the professions' pedagogies of engagement develop capacities for engaging uncertain contexts responsibly. They provide their students with the means of taking on complex roles and responsibilities with understanding.

This set of pedagogical topics is both broader and more concrete than the kinds of teaching typical in the academy. We believe, moreover, that this pioneering work points toward a valuable new *educational agenda* for higher education. We have borrowed this term from Dennis McGrath and Martin B. Spear's enlightening study, *The Academic Crisis of the Community College* (1991). An *educational agenda* refers to "the varied ways education is pictured or enacted in particular pedagogies, and assumed in the vocabularies that faculties use to explain and justify what they do" (p. 69). As McGrath and Spear go on to note, "The apparatus of agendas is useful for making explicit what is usually overlooked, hidden" (McGrath and Spear, 1991, p. 69).

To talk of an agenda connotes a plan of things to be done and ways to accomplish them. Yet any particular way of educating always excludes some other ways. How is the academic enterprise as a whole or a specific field or profession represented in teaching and assessment practices? How are these practices described and given legitimacy? These are important and illuminating questions for educators to consider. The meaning and importance of practical reasoning as an educational agenda emerges most sharply when it is posed in contrast to the educational agenda that currently dominates higher education: critical thinking.

Critical Thinking as Educational Agenda

Few terms are more common in contemporary discussions of the purpose of higher education than *critical thinking*. This concept may seem, to many readers of this book, to be an almost self-evident good and an obvious aim of serious educational endeavor at the college and university level. In fact, critical thinking is a vague and often poorly conceived notion of educational purpose, more like a slogan than a well-formed educational ideal. Despite its vagueness, however, its prominence makes it a useful point of comparison by which to make clearer the significance of the idea of practical reason. The contrast becomes clearer when analyzed in relation to what is known about how higher education contributes to students' cognitive and moral development, as we will show shortly. But the question of intellectual agendas also opens a window onto the big question with which this study has been concerned throughout: *what higher education is and should be about.* Following our examination of critical thinking, we will turn to this larger question as a way of clarifying the import of the seminar's work.

The foundational myth of higher education was given in Greek antiquity by Plato. In the middle of the dialogue we call *The Republic*, Plato's Socrates asks the reader to imagine humanity as prisoners in a dark, underground cavern. While trapped in this dark realm of illusion, one of the prisoners is somehow able to free himself enough to "turn around." He looks away from images projected on the cave walls by flickering firelight and begins an arduous climb upward, toward the world of reality, which is bathed in the brightness of the sun. There the escaped prisoner undergoes a transformative illumination. He glimpses what Plato mysteriously calls the Good, described in images as the light of all reality. Moved by what he has seen, the prisoner returns to the cave and tries to persuade his fellows to also turn around. Ominously, Plato tells us that the prisoners resist their liberator and threaten to kill him if he persists, just as the Athenians did to the real Socrates. Plato follows this potent story with a series of other parables and images, ending with an educational curriculum designed for the future Guardian class who are to rule the rightly ordered city that Socrates and his interlocutors have been struggling to imagine through their dialogue.

The critical thinking agenda has evident resemblances to the myth of the cave. Like Plato's story, advocates of the critical-thinking agenda present higher education as a quest to escape from narrow views. It is a movement up and away from concrete and local understanding, toward a wider perspective at a higher level. Critical thinking, as we shall see, is generally presented as an application of epistemology, a sort of applied theory of knowledge.

However, the transformative moment of Plato's tale is missing in the critical thinking agenda. With it goes the moral drama of the re-immersion into "the cave." The Platonic myth is marked not by a one-way journey but by a two-fold movement. Liberation finds its fulfillment in service. In the cave story, the educative movement is indeed away from the immediate, upward toward a transformation of understanding and motive in the transcendent vision of the Good. But that experience demands and receives consummation through action, in the form of the prisoner's journey back into the cave for the sake of his fellows, a journey whose risk Plato underscores. In the subsequent parable about the education of the Guardians, the movement is again bi-directional. After the arduous climb "up" to synthetic understanding through dialectical training, the future Guardians are then to spend three times as long going back "down," learning in practice how to relate their cognitively and morally transformed understanding to the concrete affairs of the city (Plato, 514a–520e, 538a–540a).

How does the critical thinking agenda play out in today's academy? There is surprisingly little clarity about what educators really mean by the idea. In a wide-ranging compilation of the available research literature, Ernest T. Pascarella and Patrick T. Terenzini suggest that the term *critical thinking* is typically understood to mean something like the ability to "identify central issues and assumptions in an argument, recognize important relationships, make correct inferences from data . . . interpret whatever conclusions are warranted based on data, [and] evaluate evidence or authority" (Pascarella and Terenzini, 2005, p. 156).

Unfortunately, Pascarella and Terenzini conclude that the available evidence indicates that while there are small cognitive gains across a variety of measures by most students during their college years, it is unclear that specific pedagogical efforts targeted toward improving critical thinking have much effect on students' performance (Pascarella and Terenzini, 2005).

A potentially more promising approach to understanding education for critical thinking has been developed by Patricia King and Karen Kitchener in a significant body of research focused on the different, though related, concept of *reflective judgment*. King and Kitchener distinguish their approach from the more familiar notion of critical thinking. They assert that, typically, "critical thinking involves many types of reasoning, including deductive and inductive logic about well-structured problems" Furthermore, much discussion imagines critical thinking as "a set of skills that can be acquired through the learning of increasingly complex behavior or rules." By contrast, an emphasis on reflective judgment means thinking in terms of the "interaction between the individual's conceptual skills and environments that promote or inhibit the acquisition of these skills" (King and Kitchener, 1994, p. 18).

Like other lines of developmental research, King and Kitchener's work depicts maturation as progress through a series of levels of ever-increasing complexity and generality of understanding. At the start of this developmental trajectory, students view knowledge as certain—as information or facts that depend on authorities or personal experience. As students mature, they proceed toward a more sophisticated view of knowledge as less certain, more complex, and always subject to further questioning. At the first level, which they call prereflective, King and Kitchener tell us that thinking is understood as imitating well-rehearsed models and following explicit rules without deviation. From there, cognitive development moves in the direction of a second level of "quasi reflective" thinking. At this level, knowledge is seen to derive from processes of reasoning. Beliefs require argument and evidence and so demand efforts to provide justification.

Eventually, at the third level of fully reflective thinking, individuals' epistemological assumptions have been revolutionized.

> [They now] recognize that knowledge is never a given but rather the outcome of inquiry, synthesis of evidence and opinion, evaluation of evidence and arguments, and recognition that some judgments are more solidly grounded than others. (King and Kitchener, 1994, p. 38)

This is the kind of thinking necessary for engagement with "unstructured problems"—situations marked by uncertainty and complexity. These are real contexts or imagined situations for which there is no single solution according to a clear set of rules. Instead, ill-structured problems open the possibility of many solutions, none of which is entirely sure to be correct. Reflective judgment is necessary—that is, an overall evaluation that takes into account often conflicting possibilities, claims, evidence, and ways of proceeding but finally decides to affirm one approach over others (King and Kitchener, 1994).

This movement through three levels, from a conception of knowledge as factual information toward a more complex view of knowledge as contextual and open-ended, describes a progress in how learners are able to understand, as well as a series of changes in how they see their world. King and Kitchener invoke John Dewey's theory of reflective thinking, pointing toward reflective judgment as a "set of flexible and growing habits"—an intellectual disposition to engage with complex and uncertain situations rather than to deny or avoid them (King and Kitchener, 1994). This understanding places King and Kitchener's agenda in between the formalism of much critical-thinking talk, on the one hand, and the engagement with context and purpose that characterizes practical reason on the other.

The critical thinking educational agenda is fairly clear in outline if fuzzy in detail. In the remainder of this section, we distill four fundamental presuppositions of the critical thinking agenda. We then discuss the implications and limitations of these presuppositions in practice. The critical thinking agenda presumes the following:

1. True knowledge consists in representations derived through valid rules of inference.

2. Students proceed from black-and-white thinking and the desire for certainty toward more subtle shades of gray and the practice of reasoned argument.

3. Logical patterns of thinking can be taught in abstraction from the particular contents and embodied concerns of action.

4. "Becoming a critical thinker" entails liberation from the contingencies of the particular.

First, the critical thinking agenda entails epistemological assumptions about what counts as true knowledge. Its fundamental assumption is familiar: knowledge consists in representations of states of affairs that can be defended on grounds of good evidence and derivation, according to valid rules of inference. Students advance toward this understanding by learning to perform the logical operations required to recognize this definition of knowledge. Second, student development is conceptualized as progress from fixed and unexamined beliefs (the familiar black-and-white thinking so often decried by academics) through intermediate stages of thinking that recognize the increasing relativity of facts to rules and contexts, until the learner finally arrives at more supple forms of thinking, able to reflect on patterns of inference. In the King and Kitchener version, this highest level moves beyond well-structured problems, in which context is already given, toward unstructured problems that require complex judgments for which no single set of rules of inference is available.

This is no small challenge. As King and Kitchener observe, students typically enter college at a prereflective level in their thinking processes. In college, students come to realize that knowledge is sometimes uncertain and that beliefs must be justified in more complex ways. This is not equivalent to full-fledged reflective thinking, but students in the main advance into at least quasi-reflective thinking. They are able to use reasoning and evidence in shaping their judgments, as well as evaluating and justifying them (King and Kitchener, 1994). It is unclear whether the inclination to think critically about situations, to be open to argument and evidence, and to engage with complexity and ambiguity develops at the same time as the cognitive abilities themselves. In other words, the development of disposition and critical virtue may be different from cognitive maturation—the formation of critical skill.

As an educational agenda, critical thinking holds out to students the prospect of movement from a simpler, more primitive state of mental capacities, often characterized as concrete and operational, toward a more mature, complex higher-order thinking that is formal or general in pattern rather than concrete and context-bound. Virtually all educational programs to develop critical thinking imagine their aim as teaching students to abstract general rules from specific contexts and thereby to inculcate the priority of analytical over concrete or intuitive thinking. This agenda overlooks the embodied, often tacit knowledge present in skillful judgment. Knowledge is reduced to formal or representational modes exclusively.

The third feature of the critical thinking agenda is the separation of the form of reasoning from its contents and of abstract patterns of thinking from dispositions and habits of comportment. Critical thinking thus appears to both educators and students as essentially an affair of training the mind in such a way that the shaping of perception and intuition, like involvement in contexts of action, is of only peripheral importance.

This conception of reasoning and knowing lies at the core of modern academic life. But it remains controversial to claim that focusing on critical thinking in this general, formal way actually delivers the intended outcome—or, indeed, if this notion is even coherent in the first place. One of the most serious objections raised to this agenda is based on the finding, supported by considerable educational research, that higher-order patterns of thinking turn out to be notoriously difficult to transfer from one learning context or one subject matter to another. John E. McPeck has argued that critical thinking abilities, far from constituting a general skill, are highly context- and domain-specific (McPeck, 1981).

McPeck goes on to insist that the most substantive definition of the term *critical thinking* that we can legitimately give is that it constitutes "the propensity and skill to engage in an activity with reflective skepticism" (McPeck, 1981, p. 152). In other words, properly construed, there is no a priori "thing" or "skill" called critical thinking, as such. Rather, we can discern the place of critical thinking as an analytical moment of broader disciplinary practices. In isolation from particular engagements, the best we can do is to identify certain commonplaces of reflective skepticism *in use,* such as when Stephen Toulmin, in *The Uses of Argument,* counsels that all disciplines embody unique standards and traditions for considering claims, their support and warrant, and the practice of rebuttal and dispute (Toulmin, 1958).[1]

Finally, the fourth feature of this agenda is perhaps its most marked characteristic. Becoming a critical thinker is usually described as moving up toward general propositions and universal patterns of argument, leaving behind concrete experience, information, and context. This process of development is pictured as unidirectional. For this reason, it seems fair to call this an up-and-away view of higher education, the purpose of which seems to be the freeing of individual minds from the constraints and limited horizons of their inherited patterns of living and thinking.

This final presumption makes the critical thinking agenda powerfully attractive for educators and students alike. It casts the educator as an emancipator. The teacher prods developing minds to grow their cognitive wings and break free of narrow horizons, to fly deep into the sky of analytical cognition. In this way, the individual is emancipated from inherited prejudice and limitation. This is liberation from the confinement of the particular, rather than a consideration of, or an engagement with, the particular. This educative journey is cast as both a maturation and a leave-taking: from the particular to the general; from the specific to the universal; from the concrete and time-bound to the timeless and abstract. What emerges is a particular view of what is "liberal" about liberal education.

The preferred means for accomplishing this task, though variously understood, is immersion into what we might call a culture of argument. (Advocates of the critical thinking agenda rarely speak in terms of participation in communities or induction into cultures or practices of thinking, however.) The critical thinking agenda resonates with the Socratic tradition's instigation of the examination of life, of the value of thinking self-reflexively.

It is striking, however, that few advocates of the critical thinking agenda have noted the problem that, as we have seen, Plato brought to attention in his exploration of education in *The Republic*. When Plato has Socrates lay out an educational agenda for the formation of the philosophical rulers known as the Guardians, he explicitly takes up the issue of their initiation into the culture of argument. Here, Socrates shifts perspective from the liberation metaphor of the cave. He suddenly warns his interlocutors about the nihilistic potential of acquiring the skills of critical argument when poorly grounded by a moral compass developed through earlier study of literature and myth. The so-called lower-order or operational thinking typical of uncritical immersion in imaginative thinking—the sort of thinking one might imagine typical of dwellers in the cave—is not something over and done with, therefore. Reverencing good ideals and drawing analogies from right models turn out to be vital, for these activities provide pre-reflective understandings of value that can withstand the winds of criticism. Otherwise, we are told, ideas of value inevitably come to appear arbitrary. (Of course, it is crucial that in the city Socrates is constructing in the imagination, those "mythical" understandings have already been "corrected" by critical reflection.)

Still, without such grounding, Socrates insists that learning the tools of argument can be disastrous for both individual and society. He analogizes fledgling dialecticians to young hounds who discover that they can tear to bits any argument, making the weaker and worse case seem the stronger and better. Thus virtue and critical skill are not the same. For this reason, Socrates goes on to say, future Guardians must not only be well formed morally before they embark on the study of dialectic. They must also follow their dialectical training with a long stint of supervised practical involvement in the affairs of the city. Only then, he argues, will their critical capacities be of benefit to themselves and their city (Plato, 538a–540a).

Historian Christopher Lasch offers a contemporary version of this critique in *The Revolt of the Elites* (1995). Lasch raises concerns about the effects of higher education on the habits of mind of those who succeed best in the kind of meritocratic competition the academy promotes. Higher education's great function is to initiate students into the "culture of critical discourse" (Lasch, 1995, p. 34). Lasch argues that critical discourse is the common coin of the academy and of the meritocratic elites who staff the key institutions of modern society. In the culture of critical discourse, innovation is valued over continuity, flexibility and variety over loyalty, technical intelligence and instrumental finesse over character, and moral cultivation and iconoclasm over reverence.

This peculiar culture creates an invidious separation from "ordinary people," Lasch worries. Because this culture is the key to elevation into superior status, possession of the credentials of critical discourse often breeds arrogance. It leads those who master it to see themselves as meritorious experts who deserve their status because they solve complex problems in sophisticated ways. However, echoing Plato's Socrates, Lasch points out that such experts tend to see themselves and their lives in strategic terms, often consumed by maneuvering for the better deal in the status competition internal to professional occupations. When embraced naïvely, Lasch concluded, this apparently sophisticated consciousness becomes the growing soil of nihilism (Lasch, 1995).

We believe that the Platonic parable of the education of the Guardians, interpreted pointedly for our time, reveals an important omission in the critical thinking agenda: its blindness to education as formation. Socrates' warning can spark the insight that practical reasoning provides at once a completion and a corrective to the agenda of critical thinking. Contemporary learning theory has provided conceptual tools to fill out this Platonic insight in ways that emphasize how all four topics of practical reasoning—*identity, community,* and *responsibility,* as well as *bodies of knowledge*—become relevant once the educational agenda is broadened to reconnect analytical thinking with the larger purpose of just human formation.

Practical Reason as Alternative Educational Agenda

Educational agendas resonate with larger culture-shaping movements at work in the contemporary world. Seen against this larger backdrop, the critical thinking agenda emerges as a script for forming particular kinds of persons who are equipped to take up a stance of criticism toward inherited ideas and values. That script is at once lofty and familiar, carrying on recognizable themes of the eighteenth-century Enlightenment. Its core intuition is that knowledge is developed by representing the social and natural worlds in objective and universal terms that surmount inherited prejudice and superstition. But the cognitive agenda is also closely linked to the formative project: developing persons who can subject all things to distanced criticism is ultimately for the sake of moral progress.

Whether the two sides of this agenda fit well together is, as we have noted, a contested issue. But overall, the resonance of the educational program with the larger cultural aims is nonetheless striking. It is around this ultimately moral aim that serious conversation between the agenda of critical thinking and practical reason might begin.

What, then, of practical reasoning as an alternative educational agenda? In the form in which the members of the seminar practice it, practical reasoning affirms an emphasis, shared with proponents of the critical thinking agenda, on developing self-awareness and the ability to subject opinions to analysis and critique. The core intuition is different, however, as is its larger resonance. Practical reason looks on knowledge, including representational knowledge, as founded on participation and engagement with the world. This is most evident in practical reason's assumption that all knowing, including all criticism (McPeck, 1981), takes place within particular knowledge communities, defined by specific cognitive practices.

This epistemology portrays knowledge as rooted in interactions that give rise to holistic recognition of pattern, rather than in analytical distinction among elements. More explicit, analytical understandings are produced through practices of interpretation. In this model, developing clarity of understanding necessarily moves in a "hermeneutical circle." The vaguely intuited whole, which is the source of meaning, provides the tacit context within which the active work of inquiring, testing evidence, and drawing inferences gets point and direction. So rather than being an up-and-away, unidirectional trajectory, education for practical reason is about establishing a conscious relationship between the implicit, holistic grounds of meaning, on the one hand, and the work of analytical thinking, such as articulating logical inferences of cause-and-effect, ranking and ordering, and inclusion or exclusion of concepts within general categories.

The educational goal of practical reasoning is the formation of persons who think and act through a back-and-forth dialogue between analytical thought and the ongoing constitution of meaning. As we have seen, the best of professional work and teaching embody just such an ongoing dialogue between these two modes of thinking. The teaching cases with which we began in the Introduction to this book already exemplified this fundamental feature of practical reason. The use of case studies enables such teachers as Hessel Bouma, Robert McGinn, and Allen Hammond to represent to their students various ways in which skilled persons use formally derived knowledge within meaningful frameworks in order to think and decide matters of judgment.

As we saw, the use of analogy proved critical in legal argument as Allen Hammond led his class to follow the circle of interpretation in judicial decisions. Students discovered that judges' efforts to solve legal puzzles engendered leaps of analogical imagination. These intuitive judgments then had to be tested out by meticulous criticism and argument, in an effort to establish substantive equity while maintaining the formal consistency of principles. In both Hessel Bouma's course on human biology and Robert McGinn's engineering ethics course, meanwhile, students confronted what King and Kitchener would call unstructured problems, whose solution required reflective judgments. In these courses, dialogue functioned to keep students in a responsive relationship to each other's concerns. Bouma's and McGinn's pedagogies of practical reason sought to ground the students' deliberation about judgment in responsibility for consequences, in order to prevent ungrounded criticism from sliding into arbitrariness or nihilism.

Pedagogies of practical reason aim at the formation of a particular kind of self: an engaged self, who has absorbed the critical perspective without becoming identified with it. Such persons use critique in order to act responsibly on behalf of shared ideals. Practical reason aims at a kind of synthetic knowing that links self-conscious awareness to responsive engagement in projects in the world. These engagements are understood as ongoing traditions of inquiry and construction that, while increasingly open to critical investigation, are valuable sources of meaning, rooted in modes of engagement in the world that cannot be fully translated into representational symbols. The agenda of practical reason could be said to be about re-grounding the ideals of the Enlightenment. This agenda grounds the meaning of critical rationality in human purposes that are wider and deeper than criticism, in part inherited and partly constructed in emerging social relationships. Thus the practical reasoning agenda resonates with the progressive aspirations of the Enlightenment project. Unlike the critical thinking agenda, however, practical reasoning values embodied responsiveness and responsibility over the detached critical expert.

Practical Reason and Contemporary Theories of Mind

Jerome Bruner, one of the pioneers of what has been called the cognitive revolution in modern psychology, has argued that modern societies depend on two broadly different modes of thinking that do not fit easily together (Bruner, 1986). Bruner called one mode of thinking *analytic,* or paradigmatic thinking (which we call here *analytical*). In this mode of thinking, things and events are detached from the situations of everyday life and represented in more abstract and systematic ways. Analytical thinking attempts to see the world through general patterns of cause and effect. Its aim is to translate particular objects or events into general concepts, as well as to discern rules for combining and manipulating these symbols with clarity and certainty. This is the ideal of thinking espoused by the critical thinking agenda for education.

Consider, for example, the great cultural authority wielded by the model of analytical or paradigmatic reason. This is exemplified by remarkable advances in the mathematical sciences' ability to measure, explain, and control natural phenomena. When students are inducted into scientific thinking, they are learning to conceive and describe events in terms of general rules and procedures. This analytical mode of reasoning is the ideal of knowledge upheld in the university, which places a premium on formal knowledge, abstracted from context and particularity. Students are often led to conclude that analytical thinking demonstrates a superior grade of knowledge, ultimately applicable to practice through formal techniques for deducing results.

Over time, this model of knowledge has become the unquestioned canon according to which intellectual disciplines are defined and criticized. It is also the model in light of which the academic disciplines are distinguished from what are considered more primitive claims to knowledge, like those derived from the experience of practice, including clinical experience. Philosopher Stephen Toulmin, a noted proponent of practical reasoning, has criticized this genealogy of the modern disciplines. Toulmin makes the strong argument that, despite its successes in technology, the methods of the modern sciences provide inadequate support for the actual use of scientific knowledge in fields of professional endeavor, such as medicine (Toulmin, 2001). In other words, the analytical mode of thinking that Bruner describes is only a part of what rationality is all about. This is a charge with merit, as we shall shortly see.

Bruner also characterized a second cognitive style, however, called the narrative mode of thinking. Here, things and events achieve significance by being placed within a broader story, or ongoing context of meaningful interaction. This mode of thinking integrates experience through meta-phor and analogy. The narrative mode is employed in the arts, both in practical situations and very heavily in professional practice, including clinical medicine. It cannot provide certainty, but it does allow the inquirer to explore and make sense of situations and contexts of action. Moreover, Bruner showed that the narrative mode of thought is closer than the analytical mode to the sources of human meaning and value, even in contemporary society. And yet, in modern culture, narrative think-ing is mostly taken for granted. In the university, narrative reasoning gets little respect when compared to analysis, its flashier younger sibling.

Bruner refined the contrast between these two types of thinking further as an opposition between two models of mind. The first, derived from the analytical mode of reason, he called information processing. The second, on which the narrative model is premised, Bruner called meaning-making (Bruner, 1990). Bruner noted that advances in artificial intelligence research have created a popular view of mental activity as akin to digital computing, running "programs" that apply rules in the processing of ele-ments or "data." Behind this metaphor stand certain modern theories of language that postulate inborn processing structures that operate much like computer programs.

Bruner, however, argued that this conception rests on an unfortunate simplification. Some kinds of human thinking are indeed forms of infor-mation processing. Analytical thinking shares some of these "digital" features, especially the use of categories and rules of inference for associ-ating data and drawing conclusions. But all this rests on a more funda-mental human capacity for meaning-making. Such sense-making grows out of the sensory-motor activities of the human organism and works by constructing analogues from sensory experience. Humans make sense of their world by shaping experience into whole patterns, like perceptual gestalts. This model of mind draws on the findings of the Gestalt theory of perception, which has shown that humans perceive not digitally (bit-by-bit) but by combining digital clues into whole patterns. Thus rec-ognition of known persons and places is almost instantaneous for humans but laborious and slow for computers, which must match every perceived element to known bits of information, one-by-one.

Holistic representational patterns enable humans to cope with situations. These patterns synthesize both emotional and cognitive significance. Furthermore, humans do this within broader systems of "distributed cognition," or communities of intensely social interaction. Within these settings, groups develop narratives to integrate perceptual and operational gestalts into larger patterns for representing both self and world in meaningful contexts. Narrative thinking, Bruner follows Jean Piaget in noting, precedes the development of conceptual thinking in children. It remains universal in human experience, and it is through concrete engagements with the world that the patterns of meaning narrative represents arise in the first place. In Bruner's conception, analysis always retains a certain dependence on narrative and underlying interactions with the social and natural worlds (Bruner, 1990). Human thinking is necessarily bi-modal, with narrative holding priority. Narrative without analysis can be naïve, but analysis without narrative is literally meaningless.

An Anatomy of Practical Reasoning: The Example of Clinical Medicine

The force and significance of Bruner's argument becomes vividly apparent in the case of medicine. No field of endeavor has been more identified in the popular imagination with the triumphs of modern science, and so there is nowhere one would least expect to encounter the dependence of analytical rationality on narrative thinking. Yet this dependence holds true, even at the heart of medicine, in the clinical decision making and interventions of physicians who strive to treat patients. In a recent study of physicians' ways of reasoning, Katherine Montgomery argues: "Despite medicine's appeal to the canons of physical science as a model for its work, physicians do not reason as they imagine scientists do." Faced with a patient, physicians do not "proceed as they and their textbooks often describe it: top-down, deductively, 'scientifically.'" Instead, they reason from cases (Montgomery, 2005, p. 46).

The starting point for all case-based reasoning, Montgomery's study shows, is neither deduction from general principles nor induction from the particulars to a universal concept. Instead, doctors form hypotheses about the possible causes of a particular patient's situation, then test those possibilities against details revealed by closer examination of the patient. This is a "circular, interpretive procedure" that moves between "generalities in the taxonomy of disease and the particular signs and symptoms of the individual case." This intellectual movement proceeds "until a workable conclusion is reached" (Montgomery, 2005, p. 47). The reasoning process at the center of this activity is the interpretive circle that we have seen used in a variety of situations of practical reasoning. The case narratives that physicians construct are not mere conjecture or poetic flights of speculation. Case narratives put conjectures to the test. They employ analytical and taxonomic knowledge through the interpretive work of isolating probable causes of illness by eliminating alternative possibilities—that is, by differential diagnosis.

The narrative mode of reasoning remains at the heart of medical practice and training. Montgomery argues that the case narrative is "the principal means of thinking and remembering—of *knowing*—in medicine." The case narrative represents nothing less than "clinical judgment . . . in all its situated and circumstantial uncertainty" (Montgomery, 2005, p. 46). It enables practitioners to makes sense of the contingent unfolding of a disease or medical situation by setting up a kind of conversation, a back-and-forth, between the patient's particular story and general analytical knowledge. Analytical modes of explanation alone simply cannot achieve the integrated forms of understanding that medical professionals produce through this kind of narrative sense-making.

The crucial point, insists Montgomery, is that case reasoning is not a holdover from the pre-scientific past. Rather, it is "the best means of representing the exercise of clinical judgment" (p. 46). As such, case reasoning is the indispensable foundation of all medical skill. Montgomery concludes that we must recognize that medicine is more than a science. It is a complex practice of healing in which "diagnosis and treatment are intensively science-using activities," though not "in and of themselves, science" (Montgomery, 2005, pp. 46, 52).

The chief accomplishment of medical education lies in its fostering of an ongoing, back-and-forth conversation between the narrative and the analytical. Medical education must provide a foundation in both kinds of learning in order to be effective. One cannot become a doctor in any responsible or meaningful sense without proper induction into the scientific knowledge and frameworks on which medical practice depends. Abstract, analytical representations of scientific knowledge provide useful scaffolding for narrative thinking, inasmuch as physicians must deploy large quantities of knowledge about human anatomy, physiology, and the like. But doctors must also be able to integrate, or re-integrate, this analytical knowledge through ongoing practical contexts, for which the final question is always *what to do* for and with *this* patient at *this* time. Resolving such questions about the doctor's action and responsibility requires the same narrative organization that posing the question does.

Like analytical capacity, the clinical habits of mind that are necessary for skillful intervention in patients' lives can be developed and trained. But the formation of such habits of practical mind requires, as every medical educator knows, complex forms of apprentice-like pedagogy. It requires the everyday modeling of expert judgment, in concert with the coaching of learners through analogous activities. This is why clinical training is so important, even in an age of so-called scientific medicine. "Clinical education," Montgomery concludes, "is finely calibrated to instill and reward the development of clinical judgment in the face of uncertainty" (Montgomery, 2005, p. 52). It is a particularly illuminating— because so highly elaborated and stylized—example of education in practical reasoning.

The Relevance of Practical Professional Pedagogies for Liberal Education

The learning sciences' understanding of cognitive development casts into high relief the relevance of the professions' practice-oriented pedagogies for re-orienting and revitalizing liberal education. Training in clinical medicine is one of the most highly developed of these pedagogies, but in the seminar we encountered other examples drawn from fields as diverse as engineering and seminary education. As opposed to the up-and-away, unidirectional picture of liberal learning promoted by the critical thinking agenda, the practice-oriented pedagogies of the professions point to the need to develop sensitivity to particular contexts, both intellectual and practical. Only by becoming familiar with how a particular field understands the salient dimensions of action—*identity, community, responsibility,* and *bodies of knowledge*—is it possible for students to develop the holistic and meaningful grasp of situation that marks professional expertise.

This process of formation is achieved through a three-fold pattern: a rhythm of moving back and forth from engagement with the concrete situation toward the use of analytical reasoning and back again toward a more informed and discerning engagement with the situation. This process is reiterated many times in effective professional education. Indeed, it is the multiple iterations that allow for improvement through feedback. The development of cognitive processes, after all, is always simultaneously a social process. It requires personal engagement with a particular community and its modes of thinking and acting. The centrality and effectiveness of feedback in helping people learn provides the rationale for formative assessment—those forms of response to student work that are intended to guide the student's ongoing development, in contrast to summative assessment—the final grades that select and ratify completed student achievement.

This three-fold movement—this back-and-forth between particular and general, narrative and analysis—occurs in all professional practice. Physicians, as we have seen, engage medical situations through a specific framework of meaning, as persons shaped by the profession of medicine. This profession is a social organization that embodies an ongoing tradition of concern with healing, including a commitment to use the best available scientific knowledge to promote that goal. Through this tradition, physicians learn to be effective agents of healing, willing and able to focus their skills and knowledge on assisting patients. Physicians are also trained in scientific analysis and problem solving, learning the detached stance of a researcher in the biomedical sciences. Perhaps most important, they are taught, through the intimate relationships of apprenticeship, habits of moving back and forth between these two cognitive positions, so as to re-engage more effectively with the therapeutic situation. *Practical reason* is the name for this whole circuit of thinking.

This three-fold circuit of practical reason describes human rationality in its widest and most dynamic sense. As the example of the professional fields suggests, the circuit is a social process, as well as an individual activity. Its power and significance have impressed some modern thinkers, most notably John Dewey, as a key to understanding humanity's evolution as a learning and inquiring species. Dewey's notion of inquiry placed the detached, analytical stance of scientific investigation as a "moment" within the larger process of human rationality. Dewey noted how science has enabled our species to better understand the workings of nature and, in certain areas, to control nature in support of human purposes (Dewey, 1929). However, the reason for undertaking the investigation in the first place, as well as its potential meaning, come only from those shared, historically rooted cultural meanings that Dewey sometimes called experience.

Dewey argued that it was a shared experience, or cultural ethos, that enabled a group of interacting investigators to perceive a situation as problematic and therefore as a stimulus to inquiry. Purposeful human activity, or *praxis* in the Greek sense, is thus the ground and also the goal of the analytical phase of inquiry. The point of inquiry is to restore, or reconstitute, the flow of meaningful activity. Analytical thinking is successful when it contributes to a fuller, more adequate narrative understanding of the salience of events. Human rationality in its full sense is ultimately practical—and therefore social, historical, and narrative—by nature (Dewey, 1938).

The great revolution in thinking that we call modern science has gradually codified and institutionalized the second, analytical phase of the circuit of practical reason. Approaching nature with objectivity and distance has proved enormously fruitful in the production of accurate information. It has also provided new powers to control and transform natural processes, as the achievements of modern technology demonstrate powerfully. The neat, bounded quality of the observer's stance is one of the charms of scientific theory. Another is the sense of certainty available in theory, so welcome compared to the unsettled uncertainty and anxiety of decision that pervades the realm of practice. The aesthetic appeal of the qualities inherent in theorizing, along with the technological powers generated thereby, have seduced some philosophers into imagining that scientific thinking exhausts rationality itself, that information is all of knowledge.

This is a serious mistake. Fixating on the analytical phase of inquiry threatens to short out the vital circuit of rationality. A more expansive sense of practical rationality can help to release this fixation. A grasp of inquiry in its full, practical sense also offers a remedy for the widespread worry that we live today awash in meaningless information, overwhelmed by the production of knowledge that, in the form of weaponry and environmental degradation, threatens human survival itself. As these threats reveal, the great challenge of our era is precisely to re-integrate the analytical phase of investigation and knowledge production with those frameworks of cultural orientation on which we depend in order to secure human flourishing in the long term. To see the problem in this way is to grasp the perspective of practical reason.

Captivated by the expanding powers of the detached, analytical stance, liberal education can fail to convey this vital sense of narrative meaning and lose thereby its historic capacity to orient and enrich the life of our culture. All the members of the seminar worried about this possibility in different ways. Dewey worried about this possibility as well. His theory of inquiry was intended to map the wider normative terrain of human rationality, such that we might avoid this analytical trap. What needs more emphasis today than in Dewey's time is the vital necessity of re-grounding the academy's legitimate concern for fostering theoretical abstraction on the meaningfulness of lived experience itself. The four topics that we developed over the course of the seminar are an example of such an effort. Attending to the demands of identity, community, responsibility, and bodies of knowledge brings alive Dewey's insight that intellectual reflection—the transmuting of meaningful experience into general concepts—is not as an end in itself. Such concepts are guides for engaging a richer terrain of experience.

This broader educational agenda and the engaged pedagogical practices on which it depends can only be sustained given the proper enabling conditions, however. Education for practical reasoning is only possible if teachers and students actually *do* have recourse to broader narratives and frameworks of meaning through which to act with growing responsibility. Even if we all agree about the value of practical reasoning as an alternative educational agenda, we may find ourselves straining for resources beyond the analytical and the instrumental. The institutions through which we undertake and undergo our lives may be so fragmented—so denuded of normative horizon—that we can scarcely imagine, much less enact, a broader sense of responsibility and vocation.

Commenting on Jerome Bruner's distinction between analytical information processing and the narrative formation of meaning, anthropologist Bradd Shore has posed a worrisome question. Shore imagines a sort of continuum along which modern institutions range. Toward one end lie institutions that embody stable and integrating models of sense-making. These include religious and cultural communities but also professions to the degree that they are communities of ethically committed practice. Such contexts provide, even at the level of perception and bodily skill or expression, "relatively stable models or schemas by means of which people can maintain a sense of fundamental stability in their apprehension of reality." Shore calls these "orienting models" for sense-making (Shore, 1996, p. 157).

Toward the other end of the continuum lie institutions such as the capitalist market, modern advertising, or many aspects of the World Wide Web. In these contexts, pattern stability gives way to an apprehension of flexibility and of contingent and transient possibility. This can be an exhilarating experience for individuals, opening new opportunities for self-expression or exploration. But the predominance of such fractal patterns of experience also poses a threat to individual growth and the integrity of experience. Shore worries that "there may be distinct cognitive limits" to how well individuals can assimilate unrelated bits of information until "experience loses its integration" and becomes flat and arbitrary (Shore, 1996, p. 158). This, of course, is a description of the leveling at the core of the postmodern condition, criticized by some and celebrated by others.

Shore's worry echoes Socrates' warning about the destructive potential of the ungrounded use of argument in Plato's *The Republic* but enlarges the scope of this warning to concern not only the conduct of individuals but the ascendant trends of contemporary culture. Shore's interpretation is significant because it tightly ties the educational process of becoming a particular sort of person to the enabling conditions for meaning-making. In order to grasp "flexibility, and contingent, and transient possibility," the individual depends on a prior sense of the coherence of self and world. Traditionally, liberal education has aspired to foster just such a sense. And, as we have seen, this is not only true of liberal education in the humanities and sciences. The professional fields must also emphasize the formation of an antecedent integrity of experience, so that students can begin to engage the world in ways that are consistent with the skillful comportment shared by a particular profession. Toward this end, the professions have developed a variety of what we have called pedagogies of engagement.

The university has become the paramount institutional context for formation in both the professions and the liberal arts and sciences. As such, the university either enables or disables the educational agenda of practical reason. It is to the university that we now turn.

Instituting Educational Agendas: What Is Higher Education For?

One of the key findings of contemporary cognitive research is how important conceptual models, or schemas, are in human thinking. Social thinkers such as Clifford Geertz have made an important criticism of what Bradd Shore calls the *psychologism* implicit in much cognitive research. Cognitive psychologists have tended to base their research on the premise that "the construction of mental models mediates an individual's encounter with a particular physical world." By contrast, Shore argues, Geertz and others reveal that

> the social environment includes a stock of shared social models that constrain and motivate the [individual's] construction of cognitive models . . . by introducing a *social* environment into the equation, the anthropologist transforms the problem of models into one involving intersubjective communication and not just adaptation. (Shore, 1996, pp. 49–50; see Geertz, 2000)

Shore calls these shared, dialogical understandings *instituted* models— models that are rooted in organized practices that help define group identities and the meaning of situations and practices. They are the stock of culture (Shore, 1996).

The educational agendas we have been examining, both critical thinking and practical reason, find their source in the instituted models of the modern university. The university is a cultural institution. Like all institutions, universities are "distributed cognitive systems"—that is, networks or webs of interaction through which humans think, deliberate, and act. The patterns of thought and experience that are "instituted" by the university fix, amplify, and sustain particular aspects of human rationality that would otherwise be merely episodic experiences in the lives of persons. The university establishes particular foci of shared attention and reference that enable individuals to imagine their lives in coordination with others. Shore calls these foci templates. In doing so, the university also marginalizes other possible concerns.

The culture of the modern university is distinguished by its emphasis on cognitive templates that frame experience in highly general, analytical terms. These universal templates make it possible to see beyond the uniqueness of particular aspects of the world, toward common aspects that bind apparently unrelated patterns of experience. They enable comparisons between objects, situations, persons, and groups that would be impossible otherwise, such as when anthropologists speak of the diverse range of human cultural expression. In this way, analysts may enter apparently alien human situations more knowledgeably and sympathetically as "cases" of a more general category.

But it is a mistake to conclude that the particular is somehow the enemy of the general or that the universal represents a necessarily higher or more real sort of knowing than engaged knowledge of the local and the specific. The educational agenda of practical reason opens another possibility. The general and the particular are not in zero-sum relation to each other epistemologically. They are tied together necessarily. Through the particular, the general achieves sensibility. Through the general, the particular achieves salience.

Consider one of the most prized aspects of critical, theoretical reason, namely, the ability to interrogate experience and ask penetrating questions that open up new perspectives on even familiar aspects of the world. As we have seen, the critical thinking agenda places the ability to do this close to the top of its hierarchy of cognitive development. But this agenda remains unable to account for the willingness or unwillingness of particular persons, or populations, to engage in this practice. It cannot, on its own terms, explain how to get students to *care* about disciplined inquiry and invest the work that is necessary for critical formation. The critical thinking agenda is left straining for the "affective factors" that might lead to "curiosity and purpose" (Kurfiss, 1988, p. 47).

Even in contexts whose aims are purely theoretical, such as the natural or social sciences, the precondition of critical thinking is engagement with the intellectual practices at hand. As Dewey reminds us, questions arise from breakdowns in the taken-for-granted assumptions of valued activities and contexts. In order to pose "critical" questions, one must first be sufficiently engaged with (and within) a context of communication or action to have made its purposes and perspective one's own (Dewey, 1920; Sullivan, 2004). Even when carried out by an individual in solitude, these practices are always rooted in social interaction, supported by institutions. Ultimately, analytical practices are forms of participation in shared social projects, such as natural scientific research. When disruptions or breakdowns occur, it is engaged participants, having internalized a disposition to attend to the aims of the practice, who can raise significant questions. Although these questions may lead to a critical or distanced stance, they remain oriented and motivated by their underlying position of engagement in the practice. Different disciplinary templates provide different analogies, so they direct attention toward various aspects of the situation, such as the distanced and critical orientation of the theoretical disciplines or the engaged and practical stance of the professional fields.

The humanistic tradition of the liberal arts and sciences is deeply committed to the development of students' capacities for the critical interrogation of experience. It shares this concern with the critical thinking agenda. Yet like the professional disciplines, the humanistic tradition has been concerned historically about engagement with the world, the situation, and other selves as well. As such, the humanistic and professional domains have much to learn from one another. As we have seen in this book, the virtue of the distinctive pedagogies of the professions is that they provide ways of teaching forms of engagement that are both reflective critically and committed practically. The four topics of the seminar—*identity, community, responsibility,* and *bodies of knowledge*—distill this insight into orienting questions for both teaching and the practice of inquiry itself. By reorienting their professional students toward this wider terrain of action, a number of the seminar's professional educators have consciously found the approaches of the humanistic tradition decisive for their teaching.

This is particularly evident in two courses that are designed to broaden professional students' understanding of the dimensions of professional competence. Gary Downey and Juan Lucena's "Engineering Cultures" is intended to lead skeptical engineering students beyond their discipline's frequent indifference to diversity of historical and cultural context. Downey and Lucena hope to help their students recognize, through guided writing assignments and discussion, the complexity of the human interests and values that engineers must engage in order to resolve engineering problems within an increasingly global workplace. Daisy Floyd's "Advanced Legal Ethics," meanwhile, contends with the challenge of enabling law students to assess their chosen profession in light of a broader horizon. She hopes to help her students develop healthier practices for integrating the technical and competitive aspects of their work with a broader sense of normative purpose and vocation.

Pedagogical perspectives that are more typical of the humanities are central to both of these courses. By leading students to take the role and viewpoints of others, thus distancing themselves temporarily from their domains of involvement, these courses teach students to conceive their own identities within a broader, more "objective" framework. But by incorporating these new understandings through writing and dialogue, the students are also enabled to consider their practical responsibilities in the world more richly: To whom and for what am I accountable? Downey and Floyd's students expand their own horizons as competent, reflective, and ethically committed professionals by engaging these questions—questions that are made possible through engagement with the perspectives and practices of the humanistic tradition.

The orientation toward practice that distinguishes the professions also provides powerful ways of expanding the scope and import of liberal arts courses. William Spohn's "Scripture and the Moral Life," for instance, introduced students to enriched practices of biblical reading that enable them to imagine and respond to the moral demands of modern life more sensitively. There, too, students' sense of self was opened as they came to include more distant others—often historically and culturally very distant others—within their expanding sense of perspectives that might illuminate the moral dimensions of experience. Spohn hoped to help his students achieve a heightened awareness of the significance of their own decisions and the assumptions underlying them. Spohn's students' sense of who they ought to become grew increasingly intertwined with the question of to whom they were responsible in their decisions and for what ends— questions that also inform good professional education.

Like the other courses examined in the seminar, the teaching practices of Downey, Floyd, and Spohn reveal a convergence of themes between professional preparation and liberal learning. One of the important implications of this line of thought is that institutional templates or bodies of knowledge are never simply tools, or neutral instruments, in the hands of individuals. Rather, institutions incorporate meanings in their practices and so are "pedagogical" and "formative" in their effects. They confer value and legitimacy on certain forms of life and thinking while marginalizing others. This is especially true for those instituted templates that require intense, intimate engagement over time. To imagine universities and colleges as culturally instituted templates that shape the experience of their participants is to open up the most far-reaching questions at the heart of the Life of the Mind for Practice seminar: What is the purpose of higher education as it is currently organized, and what ought to be the purpose of higher education?

The work of sociologist John Meyer and his colleagues provides empirical evidence that higher education's remarkable spread around the globe during the past half-century represents the diffusion of a universalizing cultural template. Meyer challenges the shibboleth that higher education's spread is simply a response to more complex patterns of work. This utilitarian assumption cannot account for the striking uniformity in both structure and content in higher education, argue Meyer and associates. Their counterproposal fits well with our analysis of educational agendas earlier in this chapter. Their key premise is that, far from being essentially utilitarian in function, higher education is best seen as a culture-forming institution. Over the past half-century, the university has grown ever more prestigious and important. It enrolls ever-larger proportions of the population, even in nations where it performs few utilitarian functions in relation to the economy. The university's growth represents the spread of a "secular canopy" that specifies what counts as a legitimate explanation of reality and forms the kinds of persons who will accept and produce such understandings so as to take part in contemporary global culture (Meyer, 2006).

As David J. Frank and Jay Gabler reveal in their illuminating study (Frank and Gabler, 2006), the globalized university emphasizes the scientific explanation of physical nature. Reality is conceived as uniform, rational, and capable of being explained and manipulated according to general rules and principles. Equally important, the university's cultural frame casts the individual as essentially a free agent, capable of comprehending the world and choosing courses of action within it in order to maximize the individual's own life purposes. Such individuals find their appropriate milieu within a universal regime of individual rights and opportunities. Higher education, Frank and Gabler argue, provides an environment in which these core features of the emerging global culture can be expounded, elaborated, applied, and internalized by students and faculty alike. This, rather than any form of job preparation, is the great purpose that drives higher education's new-found prominence wherever the assumptions of this global culture are adopted. What makes university graduates desirable for jobs in the most advanced sectors of the economy, state, and society is their successful assimilation into these modern cultural assumptions.

This is a picture of the university as a culture-shaping institution carrying on the work of the Enlightenment. Its educational agenda is everywhere remarkably the same: to teach analytical reasoning—the ability to transform thought and experience from the local to the universal and general. The university inducts students into the deep structure of science and modern attitudes toward the world. It carries as its correlate the idea that the individual who successfully enters this culture is transformed in mind. Henceforth, such persons are social "actors" in a very strong sense: entitled to criticize the present and construct lives and identities of their own choosing.

Realigning Universal and Particular: Humanistic Rhetoric as Practical Reason

The work of the Life of the Mind for Practice seminar emerges in sharp relief within this cultural frame. The university's exaltation of analytical reason leaves the "actors" that it forms with few resources for re-entering the realm of concrete social life, for living amid particulars while also striving for a wide frame of mind and sympathy. The challenges of community and responsibility that are central to such living are, at best, indistinct background to the main theme of universal, individual empowerment.

The experience of the seminar reveals unexpected resources that can help fill in the missing interconnections. The old humanistic discipline of rhetoric, which has been marginalized during the last century by the rise of the scientific model of higher education, turns out to have strong affinities with the seminar's understanding of how professional and liberal education might find mutual strength and purpose. The work in rhetoric and composition theory that seminar partner Janice M. Lauer brought to our shared exploration conceives rhetoric as a discipline of inquiry into context. It provides an intellectual connection that is often missing in the university's agenda: the way "down" from analysis to engagement with others in responsible relationship. By drawing on recent work in these fields, Lauer provides her students in composition and rhetoric with deliberate learning strategies—or heuristics—to help them implement the threefold cycle of practical reasoning in a variety of academic areas. The result is a rhetorical pedagogy for our time that adds richness to our understanding of how to teach practical reasoning.

Lauer's core proposal is that we acknowledge writing as a kind of universal medium in contemporary life (Lauer, 2003). Writing is central not only in all areas of academic pursuit but also in modern work contexts, the professions, and political activity. To bring this insight to life in the lives of her students, Lauer organizes her argument into three "writing experiences" or "acts." These acts are organized as follows:

1. The first act is Questioning. This first experience is analogous to Dewey's first phase of inquiry. This experience provides students with practical strategies for turning sources of perplexity or interest into a defined issue or topic for investigation.

2. The second act is Exploring. This is a strategy for engaging in the second phase of inquiry—that is, the moment of detached, critical questioning. Here, Lauer provides her students with practical guidance into the process of gaining perspective and insight into their topic of concern.

3. The third act is Focusing. This is the moment of judgment, in which students must decide which aspects of their topics are most salient and respond by taking up a position. Here, Lauer introduces her students to the technicalities of developing arguments as a means for communicating what they have learned, explaining their judgments, justifying their positions, and persuading others of the merit of their reasoning.

Lauer's consideration of the art of persuasion, as opposed to thinking only of logical validity, is especially notable. The rhetorical perspective, unlike formal logic, insists that we recognize that even the most abstruse cognitive endeavors are performed in relation to, and with, others. Indeed, the point of construing writing as three interconnected moments or acts—Questioning, Exploring, and Focusing—is to help her students understand that writing is *always part of an ongoing situation,* a specific "writing context" (Lauer, 2003, pp. 6–7). These three acts need not always move in sequence. On the contrary, the reiterative process of critique and revision may make one or another of the three phases dominant and repeated more than the others. The point, however, is to show students that writing is not about showing what one already knows but, perhaps surprisingly, that they can "learn something through writing" (Lauer, 2003 p. 6). That means moving the emphasis of instruction from wrestling with a pre-given thesis, for which the students struggle for the "right" answer, toward learning to confront and ask puzzling questions, and to open oneself to problematic situations and discovery (Lauer, 2003).

Lauer's pedagogy enhances her students' understanding of the "reflective skepticism" that John E. McPeck found the common coin of critical thinking (McPeck, 1981). But she provides more than an exhortation to "ask questions." The rhetorical tradition's strength was that it provided students with well-honed protocols or strategies for posing and refining questions and for discerning and defining salient topics. This was called invention (Lauer, 2004). We have already seen how the members of the seminar refined a common concern for practical reasoning by elaborating four topics that constitute, in their estimation, the fundamental terrain of responsible action: identity, community, responsibility, and bodies of knowledge. Lauer breaks down and models this kind of inquiry for her students, starting with strategies for becoming aware of the dissonances or perplexities inherent in many common understandings and contemporary situations.

For example, Lauer asks her students to think about areas in their studies where what one discipline says about human nature conflicts with the views of another, such as "some theories in my psychology class seem to conflict with my religion" (Lauer, 2003, p. 7). This conflict recalls the clashes of perspective that students experienced in Hessel Bouma's "Human Biology" course, with which we began the Introduction. Lauer provides her students with heuristics for asking what it is about these approaches that leads to this conflict, as well as why the conflict seems disturbing. What assumptions do they bring to the situation that makes the disagreement challenging to their own beliefs or hopes? This guided process of Questioning leads students to emphasize and articulate relevant aspects of the topic into which they can inquire, such as what might account for the nature and significance of an apparent dissonance between some theories in psychology and certain religious beliefs about human nature.

The second rhetorical act is Exploring. This is the phase of writing in which students assume "a somewhat detached position, allowing them to deploy critical methods based on their rhetorical knowledge" (Lauer, 2003, p. 9). Developing facility in the art of Exploring is one of the major educative benefits of the kind of composition instruction that she advocates. Lauer provides her students with practical guides to help orient—but not determine—their exploration. In the case of conflict between the theories of psychology and certain religious beliefs, for instance, students can proceed by comparing and contrasting the basic assumptions, claims to proof, and implications of both perspectives. Students may trace the changes in their own thinking as they have attempted to understand the clash between the two viewpoints. They may draw analogies to this conflict in other areas of their life or studies and develop metaphors for illuminating its stakes. As William C. Spohn does in "Scripture and the Moral Life," Lauer helps her students understand that analogy and metaphor are central aspects of how we orient our action.

This final point is central to the rhetorical perspective that Lauer models for her students. Whenever her students conduct research and ask questions, they always do so as part of a broader communicative context. Writing is always conducted in relation to some community that talks in certain ways. By refining and exploring topics of concern, her students are making an intervention in the life of this community. They are engaging in interaction. Writing, like speech, is never entirely innocent. It has effects and elicits responses from others. It also affects the writer, as when student and teacher engage one another in the process of giving feedback and making revisions. These occasions are moments of formative assessment in the richest sense: they contribute to the meaningful formation of both text and writer.

These realizations spur Lauer's students to try to understand their likely readers better. As Gary Downey and Juan Lucena do in "Engineering Cultures," Lauer encourages her students to inquire into the histories and concerns of their readers. To bring this key point home, Lauer follows contemporary composition research by stressing the actual writing contexts in response to which her students write, such as situations in the workplace, the political arena, or their personal lives (Lauer, 2003). Again, this parallels the importance of interaction with real or imagined clients that we have seen in certain professional school pedagogies. From the rhetorical perspective, exploring ideas raises challenges for the writer, not only by challenging the writer's analytical comprehension of a topic but by heightening the writer's awareness that she is entering an ongoing arena in which she will encounter others in back-and-forth debate and questioning.

The purpose of detached and critical exploration, then, is to gain the insight that is necessary for engaging responsibly in the third act of writing: Focusing. In this moment, students form judgments about what is most important, what should be said and, ultimately, what should be done. Lauer notes:

> A focus sets the stage for what you will write . . . [it is] a two-part statement that organizes a text. The first part, a subject, names the aspect of the topic under investigation; the second part expresses the point of significance, the judgment or understanding you have reached about the subject. (Lauer, 2003, p. 17)

Returning to the example of conflict between the perspectives of psychology and religion, one can imagine a student arriving at a focus like this one:

> The clash between psychology and religion about the nature of human nature (i.e., the topic of investigation) derives from important incompatible assumptions about their subject (i.e., the point of significance).

But this is not the only possibility. Another student might focus the topic like this:

> The clash between psychology and religion about the nature of human nature (i.e., the topic of investigation) is overblown. The discrepant nature of the evidence underlying the opposed positions does not permit direct comparison (i.e., a different assessment of significance).

Thus, as Barbara Stengel reminded us in Chapter One, the purpose of heuristic frameworks like the ones that Lauer provides to her students is not to *determine* students' action but to *structure* it such that they learn what it means to participate responsibly in a practice (Stengel, 2003b).

Lauer's students are now ready to compose an argument for their new judgments and understandings. They may make appeals on a variety of grounds. Lauer helps them draw on their growing understanding of context, community, and rhetorical situation, especially the nature of their readers, in order to compose arguments that are not just clear but persuasive. Lauer leads her students to consider that effective argument in actual rhetorical situations often requires several kinds of appeals. It may require appeals to shared values in order to establish a writer's credibility. Affective appeals to shared attitudes or concerns may be appropriate. Finally, logical or rational appeals, such as establishing cause-and-effect relationships or citing sources of authority, may be in order (Lauer, 2003). Each form of appeal responds to some dimension of the rhetorical situation. Lauer provides her students with examples and taxonomies of the many forms that such appeals can take, in order to help them discern the appropriate actions to take.

The logical qualities of these arguments turn out to be pivotal for students' sense of identity as rational persons. Lauer poses a set of reflective questions that help her students assess and come to terms with their own arguments and those of their peers. These questions are based on Stephen Toulmin's *The Uses of Argument,* which we cited earlier in this chapter (Toulmin, 1958). Lauer directs her students toward the reasons, assumptions, and evidence that ground their claims, as well as the ways in which their claims are qualified (Lauer, and others, 2000). By assessing their own arguments critically, as well as those of their peers, Lauer's students learn to adopt a metacognitive stance toward the meaning of their own conduct and inquiry. This critical stance is central to what it means for Lauer's students to understand themselves as rational persons.

Lauer's rhetorical pedagogy is formative in a still broader sense as well, however. As Lauer's students perform successive iterations of this process, they are provided opportunities to place the cultural assumptions with which they enter college into a more constructive and mutually illuminating relationship with both the intellectual demands of college and the practical demands of situations. The student who inquires into the conflict that she experiences when trying to square the theories that she encounters in her psychology class with her own religious beliefs does not merely learn to conduct and compose an analytical argument. She charts a broader, more insightful and more responsive identity.

As Lauer notes, the great benefit of learning to use heuristics that guide beginners consciously into the structure of a practice is that "later in the course, and in other courses, and outside academia, the strategies can be used tacitly and adapted to the writers' style and new contexts" (Lauer, 2003, p. 24). Lauer observes:

> [A] writing course that helps students to engage in practical reasoning enables them to construct understandings in their busy lives. At the end of their education, students who have inquired through writing have had the chance to grasp their fleeting moments of discovery, learning, wondering, loving, and fearing long enough to create meaning. (Lauer, 2003, p. 24)

Unlike students who have lived so fast that they fail to remember or notice what has happened to them, modern rhetorical training can enable students to become more reflective, better able to explore context, community, and identity, and more disposed toward "finding patterns and structures in their lives similar to those they have heard or read about" (Lauer, 2003, p. 24). In other words, learning to write can be more than simply the picking up of a skill. Properly taught, writing can make an important contribution toward identity. Such teaching provides formative occasions for becoming a reflective and engaged person—that elusive end to which both liberal and professional education aspire.

Lauer's teaching in composition and rhetoric illuminates the other courses that we have documented in this book in two important ways. First, Lauer helps us recover a long humanistic tradition and formative legacy that blends critical inquiry with practical engagement and responsibility. Little wonder, then, that Janice Lauer and Albert Jonsen, both of whom are expert teachers and communicators of the arts of classical rhetoric, philosophy, and the humanities, proved such important partners in the growth and formation of the seminar. Second, Lauer's teaching illuminates the deep, formative structure of the other courses that we have profiled. Our partners aspire to help their students understand that critical insight achieves significance and meaning through participation in, and taking responsibility for, the problems of their community or profession. This is why their pedagogies value cases, reflective engagement in actual work, and writing so highly. These practices populate students' imaginations, not only with diverse theoretical perspectives but with meaningful exemplars of good practice. Criticism is a fundamental aspect of what it means to chart and take up a place in one's community and to form a broader and more responsive sense of self thereby—but only insofar as the values *intrinsic to practice with others* remain of paramount concern.

There is a potential shadow side to this kind of pedagogy, if we do not remain mindful of this final insight. Discovering how to focus a topic and argue for that focus persuasively has long been the core technique taught in rhetorical education. This technique was formed traditionally through the method of arguing *in utramque partem,* for and against a topic. But how do we prevent the art of engaged action and persuasion from degenerating into relativism or the instrumental pursuit of one's own advantage? How do we help students become not merely the young hounds that Plato decried but persons with a genuine concern for the importance of critical inquiry as an aspect of judgment? How, in other words, might we teach in a way that places analytical knowing into proper and necessary relation with the concerns and demands of identity, community, and responsibility?

From the perspective of practical reason, the basis for such care and concern is not analytical technique itself but engagement in practices that are ethically, as well as technically, valued, such as civic or professional practices (Colby, Ehrlich, Beaumont, and Stephens, 2003; Sullivan, 2004). The critical stance only achieves purpose through participation in such meaning-giving practices. Educational psychologist Deanna Kuhn argues this way:

> The goal [of forming students' skills of critical judgment in a way that goes beyond mere nihilism or relativism] will not be achieved by exhortation—by telling students that a particular kind of activity is valuable, or even how or why it's valuable. A more promising adult role is that of introducing young people to activities that have a value that becomes self-evident in the course of engaging them and developing the skills they entail. (Kuhn, 2003, p. 21)

As we have noted, this formative insight has a long pedigree. It can be traced in the thinking of the ancient Stoic, Epictetus, who taught that we truly take up our "profession" as human beings only when we recognize that we are by nature both rational *and* social. We find genuine fulfillment as human beings, he argued, when we relate to others through the means of persuasion and in a spirit of cooperation (Epictetus, 1988, II). This basic Stoic insight, which views human action always in light of its place in a broader community, or *polis,* can also be traced in John Dewey's philosophy and educational thinking. Dewey counseled that lived commitments beyond the self cannot be fostered through detached critical thinking alone, though such thinking constitutes a fundamental moment in the circuit of human rationality. Rather, the enduring commitment and social interest of the student can be engaged only through participation in the values and practices of the *occupations* of students' time and place (Dewey, 1902, 1916). The fact that we remain continuously forgetful of this insight, despite its long and dignified history, is a testament to just how powerful the university's drive toward critical and universal templates of conduct remains.

———— o ————

Janice Lauer's presentation of composition pedagogy as practical reason provides a good point at which to conclude our exposition of the lessons of the seminar. "Unless writers can express what they want to understand and don't grasp yet about a subject," Lauer writes, "they can't begin the process of inquiry well" (Lauer, 2003, p. 4). It is a humbling reminder that the seminar organizers themselves started too abstractly, by giving our partners a pre-formulated thesis that they were to "prove" through their own teaching. It was only through failing on that path that we were able to learn, from our partners, that the way toward understanding in the realm of practical reason lies necessarily through mutual engagement. In practical reasoning, all are participants, seeking to discover together the meaning of identity, community, and responsibility for animating the subject matters of the professional and liberal arts. In our final chapter, we return to the question of how this large lesson from the seminar experience might become *practical* for others as well.

ENDNOTES

1. Regarding Toulmin's *The Uses of Argument*, see also Kurfiss, 1988.

CONCLUSION

TAKING FORMATIVE ACTION

HOW SHOULD THE ACADEMY RESPOND PEDAGOGICALLY to the practical demands of judgment in the world? How might the institutional divisions that prevent such responsiveness be overcome?

In *A New Agenda for Higher Education,* we have addressed these questions in four stages. First, we turned to the actual teaching of faculty who represent a wide variety of professions, disciplines, geographical locations, and institutional contexts. We witnessed the ways in which they work to sustain a broad conception of academic purpose within their respective fields, in order to foster informed practices of responsible judgment in the lives of their students. These teachers wrestle with a common predicament: the challenge of teaching for responsible judgment through academic contexts that devalue practice at the expense of universality and generalized critical thinking. We hope that you have recognized your own values in the lives of these teachers.

Second, we told the story of what happened when The Carnegie Foundation gathered these diverse teachers together through the Life of the Mind for Practice seminar. We hoped to foster a common dialogue across fields so that we might better understand the stakes and possibilities of their shared predicament. The seminar was successful. It engendered collaboration and the formation of a shared discourse. But we also discovered how difficult cross-professional community building really is within the contemporary academy and how liberating an experience it can be for faculty. We hope that our narrative of the seminar experience can serve as the basis for new models of collaborative faculty development across disciplines and professions. Such new models would be oriented toward the discovery of common predicaments, common purposes, and new opportunities for institutional renewal.

Third, in the last chapter, we distilled the key concepts and the common language that emerged over the course of the seminar. We presented an argument for why this new discourse, which is grounded in a long tradition of practical reason, offers a new agenda for contemporary higher education. This was the "analytical" moment of the book. We discerned underlying relationships between the diverse teaching practices and agendas of our seminar partners. We also criticized the institutional ground on which our partners struggle to chart lives that are responsive to the call of responsible judgment. But the formation of a new critical standpoint is not the final destination of our journey. We must put this renewed perspective to work. Analytical insight must be enacted through new forms of practical conscience.

We now address the question of what the seminar means for your own campus. These final pages are a call to action. Our purpose is to offer practical orientation regarding how faculty collaboration, focused on the problem of teaching for responsible judgment, might be pursued in your own local setting. We do not offer certainty. We do not offer recipes for deducing right action. Rather, we hope to orient you in the proper direction and to point out necessary considerations, possible pitfalls, and emerging possibilities. We hope that these final pages will be useful in the formation of campus initiatives, the character of which we cannot anticipate but which might find inspiration and resources for moving forward in the example of our work.

What Is Possible?

The goal of this book is to chart a new path toward the renewal of personal and institutional purpose in the contemporary academy. Having enshrined abstract argument and critical thinking at the center of academic life, our academic institutions continue to look on the situated and the particular as cases of the "fallenness" of the practical. We are still disposed to view the world of practice as unredeemed by the sacred objects of universalized argument, to which we have been trained to devote our lives and our loyalty. We have forgotten the practical ground on which our academic institutions are built.

At least three sources of academic isolation sustain this state of affairs. First, despite the growing and increasingly consequential "scholarship of teaching and learning" movement, teaching remains too often a private practice performed by sole academic proprietors, rather than a public and scholarly practice through which insight is developed progressively over time. Second, as the case studies in this book demonstrate, teachers whose work embodies a strong concern for the formation of practical responsibility often work against the grain of their own departments, disciplines, and institutions. Finally, the cross-disciplinary and cross-professional engagements that might foster new insight into practical action as a pedagogical concern are rare. This is particularly the case where the institutional divide between the professional schools and the disciplines of the liberal arts and sciences is concerned. The cumulative result is that teachers who mourn the loss of practical responsiveness in academia must chart their pedagogical paths without collective support and dialogue and without access to a shared discourse for orienting their pedagogical lives in a growing fashion. This is a particularly striking instance of what Stanley N. Katz calls the professoriate's long lost "sense of belonging to an ascertainable and manageable community of teacher-professors" (Katz, 2006, p. B8).

The Life of the Mind for Practice seminar offers an alterative to this state of affairs by redirecting our attention to the structure of responsible action itself. By bringing to the surface the motivating values and purposes that underlie teaching for responsible action within an array of fields, the seminar proved an exciting opportunity for fashioning new connections between faculty and disciplines. By engaging the perspectives of others, our partners were able to adopt a renewed perspective on their teaching and the structure, possibilities, and limitations of their own disciplines. In the process, the seminar enabled an experience that several of our partners said was among the most enriching of their professional lives.

Neither lasting pedagogical innovation nor renewal of academic purpose can be achieved by individual practitioners who are condemned to act in isolation. Dialogue is central to meaningful faculty formation, as are the institutional conditions for sustaining and deepening dialogue. This requires the action and growing commitment of a broad network of academic actors. Who are these people, what do they want, and how can the model of faculty formation espoused in this book help them achieve their values in new and more integrated ways?

Who Is Involved?

The practices of faculty formation that we have documented in this book involved many actors. These included faculty from across the professions and disciplines. But this work also required organizational leadership and administrative support. Each of these stakeholders has a unique role to play, and each can draw different practical implications from our collective work. In this section, we address several of these audiences in turn. We suggest how different academic actors might benefit from our work, toward a broader understanding of both individual and collective purpose.

Faculty

Faculty teaching is at the center of this book. In the end, the purpose of this entire endeavor is meaningful student formation in the practice of integrating analytical insight with practical judgment and action. But this goal cannot be achieved without mindful, integrative pedagogical effort by faculty, both within and outside the classroom. In order to realize fully our responsibilities for *student* formation, we must consider the problem of *faculty* formation. Faculty must learn how to model critical engagement with the possibilities and limitations of their own disciplines in order to point toward broader, more integrative forms of engagement in the world.

One important implication of the seminar for faculty is that growth and formation over time in the art of teaching for practical judgment is premised on meaningful dialogue and collaboration across disciplinary and professional boundaries. This truth is easy to forget in the contemporary academy. Our prospects for advancement and recognition are premised primarily on publication and specialized identification *within* our disciplines, rather than across and among them. Disciplinary formation is important. Faculty must be steeped in the practice of their disciplines and bring that practice to life for their students. But the purpose of higher education is not just to reproduce the disciplinary guilds. The purpose is to produce engaged and consequential *persons* who will take up a place and a stance in the ongoing formation of their society and culture. We may look to our disciplines for insight, but we must also learn to look beyond ourselves. As seminar partner William Spohn reminds us, in the spirit of H. Richard Niebuhr and Josiah Royce, only through responsiveness to the call of the world upon our action and our conscience do we achieve a self and a cause (Spohn, 2003).[1]

This requires new models for encouraging and sustaining faculty engagement across disciplines and professions. The seminar offers a model of how genuinely cross-disciplinary and cross-professional engagement and collaboration might foster the recognition of common pedagogical ends that exceed the purview of any single discipline or school.

The seminar offers a way forward, toward the overcoming of disciplinary isolation.

The seminar provided faculty with a new set of salient perspectives, through which our partners could objectify and interpret the values and practices of their own disciplines critically. In this way, our partners deepened their understanding of how they might model critical and integrative action for their students. We could call this a powerful case of teaching and modeling critical thinking. But this form of pedagogy far exceeds what we usually mean by the term. What is at stake is the reformation of the meaning of the disciplines themselves, as they are illuminated practically through concrete acts of judgment and responsibility. Critical thinking is a necessary but partial aspect of a larger formative horizon.

The faculty case studies that we present in this book are intended to offer exemplars with whom you might keep imaginative company (Booth, 1988). They also represent potential colleagues. We hope that you will recognize something of yourself in their stories of struggle and integration and find new, congenial language through which to give voice to your own pedagogical aspirations and predicaments. These case studies hold out the promise of new forms of professional solidarity and conscience that exceed the boundaries of particular disciplines and find their ultimate end in the calling of action and judgment.

Graduate Students

The Life of the Mind for Practice seminar offers a new form through which to imagine the formation of graduate students. There is no better time to introduce future faculty to a broader conception of academic responsibility than from the opening moments of their doctoral formation. And yet, such a reframing of academic purpose is also profoundly untimely. Everything weighs against it. Graduate students know very well that their prospects lie not with the enlargement of their calling at the level of the engaged academy but with its specialization and narrowing at the level of the methodological enclave. As the work of the Carnegie Initiative on the Doctorate reminds us, we neglect the formation of graduate students as teachers routinely during the process of doctoral education (Golde and Walker, 2006).

Imagine a doctoral program that draws on the example of the seminar. Imagine that graduate students in this program receive a pedagogical apprenticeship in both the practice of teaching and the art of cross-disciplinary reflection and dialogue on the purposes of that practice. Such a program would far exceed the narrower research imperatives that usually structure graduate education in the contemporary academy. And yet how many of us, looking back on the insufficiency of our own preparation for the pedagogical responsibilities that we now uphold, would not jump at the chance for such apprenticeship?

Such a program would do much more than prepare graduate students to teach well. It would also deepen their understanding of their chosen fields. Graduate students would be led to recognize both the possibilities *and the limitations* of the ways in which their chosen fields are normally pursued pedagogically. They would be introduced to more reflective, critical, and constructive appreciation for the meaning of their disciplines for the lives of self and other. Such graduate students, as they embark on their academic careers, would not only pursue their fields from the inside. They would also assess the ongoing formation of their fields from alternative perspectives and remain mindful of the broader purposes to which their chosen disciplines ought to respond.

Administrative Leadership and Support

We believe the agenda of practical reason will be especially valuable to deans and chief academic officers—those leaders finally responsible for ensuring faculty development. In particular, we believe that this agenda holds great promise for the enrichment of institutional identity and the relationship between institutions and their publics.

What, you might rightly ask, is in it for you as an academic leader? We recognize that administrative leaders face competing goals and agendas advanced by different stakeholders in their institutions. Faculty want academic rigor and opportunities for career advancement. The public looks for evidence of "value added" in return for their investment in the institution's well-being. This value added is formidable indeed: liberal learning must be "relevant" to practice and, simultaneously, must dignify and develop the critical capacities and moral commitment of future professionals, business leaders, citizens, and other public actors.

The agenda of practical reason provides administrative leaders and chief academic officers with an integrated rationale for pursuing the continuing development of faculty in response to today's demands. At a minimum, this new agenda gathers in a common framework the diverse efforts to fuse practical engagement and liberal learning that may already distinguish your campus, such as residential learning communities and service- and community-based learning. The agenda of practical reason provides a compelling account of how these efforts contribute to the formation and integration of knowledge, practical competence, and moral responsibility in the lives of your students. This account takes seriously the legitimate demands of the public but also reaffirms the value of liberal education and the intrinsic meaning of faculty work.

Toward this end, the agenda of practical reason also provides a rationale for breaking down well-worn institutional barriers to creative engagement across fields and specialties. We have emphasized the potential contribution of the professional fields to teaching practices in the arts and sciences. This is because however academic their aspirations, professional programs recognize that understanding alone is not enough for professional students. Such programs have to go beyond critical thinking to look for evidence that their students can take informed action on behalf of clients, according to the standards and moral purposes of their profession. The professional pedagogies that foster this kind of student formation are an untapped resource for teaching in the disciplines. But the reverse is also true. We found that the professional program faculty who are most alive to this kind of teaching also recognize and draw on the liberal arts disciplines to accomplish this task.

This realization of mutual benefit across the professional-disciplinary divide has been a principal theme of this book. We believe that it represents a breakthrough of potentially great importance. Taken seriously and systematically, it points toward a profound transformation of the culture of teaching and learning in the academy. The goal of blending critical intelligence and knowledge with practical skill and moral commitment through action is the hallmark of the value added by the pedagogy of practical reason. It provides, we think, a powerful new framework within which to pursue the enduring educational aims that define higher education.

Practical reason, as we have sketched it here, provides a way to energize faculty from across institutional divides around a new educational agenda, one that is substantive yet less dependent on particular claims to "turf" than either demands that the liberal arts be made practical or that professional training become more critical. This is especially likely to matter in the traditional humanities disciplines that perceive themselves as besieged by threatening calls for their teaching to be more practical. The fear and skepticism that underlie this siege mentality are often justified, insofar as critics of the humanities espouse a narrowly instrumental vision of higher education that reduces the relevance of the humanities entirely to the needs of the labor market.

The enriched educational agenda that we suggest offers leaders and faculty in the humanities a new language for articulating the practical meaning of their teaching in a way that is true to the social and cultural values of liberal education. This does require new forms for thinking about the pedagogical mission and practice of the humanities. But it does not require giving up the character and quality of humanities research. Indeed, it places the liberal arts and humanities on an equal footing with the professions and the sciences within an integrated vision of student formation that is responsive to the challenges of identity, community, responsibility, and knowledge.

None—or little—of this is likely to develop without clear and consistent leadership, however. Academic leaders, especially department chairs, deans, and chief academic officers, are critical for supporting the concrete activities that will enable faculty to forge new connections between their academic institutions and the public world through teaching. Administrative leaders must promote congenial conditions for engagement across personalities and disciplinary orientations. Leaders must support concrete activities that will enable faculty to enter imaginatively into the perspectives, purposes, and predicaments of their colleagues. This book provides a model of how such work might proceed.

Campus Centers of Teaching and Learning

The Life of the Mind for Practice seminar offers a variety of new conceptual and organizational tools for the conduct of serious pedagogical inquiry within campus centers of teaching and learning. At its greatest potential, moreover, the model of practical responsibility and interdisciplinary engagement offered here can provide directors of such campus centers a new language for articulating the value of the services they provide on campus.

Campus centers of teaching and learning are distinctive places that provide faculty with opportunities to inquire into the meaning and conduct of their own teaching practices in a systematic fashion and with external support. Campus centers have been key players in fostering support and legitimacy for the scholarship of teaching and learning across the United States, and their number is on the rise (Huber and Hutchings, 2005). These centers constitute one natural setting and existing infrastructure for the kinds of collaborative pedagogical inquiry and leadership discussed in this book.

Campus centers of teaching and learning come in many forms (Cambridge, 2004). Some play a central role in the formation of faculty practice and identity on a campus. Others exist at the margins of campus life. Some offer independent services, while others pursue their work in partnership with existing, ongoing faculty development projects. Some conduct their work beyond the formal decision-making structure of the larger institution, while others are more tightly integrated with institutional policy and priorities (Cook, 2004). Campus centers will draw different lessons from the work of the seminar, depending on how they are situated.

This book offers directors of campus centers of teaching and learning a new language and set of exemplars through which to articulate to their colleagues in the faculty and administration *why* these centers ought to occupy a central and integrative place in the life and mission of a college or university. Campus centers frequently offer a rare location for gathering a diverse community of disciplinary perspectives in a single place that is beholden to no single department or school. They can operate as an honest broker between perspectives and pedagogies. They can provide a common ground on which multiple teachers can learn to imagine one another's predicaments and recognize new dimensions of their own teaching. Campus centers can also foster the reflective pedagogical training of graduate students across fields, in order to help produce a new generation of faculty who are mindful of engagement and practical judgment as fundamental ends of higher education. Furthermore, because collaboration bears its most important fruit in practice and discourse only over time, campus centers can ensure the stable operation of interdisciplinary faculty formation projects.

How Must You Consider Faculty Formation?

If recovery and renewal of academic purpose is possible, then what are the conditions of that possibility? What must you consider in order to make this possibility a reality? The model of faculty formation that we espouse requires that you attend to four key considerations as you work to develop and sustain your own initiative. Keep these in mind as you proceed. Faculty formation, directed toward pedagogies of responsible judgment and practical reason, is

1. A *developmental* challenge
2. An *institutional* challenge
3. A *dialogical* challenge
4. A *situated* challenge

Let us discuss each of these concerns in turn.

A Developmental *Challenge*

Faculty formation is a temporal process. It is concerned with the unfolding over time of new forms of dialogue, discourse, and practical purpose. The point is to learn to tell a new, more integrated narrative of the relation between faculty action, disciplinary identity, and institutional mission.

This takes time. It takes time to foster new forms of discourse and conscience. It takes patience to foster mutual trust and recognition, such that faculty might engage the unique pedagogical predicaments and perspectives of their peers. It requires sustained work in the lives of faculty. Faculty must devote themselves to collaborative dialogue with others, narrative writing, and reflection on the purposes of their teaching.

The kind of faculty formation that we imagine also requires that faculty engage critically and imaginatively with the dominant practices, founding purposes, and practical meaning of their respective disciplines. This is more difficult than it sounds but also more liberating. The intended product is not yet another list of competencies that we hope students will develop. Such products are, at best, only an administrative and reductive facsimile of the lived demands of action in the world. They comment on action from the outside but do not *orient* action.

What we are after is renewed understanding of the very *structure* of responsible action within and across disciplines, whether the layered institutional life portrayed by teacher educator Barbara Stengel or the socio-technical situations presented variously by engineering educators Gary Downey and Robert McGinn. The purpose is to enable diverse faculty to draw on the perspectives of one another. In this way, faculty can enable one another to discover new and better ways to model responsible judgment pedagogically in the lives of their students and to bring the orienting concerns of identity, community, responsibility, and knowledge to life. But the goal is not only better teaching. An integrated vision of higher education that is insightful liberally, informed scientifically, and responsive practically is also at stake. Our students deserve nothing less as they look ahead to lives of unpredictable change and complexity.

Do you agree that these concerns ought to be central to the pedagogical life of your campus? If so, then you must consider how to enable faculty to invest their energy productively, such that their pedagogical work might become a meaningful and integrative locus of activity in their already busy lives. Any effort to build on the example of the seminar must safeguard the time in faculty's lives for sustained narrative engagement and dialogue.

You must also maintain a realistic and patient perspective about what is involved in doing this work, which involves hard questions about the institutions and disciplines through which faculty live their professional lives. It can be exciting in its possibilities. It can also be threatening in the crises of legitimacy that these possibilities might portend for the individual. Never forget that this work is a problem of community and conscience building over time.

An Institutional *Challenge*

The contemporary academy values that which is most generalized and abstract, at the expense of the practical and the situated. It is through this drive toward the universal that the university has carved out its worldwide position as an institution that confers legitimacy and authorizes persons through its credentials and claims to knowledge (Frank and Gabler, 2006; Meyer, 2006). To inquire into the grounds of responsible action through pedagogy is to work radically *against the grain* of the dominant structures through which faculty are positioned and perhaps also to risk illegitimacy in the eyes of colleagues and even students.

This predicament raises several considerations. First, how do you find responsive faculty who are willing to devote their time and energy toward the possibilities and the burdens of this work? Who is already coping with the limitations of the dominant academic paradigm? We are mindful that all of the faculty who participated in the seminar were, to quote one of the members, "ringers" within their respective disciplines. How did we find these distinctive individuals?

The faculty you seek are eager to find others like themselves. They crave committed intellectual partners with whom to develop a broader perspective toward the possibilities of their teaching and the formation of their own sense of academic purpose. In this hunger lay the germinal conditions for new forms of public trust, solidarity, discourse, and conscience. But faculty may not know where to turn or where to start. The institutional means for charting such paths and partnerships are not forthcoming.

There is no substitute for networking and trusted advisers. A few of the faculty who participated in the seminar—Hessel Bouma, Daisy Hurst Floyd, and Elizabeth McKinsey—were already known to the Carnegie Foundation because of their previous work as scholars in the Carnegie Academy for the Scholarship of Teaching and Learning, or as visiting scholars. For the most part, however, we simply asked faculty whom we trusted about who does interesting pedagogical work on their campuses or in their disciplines. One important resource was our ongoing work within the broader Preparation for the Professions Program, which had cultivated relationships with experts in the various professional fields whose judgment on matters of pedagogical mission and innovation we trusted. On your campus, the director of the campus center of teaching and learning is likely to have particularly deep and cross-disciplinary knowledge of who is working to develop innovative pedagogical practices.

If this seems an improvisational and unpredictable process, it is. Your goal is to foster connections between individuals and fields where no such connections are forthcoming. The institutional and collegial networks that might help you identify responsive faculty more efficiently may not exist. Your purpose is to build them. We hope that the work documented in this book will help to make these potential communities more discernable in practice.

Luckily, you need not build these networks from whole cloth philosophically. This book is also an effort to return the long-standing Western tradition of practical philosophy to the center of the academic mission. This orientation is present in the best liberal education, as well as the best professional education. It has continued to haunt the formation of the contemporary research university in countless ways, whether through public demands that professional schools attend to the development of professional responsibility, public criticisms that the traditional disciplines are not "practical enough," or such intellectual movements as the periodic resurgence of philosophical pragmatism in the face of academy orthodoxy.

In the end, our students must become more than critical thinkers. They must become responsible agents who take up a place in the life of their times. They will be called not only to bring theory to bear through situations but to develop coherent and defensible narratives of self. Analytical reasoning is only meaningful insofar as it responds to broader deliberations over narrative context and purpose. That we ended up turning to narrative practice for inquiring into our respective syllabi is not a surprise, in retrospect. We must be concerned with the formation of faculty practices as surely as student practices.

Narrative offers a particularly powerful genre for refashioning academic purpose in terms of practical reason and responsible judgment. Currently, the canonical genre of engagement in the contemporary academy is abstract intellectual argument, performed through what many commentators have called a "hermeneutic of suspicion." Particular events, stands, and claims are broken apart and analyzed for their historical contingency or reduced to underlying causes or universals. This genre exemplifies one aspect of the formative power of the academy—but only a partial aspect. In order to engage the question of how to educate students for lives of responsible judgment, the academy must also foster genres of engagement that exceed the dis-integrative power of critical thinking within the disciplines. It must recover the integrative power of practical action and narrative.

The syllabus narrative exercises employed in the seminar encouraged faculty to think of their pedagogical efforts not just as the dissemination of abstract bodies of knowledge but as the creation of *situations* to which students must respond. The relevance and purpose of these *particular* situations, over and above other possibilities, is grounded in each faculty member's underlying conception of the meaning of his or her discipline, its possibilities, and its limitations. Understood in narrative terms, course syllabi raise key questions about action in the world. What do you hope to become? How are you situated? For what and for whom are you responsible? What is the meaning of the disciplinary bodies of knowledge that might be brought to bear? By asking these fundamental questions of themselves, faculty learn to discern the forms of practical responsiveness that they hope to model in the lives of their students.

We have included the assignments that we drafted and engaged over the course of the seminar in the back of this book as Appendix Two. These resources can serve as models for your own reflection and conduct. These precedents may be tailored to respond to the demands of particular professions, disciplines, or special areas of institutional concern. They may also be tailored to the particular identity and mission of your institution, in order to foster collaborative inquiry into individual teaching practices as an expression of common institutional values. These options and more are available to you.

A Dialogical *Challenge*

Meaningful dialogue is built on analogy. The formation of common values and appreciation cannot be legislated or argued into existence from the outside. It takes well-organized occasions for entering imaginatively into the pedagogical life of others and learning to articulate their predicaments and values fairly. By participating in the perspectives of others, new dimensions of one's own pedagogical practices are disclosed. Trust, insight, and recognition are not built from scientific deduction but through the back-and-forth rhythm of good-faith engagement and the development of meaningful analogies between self and other.

The model of faculty formation that we espouse requires that teachers are enabled to serve as pedagogical exemplars in each other's lives. As the seminar demonstrates, these exemplars may come from unexpected places. Engineering and religious studies professors have much to learn from one another. So do professors of law and teacher education, or professors of English and medical education. The less habitual the relationship, the better.

The transformation of faculty conscience and institutional mission is grounded in the most basic acts of self-revelation and recognition between self and other. The key is to draw the attention of faculty to their *narrative* engagement with the challenges of their disciplines as teachers and persons, rather than as disciplinary strangers. Faculty who are concerned for the place of the practical and the normative in the intellectual life of the academy quickly discover that they share a common predicament, regardless of discipline. They also discover common intuitions about the purposes of higher education. By grounding your inquiry in the practice of discerning analogies, these common predicaments and values can be fashioned, with effort, into objects of public dialogue and shared discourse.

Your own institutional work might look very different from that of the seminar. But the most far-reaching implication of our work must be kept in mind. Teaching for responsible judgment is a challenge that is equally as important for the professions as it is for the arts and sciences. Each side of this institutional divide brings unique and important perspectives, insights, and pedagogical forms to the table. The professions focus our attention on the particular, institutional responsibilities that our students are likely to undertake in their lives. Toward this end, the professions have devised several important pedagogical forms, including the case and the clinic. The liberal arts and sciences, meanwhile, illuminate the natural, physical, social, and cultural contexts through which students' lives will be undergone. Likewise, the disciplines have devised pedagogical forms appropriate for this aim, including the lab, the seminar, and the ubiquitous tasks of writing and composition.

The broadest transformative power of this work for your institution lies in fostering common cause and discourse across the professions and the disciplines. The mutual alienation and competition for resources that estrange these domains from one another prevent the recognition of common interests and broader institutional change. Moreover, this estrangement obscures deeper ways in which these multiple domains might serve as resources and exemplars *for one another* in a genuinely formative way. Rapprochement between the professions and the liberal arts and sciences promises more integrated scholarly and pedagogical lives for faculty—and more integrated processes of educational formation for our students (Huber and Hutchings, 2004).

A bit of technical advice on the practice of dialogue is also in order. The purpose of dialogue is to discern common purposes and predicaments that have remained only tacit and implicit. As a result, the importance of *documentation* for your work cannot be overstated. In the early days of the seminar, we assumed that our primary purpose in documenting our work would be to keep track of key insights and develop them as fully as possible. When our initial attempts to foster dialogue did not take off, however, we realized that we must document not only distilled insights but, even more important, the formation of the seminar dialogue *itself* over time.

Beginning with the second session, we did exactly that. We kept meticulous and careful notes that preserved both the emergence of analytical insight *and* the practical rhythm of our discussions. This documentation enabled us to reflect not only on the meaning of key ideas but also on the ways in which our discussions *changed* over time through dialogue with one another. The syllabus narratives that each of our partners drafted, meanwhile, provided further occasions through which individual faculty might integrate and express the practical meaning of these changes for his own her own teaching. The narratives made public new ways in which this teaching might relate to analogous work in other fields.

Document everything. Although our method of choice was detailed note-taking, you might just as easily employ audio or video recording technology, singly or in some combination. We also kept a detailed electronic library of all work-product: writing, assignments, agendas, narratives, and so forth. You may also encourage faculty to explore the documentation of their individual courses through any of the emerging online platforms that have been designed to sustain the scholarship of teaching and learning.[2] The purpose is to provide as many different forms as possible for representing publicly the growth of common understandings and discourse. Diverse representations of the growth of the group will preserve your partners' irreducible particularities while enabling them to communicate with and act in terms of one another. The goal is to make the process of faculty learning and formation *itself* transparent and available for further dialogue and reflection.

This documentation will also be of great importance as you expand the institutional reach of your work. Through rigorous documentation, you will be able to tell an integrated story to others about what happened, what can be learned, and why it is important. From an organizational standpoint, you will also be in a better position to discern what works, what does not, and why. You will be able to discover important aspects of your lives together over time that you would never have been able to discover otherwise with only fading memory as a guide.

A Situated *Challenge*

Pedagogical action is not oriented toward students in general or toward a discipline in general. It is oriented toward *these* students, in *this* place, at *this* time, in the matter of *these* concerns. General disciplinary knowledge is necessary for this engagement. But it must be brought into a productive and mutually illuminating relationship with the demands of the particular.

Likewise, the examples, cases, and models that we offer in this book are not directed primarily toward the formation of a new ideal of the purposes of the university in and of itself. The purpose is to enable you to place an enriched idea of the university into a more productive and mutually illuminating relation with the purposes and identity of your particular campus. The analytical frameworks that we offer in this book, such as our four topics of responsible judgment—*identity, community, responsibility,* and *bodies of knowledge*—are not intended as a ready-made discourse for use in your own efforts. You may accidentally identify a cohort of faculty with whom this language resonates immediately. More likely, however, dialogical inquiry into the particular challenges and responses of individual teachers will be necessary in order to illuminate the *relevance* and *practical meaning* of this framework for the ongoing lives of faculty.

You will find our analytical frameworks much more powerful and consequential if you approach them as starting points for discussion. These frameworks offer a language for translating between multiple disciplines and professions. Ideally, local faculty will reshape and refine this language in accordance with the distinctive values and mission of their particular institution. This is tremendously important for two reasons.

First, this continuous growth of discourse will foster new forms of solidarity and conscience among a core group of faculty. It will foster renewed citizenship within your academic community, both toward your local institution and toward your partners' respective fields. These faculty, who are already disposed toward the innovation of their fields, will find their sense of call to action confirmed, refined, and articulated more carefully. Their action may also cultivate richer connections between the institution and its practical stakeholders. This book offers exemplars of responsible practice from which to draw inspiration and new ideas.

Second, only by developing our analytical frameworks further, in light of the distinctive values of your own institution, will your group be able to communicate the meaning and importance of your work to skeptical colleagues who hold fast to a more delimited conception of higher education. Only in this way can your work achieve true legitimacy. If broad institutional renewal is your ultimate goal, then the language that embodies your purposes cannot come entirely from the outside. It must also grow organically from inside the life of the institution itself.

Mindful *and* Responsible

How are we called, as educators, on behalf of both a public trust and the trust that we place in the hands of our students? Who should we hope to become as we answer this call? How might we think anew about the meaning of the bodies of knowledge and interpretive frameworks that distinguish our disciplines and professions as traditions through which to answer this call?

At their best, processes of faculty formation such as those documented in this book can foster renewed and sustained reflection on the responsibilities of faculty and institutions toward the future lives of our students and our diverse publics. The Life of the Mind for Practice seminar reminds us that the academy is not only called to break apart the world into its constitutive relations and causes through critical thinking. Too often, we are seduced into mistaking the evolving bodies of knowledge that distinguish our respective fields—those sacred objects toward which we academics devote so much of our lives—for pedagogical ends in themselves. We mistake analysis and critical thinking, which are disintegrating ends, for judgment and responsibility, which are integrating and consummating ends.

Our students will be called to take up concrete places and stances in the lives of others. They must learn to discern the practical salience of academic insight through integrative acts of responsible judgment in the world. What critical thinking pulls apart, responsible judgment must re-connect. The calling of higher education does not end with theory and interpretation. It culminates in the active formation of new narratives of individual and collective identity and responsibility. May our students' future practices be both mindful *and* responsible.

ENDNOTES

1. See Niebuhr (1963) and Royce (1908/1995).

2. The Knowledge Media Laboratory of The Carnegie Foundation for the Advancement of Teaching has been active in this arena through the development of the KEEP Toolkit [http://www.cfkeep.org/]. See Iiyoshi, Richardson, and McGrath (2006).

Appendix 1

PARTNER SYLLABI

"Human Biology" (Fall 2007)

Hessel Bouma III, Biology Department
Calvin College, Grand Rapids, Michigan

Course Schedule

Biology 115B, Human Biology
Health Education 115B, Essentials of Anatomy and Physiology
Fall Semester, 2007
Professor Hessel Bouma III
SB-010

Date	Topic	Assignment	Lab Exercise
September	5	Introduction	no lab
6	Nature of science & biology	Chapter 1	
7	Created "in the image of God"	Reader #1	
10	Chemistry of life	Chapter 2	Exercise #1
12	Chemistry of life (continued)	Chapter 2	

(Continued)

NOTE: *All syllabi copyright © the author(s). Reprinted by permission.*

Date	Topic	Assignment	Lab Exercise
13*	Making moral choices	Reader #2	
14	Cell structure & function	Chapter 3	
17	Cell structure & function (continued)	Chapter 3	Exercise #2
19	Organization & regulation of body systems	Chapter 4	
20*	Animal experimentation	Reader #3	
21	Cardiovascular system: Heart & blood vessels	Chapter 5	
24	Cardiovascular system (continued)	Chapters 5	Exercise #4
26	**FIRST TEST**		
27	Cardiovascular system: Blood	Chapter 6	
28	Lymphatic system & immunity	Chapter 7	
October 1	Digestive system & nutrition	Chapter 8	Exercise #5, Part 1
3	Digestive system & nutrition (continued)	Chapter 8	
4*	Human experimentation	Reader #4	
5	Respiratory system	Chapter 9	
8	Urinary system & excretion	Chapter 10	Exercise #6
10	Skeletal system	Chapter 11	
11*	Euthanasia, Part I	Reader #5	
12	Muscular system	Chapter 12	
15	Nervous system	Chapter 13	Exercise #7
17	**SECOND TEST**		

Date	Topic	Assignment	Lab Exercise
18	Senses	Chapter 14	
19	Senses (continued)	Chapter 14	
22	Endocrine system	Chapter 15	Exercise #5, Part 2
23–24	ACADEMIC ADVISING/READING RECESS		
25*	Euthanasia, Part II	Reader #6	
26	Endocrine system (continued)	Chapter 15	
29	Reproductive system	Chapter 16	Exercise #8
31	Reproductive system (continued)	Chapter 16	
November	1*	Reproductive choices	Reader #7
2	Reproductive system (continued)	Chapter 16 supplement	
5	Reproductive system (continued)	Chapter 16	Exercise #9
7	Development & aging	Chapter 17	
8*	Abortion	Reader #8	
9	Development & aging (continued)	Chapter 17	
12	Patterns of chromosome inheritance	Chapter 18	Exercise #10
14	**THIRD TEST**		
15*	HIV/AIDS	Reader #9	
16	Cancer	Chapter 19	
19	Patterns of genetic inheritance	Chapter 20	Exercise #11
21	Patterns of genetic inheritance (continued)	Chapter 20	

(Continued)

Date	Topic	Assignment	Lab Exercise
22–23	THANKSGIVING BREAK		
26	DNA biology & biotechnology	Chapter 21	LAB PRACTICAL
28	DNA biology & biotechnology (continued)	Chapter 21	
29*	Genetic engineering & gene therapy	Reader #10	
30	Human evolution	Chapter 22	
December 3	Human evolution (continued)	Chapter 22	Exercise #12
5	**FOURTH TEST**		
6	Global ecology & human interferences	Chapter 23	
7	Human popula-tion, resources & conservation	Chapter 24	

Small group discussion; meets in Commons' Knollcrest Room (across from Uppercrust)

Exam: Biology/HE 115B exam is scheduled for Tuesday, Dec. 11, 1:30 P.M.—4:30 P.M.

Textbooks:

Mader, Sylvia S. *Human Biology,* 10th edition. New York, NY: McGraw-Hill, Publishers. 2008.

Bouma III, Hessel. *Christian Perspectives on Moral Issues in Human Biology.* Copy Center. 2006–07. (color cover on white background)

Lab Manual: Biology Department Staff. *Biology 115: Human Biology Laboratory Manual,* 2006–07 Edition. (yellow cover)

Course Grade

Your course grade will be based on the best three of four lecture tests (100 pts each = 300 pts total) + 100 pts reader assignments + 150 pts lab grade + 150 pts exam grade = 700 points total. As an extra credit option worth up to 25 points, students may donate a unit of blood or write a short paper regarding blood donation (=725 points total).

Laboratory

The Course Schedule on the reverse side of this page includes the schedule of laboratory exercises, week by week. Students should read the exercise over *before* laboratory to be familiar with what we will be doing in lab.

1. Lab Attendance: Your attendance in laboratory is *mandatory*. Should you miss lab, you must make it up the same week in another lab. You must make prior arrangements with your lab instructor to be sure there is space available for you.

2. Lab Grades: You will be given a lab grade which will comprise approximately one-fifth of your final course grade. Under no condition will the lab grade be dropped. Your lab grade will be based on a combination of worksheets for various exercises, quizzes over the previous week's lab, participation, and a lab practical final at the end of the semester over the anatomy portions of the laboratories.

3. Lab Schedule and Lab Instructors:

Time	Monday	Tuesday	Wednesday	Thursday	Friday
8:00					
9:00					
10:00					
10:30					
11:30					
12:30					
1:30					
2:30					
3:30					
4:30					
5:30					

4. Animal Dissection: Much of what we know about human biology comes from animal experimentation. In the Moral Issues component of the course, we will discuss some of the ethical aspects of animal and human experimentation. While we will not perform any experiments upon live animals, we will be learning about human anatomy by studying the digestive, respiratory and urogenital systems through fetal pig dissection. If you believe you are opposed in principle to dissection work with animals, the instructor will assist you in finding another course to meet your needs.

Course Goals

1. Introduce students to the basic concepts of human biology.
2. Introduce students to the basic scientific methodology of human biology.
3. Equip students to apply basic concepts of human biology to understanding their health, sicknesses and diseases.
4. Help students integrate their learning in human biology with their other academic disciplines in developing their worldviews. This is intended to prepare students to deal with difficult bioethical issues they, their loved ones, and clients may face, and to be better prepared for civic engagement in their faith traditions and society.

Attendance

Students are expected to attend class faithfully. Although the instructor does not directly calculate attendance into the final course grade, there is a distinct correlation that exists between faithful class attendance and one's performance on tests because both the lectures and the tests emphasize what is important for a student to know about the scheduled topic. Furthermore, good stewardship of our time, talents, and finances dictates faithful class attendance. The instructor's expectation is that students should attend faithfully unless there is a very good reason on occasion to be elsewhere.

Attendance in the "Moral Issues" small group discussions and laboratory is mandatory. Both involve experiences which cannot be "made up" at a later date or by obtaining notes from a classmate; your absence deprives your group or lab partners of your input and assistance. In the

"Moral Issues" small group discussions, students will receive 5 points each week for coming prepared, on time, and participating in the group discussions, and up to 10 points each week for their pre- and post-discussion writing assignments; students who miss more than one small group discussion during the semester will lose 5 points for each missed session.

Lectures

The Monday, Wednesday, and Friday class sessions typically are didactic lectures in which the instructor uses PowerPoint presentations. Taking notes is a valuable learning tool. There is no need to copy down all the text on a PowerPoint slide. Listen carefully and take notes on the important points. Be sure to note the figures on which class time is spent, and focus your studying on understanding the structures and processes depicted by such figures. If you miss some details on a PowerPoint slide (or miss class), you may stop by the instructor's office where a copy of the current and previous lectures' PowerPoint slides will be in a plastic binder in the mail slot on his door. These hard copies are not to leave the area; you may use them to copy over the details into your own notes.

As we mature into adulthood, most peoples' attention spans increase up to approximately 20 minutes. To expect rapt attention any longer is pushing it, yet most college courses are offered in 50- or 75-minutes time slots. The instructor will use "2-Minute Quizzes" interspersed in the lectures to stimulate thinking, collaborative learning and concept development, and to reset our attention clocks.

Given the size of the class (up to 48 students) and the material we ought to cover, the lecture portion of the class does not lend itself to much discussion other than of the 2-Minute Quizzes. The Moral Issues portion of the class on Thursdays encourages much more discussion of difficult contemporary issues.

Instructor Contact/Office Hours

The instructor is available both immediately before and after class for brief questions. He will strive to maintain regular office hours on most Tuesdays from 10:30–11:30 A.M. and Thursdays from 8:00–9:00 A.M. On days when other obligations preclude being available during these office hours, a note will be posted on his door. If no note is on his office door and the light is on in his office, he has stepped out of the office and should be back shortly.

Course Work Load

For each hour in lecture and small group discussion, the average student should plan on spending an additional two hours of study time. Your actual time will vary according to your studying proficiency, abilities, and desire to do well. As a general rule, each 2-hour laboratory session, if used wisely, will require no more than one additional hour of study time.

Test Policy

Biology/Health Education 115B will have four 100-point tests. The three highest tests will be factored into your final course grade; the lowest test will be dropped. The purpose of the "drop test" is to allow for any extenuating circumstances (e.g. a death in the family, illness, etc.) to occur which might impede your ability to do your best on a scheduled test. *Students may arrange with the instructor to take any test up to 47 hours earlier than scheduled, but under no circumstance may a student take a test later than scheduled.* This policy allows students to anticipate potential conflicts and arrange to take the same test earlier; obviously, students who take a test earlier should not tell classmates what is on the test. To maximize the learning which occurs with tests, the instructor will make every effort to hand tests back in the next class period.

How To Study

In preparation for each regular class period, read the material as assigned for that day on the Course Schedule before coming to class, but you may read it superficially. After class, re-read the assignment, now in depth for full comprehension, focusing particularly on the material emphasized by the instructor in class. Highlight or underline the significant parts of each section. Be sure to look at the figures closely and read the figure legends too; try to imagine the active processes being depicted in the figures and how you would describe the processes in your own words. Concurrently, work through your Study Guide as we progress from chapter to chapter. In science courses in particular, it is very important: *Avoid getting behind.*
   In preparation for tests, review:

1. Your notes thoroughly several times over the week preceding the test,

2. The highlighted or underlined sections of your textbook, the terms in bold type, and the more significant figures (those on which we spent the most class time),

3. The types of questions and subject content and depth which appeared on the instructor's test over similar material during previous semesters (copies of the instructor's previous tests can be obtained from the front desk of the Hekman Library where they are on 2-hour reserve in the Reserve Reading materials),

4. The items in the Understanding Key Terms, Testing Your Knowledge of the Concepts, and Thinking Critically about the Concepts sections which appear at the end of each chapter and pertain to what we covered in lecture.

The instructor will also make every effort to conduct a review session from 8:00–9:00 P.M. on the Monday evenings before a test. Students are encouraged to review their notes thoroughly before a review session and bring questions for clarification to the review session.

In preparation for the "Moral Issues" small group discussion sessions, read the assignment fully prior to the discussion session. Find the discussion question which has been assigned to your small group for that session, and write a substantial one (or more) paragraph, thoughtful response to it. Bring this to class to share with your small group. After discussion, you will need to write a second response consisting of at least two (or more) paragraphs summarizing the ideas of your small group's responses to the question and rearticulating your response in light of your further thinking and reflection based upon the group's and the class's discussion of your question.

Learning Abilities/Disabilities

We have been created as marvelous beings, in many ways similar, but in some ways unique. College students are gifted with the capacity to learn in different ways; some can adjust—with differing degrees of difficulty—their ability to learn best according to an instructor's teaching style and expectations. For some, the ability to adjust is more difficult and may require special individualized assistance. The instructor is committed to enabling students to learn human biology to the best of their abilities and welcomes students' suggestions towards that end.

Any student with a documented learning disability needing academic adjustments or accommodations is requested to speak with the instructor about those needs, preferably in the first two weeks of the semester to facilitate implementation. Calvin College too, will make reasonable accommodations for persons with documented disabilities. (Students with documented disabilities should notify the Coordinator of Services for Students with Disabilities located in Hiemenga Hall #455.)

Tutor Assistance

Through the Student Academic Services Office (located in Hiemenga Hall #446), the college provides upperclass persons who will tutor students struggling with Biology/Health Education 115. A tutor meets one-on-one with a student for one hour/week to go over difficult concepts. This can be quite helpful, but only if the student is motivated, prepares diligently for his or her tutoring sessions, and is faithful in class attendance. Tutors are neither substitute teachers nor substitutes for personal study. If you think you might benefit from this service and are motivated to do your best, consult your instructor first. If he concurs, obtain a Tutor Request Form from the Student Academic Services office, fill out the application with your schedule, obtain the instructor's signature, then return it to the SAS office. Students who receive tutor assistance must attend class, small group discussions, and laboratory faithfully and prepare diligently for tutoring sessions, or forgo the services of a tutor.

Personal Electronic Devices in Classes and Labs

Personal electronic devices (e.g. cell phones, iPods, MP3 players, CD players, etc.) can be marvelous forms of technology under appropriate circumstances, but can be a significant distraction in educational settings to both the user and others. With the exception of hearing aids, all personal electronic devices must be turned off and are not to be used during classes (including tests and the final exam) or laboratory sessions. A simple, nonprogrammable calculator may be used on tests and in laboratories, but it should not be part of an electronic device capable of emitting electronic sounds.

Optional "Extra Credit" Opportunity

ASSIGNMENT. Either: 1) successfully donate one unit of your blood and learn about some basic procedures of blood donation, or 2) write a 3-page paper on one of the following topics:

a. Why I cannot donate my blood (if it is for biomedical reasons).

b. How donated human blood is processed or used safely.

c. Techniques used to minimize the risk of collecting donated blood contaminated with a hepatitis virus or the human immunodeficiency virus (HIV or "AIDS virus").

Deadline. You must complete the assignment by the last day of regular classes at the end of the semester.

Rewards. In addition to the immense satisfaction of having helped to save peoples' lives, you will receive an additional grade up to 25 points. Your final grade will be calculated with and without the extra 25-point grade; whichever is highest will be used for determining your final course grade. In addition, through the Service-Learning Center you can earn one hour of credit on your service-learning transcript each time you donate a unit of blood; you can do this through your KnightVision account.

HOW TO COMPLETE THE ASSIGNMENT

A. If donating blood:

1. You must successfully donate one unit of blood (or plasma) either to the Michigan Community Blood Center Program or an alternative blood center. The Michigan Community Blood Center Program is scheduled to be at Calvin College, 11:00 A.M. to 5:00 P.M. in the Chapel Undercroft on Tuesday, Wednesday, and Thursday, September 25–27, and November 27–29. You can either drop in to donate on a first-come, first-serve basis, or you can stop by the Service-Learning Center the week before the Michigan Community Blood Center Program is on campus to sign up for scheduled slot to donate. Alternatively, you can visit the Blood Center, Monday through Saturday, at 1036 Fuller, N.E. Of course you are welcome to donate to any blood center providing you complete the same requirements and form. In addition, you must answer some simple questions regarding the basic procedures of blood donation.

2. On the reverse side of this page is a form to be signed by the person who draws your blood, <u>after</u> your unit has been drawn. Simply turn this form in to your instructor. You will automatically receive 20 points plus immense satisfaction for your "gift of life;" another 5 points can be earned by your answers to the simple questions on the form.

B. By writing a paper:

1. Research your paper topic in the library or with reliable, quality web sites. You should consult the computer reference system of the Hekman Library and electronic databases (e.g., Readers' Guide, General Science Abstracts, etc.) for periodical literature.

2. Your paper should be three pages, double-spaced, and typed. Include a single-spaced list of references at the end of your paper. References should be recent (preferably less than five years old).

3. Turn your paper in whenever you complete it, but no later than the last regular day of classes in the semester.

4. Your paper will be graded for scientific information pertaining to human biology as well as grammar on a 25-point scale. Be sure to integrate what you have learned in class about blood and human health into your paper.

○

BLOOD DONATION FORM

BiologY/HE 115, Human Biology
Calvin College

This is to certify that _____ has
                                                    (student's name)

successfully donated one unit of blood (or plasma) to the Michigan Community Blood Program on _____.
                                                                                        (date)

(signature, Michigan Community Blood Center Program phlebotomist)

(To the student: Return this signed form to your Biology 115 lecture instructor for 20 points credit on your "Extra Credit Blood Assignment."

○

Briefly answer the questions below for the additional 5 points credit.

1. List five conditions for which you would have been disqualified from donating blood.

    a.

    b.

    c.

    d.

    e.

2. What tests are done on *you* to determine if you are a suitable donor?

3. What is done with the blood from your finger prick? Why? What is your hematocrit value?

4. What is the material on the gauze pad used to clean your arm before blood donation? Why is this substance used?

5. Will you donate blood again? Why or why not?

"Issues in Jewish Ethics" (Spring 2003)

Elliot N. Dorff
Ziegler School of Rabbinic Studies
American Jewish University, Bel-Air, California

Goals of This Course

1. Gain some knowledge of Jewish and general ethical theories.

2. Learn about the problems and methods of deriving moral guidance from the Jewish tradition.

3. Analyze some specific moral issues from the standpoint of the Jewish tradition.

4. Develop the skills to carry out a Jewish analysis of a moral issue on your own.

Requirements

The Ziegler School of Rabbinic Studies requires class attendance—and so do I! There will be a final examination and a paper required. The paper assignment is this: choose any moral issue and provide a Jewish analysis of it. Specifically, explain why it is a problem in the first place; then bring to bear any Jewish (classical, medieval, and modern) and general writings that you think are relevant to understanding or resolving the issue, including at least two who would respond to the issue in different ways; and then describe how you would respond to the issue, together with what you see to be the strengths and weaknesses of your approach. I have set the due date for this paper at midterm (specifically, March 20) so that you have enough exposure to moral reasoning to know how to do this kind of analysis well and you also have time to do this before the rush at the end of the semester.

Format and Pacing

Students will be expected to read the material assigned for each session, as listed in this syllabus, and to come to class prepared to discuss it. Please bring the readings assigned for each session to class since we will be referring to them during our discussion.

I have indicated the amount of time that I plan to spend on each topic in the syllabus. The allotment of sessions is not hard and fast: I fully expect that there will be some topics that will require more time than I have apportioned, and some less. But we will adhere to this schedule more or less so that we do not get bogged down in any one topic, however interesting it may be. If necessary, I will tell you in class to skip one or more of the assignments on this admittedly ambitious list. Hopefully, long after this course has been completed, you will continue to read about other approaches and other topics in Jewish ethics. Until and unless I tell you to skip any of the required readings on this syllabus, though, please read them in the order that they appear here.

Unfortunately, there are two Thursdays I will need to be out of town, and so there will be no class session on these dates: February 6 and March 27. In addition, since there are many people in the class who will be ordained this May (an early congratulations!), and since they will be in New York for job interviews on February 27th, there will be no class that day either. The Ziegler School of Rabbinic Studies, under which this course is being offered, has officially canceled the February 27th class. During our first session, we will establish make-up dates for the two classes that I must miss. Since I am writing this syllabus before our first class, I do not know when those make-up sessions will be, and so I have indicated the assignments for those two sessions on their scheduled dates. My sincere apologies for any inconvenience that my commitments out of town will cause you; I know that you all have busy schedules, and I have tried to keep these interruptions in our usual schedule to a minimum.

Evaluation

Since the final examination will be cumulative, covering the entire semester, it will count twice toward your semester grade, and the paper will count once (for those of you taking this course for a letter grade). While I will not keep a record of everything each person contributes to class discussion, I will use my general impression of your participation to make the difference between two grades that could legitimately be awarded you on the basis of your written work.

Evaluation goes in both directions. At the end of each semester, then, I shall ask you to fill out a written evaluation of the organization, topics, and readings of this course. I would appreciate it if you would keep brief notes for yourself on any aspect of the course that you especially liked or disliked so that you will remember that when it comes time to fill out those evaluations. (You are, of course, welcome to share such reactions with me during the semester as well!) I am sincerely interested in improving the course in whatever way I can.

Books

Students should buy the following books. The abbreviation that refers to each of them in the syllabus below is listed immediately after the book here:

John Arthur, ed., *Morality and Moral Controversies,* 6th edition. Upper Saddle River, NJ: Prentice-Hall, 1996). ("Arthur")

Barry D. Cytron and Earl Schwartz, *When Life Is In the Balance: Life and Death Decisions in Light of the Jewish Tradition* (New York: United Synagogue, 1986). ("Cytron")

Elliot N. Dorff and Louis E. Newman, *Contemporary Jewish Ethics and Morality: A Reader* (New York, Oxford, 1995). ("CJEM")

Basil F. Herring, *Jewish Ethics and Halakhah for Our Time: Sources and Commentary,* (New York: Ktav, 1984). ("Herring")

Elliot N. Dorff, *"You Shall Strengthen Them:" A Rabbinic Letter on the Poor* (New York: Rabbinical Assembly, 1999). ("Poor")

The University's bookstore was asked to order all of these books for you.

Topics and Assignments

I. INTRODUCTION: SECULAR AND JEWISH THEORIES OF ETHICS

JANUARY 23: INTRODUCTION TO THE FIELD OF ETHICS

The distinctions between morals and ethics, laws, customs, religion, and sentiment. Moral absolutism, relativism, pluralism. Morality as consequences; morality as act and intention; morality as character.

Arthur, pp. 60–71, 81–88.

CJEM, pp. 79–93.

JANUARY 30: JEWISH ETHICS: METHODS TO DERIVE MORAL GUIDANCE FROM THE JEWISH TRADITION

CJEM, pp. 129–193; 219–245

II. MATTERS OF LIFE AND DEATH

FEBRUARY 6: EUTHANASIA

Arthur, pp. 236–267.

Cytron, pp. 133–156.

CJEM, pp. 350–381.

FEBRUARY 13: TRIAGE AND SUICIDE; DRUGS AND SMOKING

A. Triage and Suicide

Arthur, pp. 377–380.

Cytron, pp. 43–73; 99–132.

Statement of the Committee on Jewish Law and Standards on Assisted Suicide.

B. Drugs and Smoking

Arthur, pp. 380–404.

Herring, pp. 221–243.

FEBRUARY 20: VIOLENCE AND WAR

Arthur, pp. 103–121.

Cytron, pp. 193–216.

CJEM, pp. 403–421, 441–454.

MARCH 6: CAPITAL PUNISHMENT

Arthur, pp. 122–152.

Cytron, pp. 157–192.

Herring, pp. 149–173.

II. SEX AND FAMILY LIFE

MARCH 13: LOVE AND SEX

Arthur, pp. 553–636.

CJEM, pp. 271–314.

Herring, pp. 175–196.

MARCH 20: ABORTION

Arthur, pp. 190–235.

Cytron, pp. 75–98.

Herring, pp. 25–46.

CJEM, pp. 382–402.

The assigned paper is due.

MARCH 27: PARENTS AND CHILDREN

Arthur, pp. 637–653.

Herring, pp. 197–220.

IV. ISSUES IN SOCIAL ETHICS

APRIL 3: EQUALITY AND DIFFERENCE: GENDER AND RACE

Arthur, pp. 457–464, 486–508, 510–531.

CJEM, pp. 315–326.

APRIL 10: CIVIL DISOBEDIENCE

Arthur, pp. 236–267.

Herring, pp. 121–148.

Final exam will be distributed. For graduating seniors: due May 8th. For all others: due May 14th by 5:00 P.M.

(APRIL 17 AND 24 – PASSOVER – NO SESSIONS)

MAY 1: POVERTY

Arthur, pp. 288–315.

CJEM, pp. 336–343.

Poor, entire.

MAY 8: ENVIRONMENTAL ETHICS

Arthur, pp. 154–189.

CJEM, pp. 327–335.

Final exam due for graduating seniors. For all others: due on May 14, 2003, by 5:00 P.M.

"Engineering Cultures" (2007)

Gary Lee Downey and Juan Lucena
Science and Technology Studies/History
Virginia Tech, Blacksburg, Virginia
Liberal Arts & International Studies
Colorado School of Mines, Golden, Colorado

This course is taught in two classroom versions and one online version. The large enrollment classroom version (ca. 150 students) consists of two plenary lecture-discussions and one small-group recitation (ca. 25 students) each week. This version is used at Virginia Tech to reach large numbers of students and to train new instructors. The small-enrollment classroom model (ca. 20–40 students), used at both Virginia Tech and Colorado School of Mines, meets 2–3 times per week. The online version, used at Virginia Tech during summer sessions, alternates between asynchronous multimedia lectures and synchronous class meetings using CentraOne© software. Typically more than half of its students are away from campus, including many out of state or even out of the country.

LEAD INSTRUCTORS

Gary Downey, Alumni Distinguished Professor, Science and Technology Studies, Virginia Tech

Juan Lucena, Associate Professor, Liberal Arts & International Studies, Colorado School of Mines

RECITATION INSTRUCTORS (1995–2007; PH.D. STUDENTS OR QUALIFIED M.S. STUDENTS IN THE GRADUATE PROGRAM IN SCIENCE AND TECHNOLOGY STUDIES)

Donna Augustine, Frankie Bausch, Thomas Bigley Benjamin Cohen, Wyatt Galusky, Krista Gile, Chris Hays, Brent Jesiek, Theresa Jurotich, Jane Lehr, Juan Lucena, Jonson Miller, Amy Nichols-Belo, Robert Olivo, Sunita Raina, Sharon Ruff, Nicholas Sakellariou, Lai-ju Zhang

Thomas Bigley, Chris Hays, Brent Jesiek, Liam Kelly, Jane Lehr, Jonson Miller, Robert Olivo, and Sharon Ruff have all taught small classroom and/or online versions of the course. Thomas Bigley, Brent Jesiek, and Jane Lehr have been lead instructors for the large-enrollment course. Juan Lucena has taught versions of the course at Embry-Riddle Aeronautical University.

Brent Jesiek, Jane Lehr, and Sharon Ruff have developed additional modules for their courses on gender and social responsibility.
Juan Lucena has extended the geographical reach of the course by developing the new course, Engineering Cultures in the Developing World.

Syllabus

Note: This syllabus is drawn primarily from the large-enrollment version taught at Virginia Tech. In order to be helpful to readers, it replaces the typical schedule of classes and recitations listing topics, readings, assignments, and exams with (a) an overview of the topics available in the multimedia content online and (b) a sampling of homework assignments, topics for online threaded discussions, online quiz questions, exam questions, and the critical reflections assignment.

LEARNING OBJECTIVES. The main goal of Engineering Cultures is to help engineering students and working engineers learn to work better with people who define problems differently than they do. Course modules travel around the world, examining how what counts as an engineer and engineering knowledge has varied over time and from place to place. We explore the historical emergence of engineering identities and the meaning of engineering work in several national contexts, all to better understand differing engineering perspectives that live in the present.

Students takes initial steps toward achieving 'global competency' by coming to recognize and value that they live and work in a world of diverse perspectives. In addition to better understanding the origins of their own perspectives, participants gain concrete strategies for understanding the cultural differences they will encounter on the job and for engaging in shared problem solving in the midst of those differences. When course modules work best, they help students figure out how and where to locate engineering problem solving in their lives while still holding onto their dreams.

Non-engineers are welcome to enroll and participate in the course. We make appropriate adjustments in course requirements. Students from the sciences will find many analogies with experiences in their fields. Students from the humanities and social sciences will be able to use this course to practice positioning themselves in a world of different perspectives, using engineers as case examples.

COURSE LEARNING STRATEGIES. In highly structured undergraduate curricula, engineering students learn to apply a rigorous and valuable methodology for solving mathematical problems. Yet the problems students solve tend to be "given." In the working world, engineers must regularly engage and work with people who define problems differently than they do. The standard method of engineering problem solving applies only to the individual problem solver or integrated team seeking one problem definition. It offers no guidance to collections of problem solvers who define problems differently from one another.

This course offers three strategies to help you prepare to work productively and collaboratively amidst contrasting problem definitions. First and foremost, you will achieve a higher level of understanding of the sorts of differences among engineers and non-engineers you will encounter around the world. In each country we examine, we ask: What does it mean to be an engineer? What counts as engineering knowledge? Where do engineers do their work? Second, the homework assignments, exam questions and discussion section activities are all geared to help you practice positioning yourself in a world of different perspectives. Third, the course offers an extension of the engineering method called *Problem Solving with People,* which locates collaborative problem definition at the core of engineering practice alongside mathematical problem solving. You can both try this method out within the course and, if you find it interesting or helpful, carry it with you to other contexts.

COURSE STRUCTURE. The main structure of this course consists of two plenary lecture-discussions and one small-group recitation each week. The purpose of this structure is to maximize the chance the course can achieve two conflicting goals simultaneously: (1) advancing the learning of 150 students in one class [approximately 275–300 request it each semester] while (2) providing numerous opportunities for the give-and-take of small-group discussions. We have designed the discussions, as well as the assignments built around them, to give you practical experience at positioning yourselves in worlds of different perspectives. The four instructors design the course together and work closely together in managing the course throughout the semester.

Course content consists of seven modules. Note that no textbook exists for this novel course. Rather, course readings consist of an imperfect selection of materials from both academic and popular literatures. All pass through the required content for each module, but none cover that content sufficiently. Lecture-discussions and lab/recitations devote considerable time to filling in the rest of the story, so that in any given location you will understand what it means to be an engineer, what counts as engineering knowledge, and where engineers do their work.

COURSE REQUIREMENTS. See your Blackboard site for the course Master Schedule and your recitation Syllabus. You need to purchase one book, Graham, Loren, *The Ghost of the Executed Engineer*. All other readings are available both in a printed packet and as pdf files to download. We recommend obtaining the printed packet.

Your major responsibility is to keep up with the reading assignments. Come to lectures and recitations ready to raise and answer questions and to discuss the material. Your final grade will be based on both your level of performance and your level of commitment to the learning process.

Exams consist of short-answer and paragraph-length questions. See your Blackboard site for copies of old exams. On exams, the material of highest priority is that which was both in the reading and discussed in class. Next highest is material discussed in class but not in the reading. Third is material discussed in the reading but not in class; in this case you will be responsible only for general ideas.

Recitation assignments include threaded discussions, homework assignments, discussion participation, learning assessments, and reflections assignments.

THE COURSE OFFERS A TOTAL OF 400 POSSIBLE POINTS, DISTRIBUTED AS FOLLOWS:

Threaded Discussions: 8 × 10 pts. = 80 pts.

Homework Assignments: 4 × 10 pts. = 40 pts.

Discussion Participation: 9 × 5 pts. = 45 pts.

Learning Assessments: 4 × 5 pts. = 20 pts.

Reflections 1, 2: 15, 20 pts respectively = 35 pts.

Exams: 3 × 60 pts. = 180 pts.

Total = 400 pts.

GRADING POLICIES. We guarantee the return of homeworks within one week and exams in two weeks. All four of us grade exams. Recitation instructors grade the homeworks, reader responses, and reflections assignments.

We re-grade assignments without prejudice according to the following policy. Within one week of receiving a graded assignment, you submit a written request for re-grading with an explanation for why you think you deserve more points. Whoever graded that assignment will review it and respond in writing with a decision. If you still have concerns, you submit that request directly to Gary, who will then respond in writing with a final decision.

The course works on a 90–100, 80–90, etc., scale for final grading. We do award +'s and −'s. In exam grading, we will curve students up if we judge the exam to have been too difficult. We never curve students down.

In order to minimize inequities among the grading practices of discussion section instructors, at the end the semester we curve their grades as follows: On each exam, we calculate a median score for each instructor. At the end of the semester, we total all the medians. Any point differential is added to the lower scores to bring them up to the score of the highest instructor. We will inform you only of the amount of this curve, not the running total of medians.

This course has no extra-credit assignments.

ACCOMMODATIONS. We are happy to accommodate students with documented disabilities. Please let us know as soon as possible.

SCHEDULE OF CLASSES. (from online course; multimedia presentations available at www.cpe.vt.edu/engcultures)

INTRODUCTION
- Culture as dominant images
- Dominant self-image of engineers: Rational problem solver, no politics
- A Method for Engineering: Problem Solving with People
- Conclusion: Are you willing to put your perspective at risk in the context of other perspectives?

GERMAN PERSPECTIVES
- Class #1: Emergence of Two Dominant Images
- Three questions; Rise and fall of the Holy Roman Empire; From arts to reason; Two dominant images of engineers; Rise of industry under the 2nd Reich
- Class #2: Rise of Industry and Scientific Technology
- Greater status in the Weimar Republic; German resistance to patents; Engineers and National Socialism; Engineers became pillars of post-WWII German society

○ Class #3: Rise to Prominence

○ German education; high percentage of engineering students are men; Germany, competitiveness, and globalization

FRENCH PERSPECTIVES

○ Class #1: Rise of the Centralized State

Three dominant images; Dominant patterns among engineers; Development of coherent French identity; Concentration of authority in the monarch; Louis XIV: 1643–1715; A changing context for the state; Enlightenment: nature as mechanism; Philosophes: extend reason to useful arts

○ Class #2: Emergence of the State Engineer

Two related hierarchies; Emergence of engineering in the military; Significance of education; French Revolution; École Polytechnique; Grandes Écoles; Who should lead society toward perfection?; Fifth Republic

○ Class #3: Two Overlapping Hierarchies

People with practical knowledge and training?; Écoles des Arts et Metiers; Positioning French industry; Direct sponsorship after WWII; École Centrale des Arts et Manufactures; Building careers in industry; A student's pathway; Engineering education; Pressures for change after the Cold War

JAPANESE PERSPECTIVES

○ Class #1 Introduction: A World without Individuals

Some dominant cultural images in Japan

○ Class #2: Life as an Engineer in Japan

What's it like to work as an Engineer in Japan; Introduction to Chikako Takeshita; Engineering training; Beginning employment; "Salarymen"; Identifying oneself in conversations; Trust and acceptance in business; Working in the midst of hierarchy; Make sure you suffer; What does group effort mean?; Group mentality in the engineering workplace; Everyday experiences; American stereotypes about engineers in Japan

○ Class #3: Cultural History and Personhood in Japan

The Japanese live with anxiety; Pre-colonial organization; Meiji Restoration; Japanese expansion to avoid subservience;

Ie = household; Uchi = center of belonging; Examples of
Ie; Becoming a mature person; The "heart" in two cultures;
Obligations to parents: the foundation of all rewarding
relationships; What does it mean to be "sincere"?

○ Class #4: Morality in Japan

The Japanese are "unprincipled"; No recognized separation of
the moral order from the actual; What then is the ultimate goal
in everyday life?; Religions in Japan: Buddhism, Shintoism;
Japan is now changing rapidly

BRITISH PERSPECTIVES [NOTE: VERSION 2.0 OF THIS MODULE
INCLUDES ONE CLASS ONLY]

○ Class #1: Emergence from the shop

Main points; A solution to the Victorian Paradox—19th
century; Three quotes about the apprenticeship system;
Training inside "cells"; Professional societies to increase status;
Development of academic education; Minimal relationships
with government; Current issues

SOVIET AND RUSSIAN PERSPECTIVES

○ Class #1: Engineering with Politics

Soviet Union was built as an alternative to capitalism; Engineers
and engineering work always had political meaning

○ Class #2: Dreams of an Alternative to Capitalism: Marxism,
Socialism, Anarchism

Tsarist Russia; Engineers under the Tsar?; Peter Palchinsky;
1905 Revolution; 1917 Revolution(s); Socialism; Marxism;
Anarchism; History of Anarchist Theory; Politics Influencing
People's Lives; Tensions by 1917

○ Class #3: Palchinsky 1, 2, and 3: Tsarist Russia, the Provisional
Government, and the Soviet Union under Lenin

Palchinsky 1: Tsarist Russia: Included workers in his study of
mining production; Humanitarian Engineering; Palchinsky
returns to work under the Tsar

Palchinsky 2: Provisional Government: Tsar abdicates, Duma
appoints provisional government; Rise of the Bolsheviks

Palchinsky 3: The Soviet Union under Lenin: Palchinsky
becomes a risk again; Palchinsky serves the Leninist government;

Engineers see a big opportunity!; Lenin's approach to a state-run economy; Tension between functional and regional planning; Engineers seek prominent roles; Similar to the "Technocracy Movement" in the United States; Tensions between engineers and the Communist Party.

○ Class #4: Palchinsky 4: Stalinism and beyond

Rise of Stalin; Eliminate bourgeois specialists; Unique technocracy under Stalin; Forced industrialization; Examples of large-scale projects; Narrowing definition of engineering work; Narrow engineers no longer a threat to Stalin; A country run by engineers but . . . ; Conclusion

U.S. PERSPECTIVES

○ Class #1: The civil engineer as Lone Ranger

Introduction: excavating disciplines; Developing a workforce of civil engineers: Early association with government: 1810s-1840s; Development of civil engineers: British model; Development of civil engineers: French model; Civil engineers as professionals?; A Lone Ranger in two ways;

Example: "Building Turnpikes in Early Virginia"; Problem: Building a road before the Civil War; A "mixed enterprise" system; The Principal Engineer of Virginia; Engineering problems in road-building; Ambiguous authority of the Principal Engineer

○ Class #2: The Morrill Land Grant Act and case study of a land-grant institution

Introduction; Congress passed 3 key acts in 1862; General provisions of the Act; Educational provisions of the Act; Rapid expansion in the # of schools; Allocating the funds in Virginia; Initial mission: to serve "industrial classes" broadly; Struggle to get beyond practical education; New effort to make agriculture equal with engineering; Emergence of new engineering fields to help Virginia industrialize; Post-Sputnik focus on engineering sciences and research; Conclusion: Evolution of a mission to serve

○ Class #3: Born in the shop: American capitalism, mechanical engineers and their descendants

Evolution of American capitalism: Pre-industrial America, pre-1810; Machine shops 1810s–1840s; Manufacturing shops

1840s–1880s; Rise of corporate capitalism 1880s–1920s; "Fordism": Corporate capitalism 1920s–1960s; Multinational capitalism 1960s-present

Emergence of mechanical engineering and other disciplines: Millwrights in pre-industrial America, pre-1810; Skilled mechanics in machine shops, 1810s–1840s; The ME emerges, 1840s–1880s; Engineers become salaried professionals, 1880s–1920s; Two descent lines in engineering; Conclusion: Mechanical engineering is the major source of new fields

○ Class #4: Origin of the tension between design and manufacturing

Introduction: history as excavation to understand the present; Design vs. manufacturing; Emergence of the separation of design from manufacturing; General Motors purchases DELCO in 1916; DELCO and engine design; Locating DELCO in General Motors; DELCO champions copper-cooled engine design; Resistance from engineers in the divisions; Full-fledged controversy; So what was going on here?

SAMPLE HOMEWORK ASSIGNMENTS (INFORMAL WRITING, 500 WORDS). *HW: The Images that Challenged Me (for week 1)*

In 4–5 paragraphs, identify and describe the images that challenged you as you were considering and deciding to pursue a degree in engineering. Wander outside of yourself and identify the source(s) of those images. Then go back inside and figure out how they challenged you. How, for example, did these challenges combine or conflict with other challenges to shape your pathway? What images are challenging you now?

The purpose of this assignment is to help you begin analyzing yourself in social terms. Those of us who have been raised in the United States tend to describe our histories as sequences of decisions or judgments we made ourselves, since we see ourselves as autonomous individuals. We tend to see anything else that is contributing to our pathways as outside forces impacting on us. Images, however, live inside us, making the inside-outside distinction more difficult to sustain. There are other ways of thinking about our identities as people.

Note: We are introducing here the course's main method of analysis, which we use repeatedly as we travel around the world. It may take you some time to get the hang of it. We'll work with you. Remember, by "images that challenge you" we are not referring to the series of decisions you made in deciding to become an engineer, difficult courses, etc. Instead, focus on images you carried around in your head—of engineers, yourself as an engineer, yourself at the time, your goals and ambitions, your fears, etc.—as well as the sources of those images—parents, friends, relatives, teachers, television, books, etc.

If you are not pursuing a degree in engineering, please articulate the images that led you away from engineering and toward that which you are now pursuing.

HW: *Traipsing Through Europe*

In this module, we are taking a quick survey of European engineering traditions, looking at similarities and differences among British, French, and German patterns. As we are seeing, each pattern relates to distinct, and evolving, dominant national images of what counts as progress.

For this homework assignment, draw on readings and class discussion and construct a three-way dialogue. The conversants in the dialogue include representatives from two of the three countries and yourself. Assume the others are classically trained in their respective countries. Then, take some time and discuss amongst yourselves the differences in images you all share, how these might have come about, and especially how the other two might be impacting you right now. Feel free to include, in absentia, the third country's engineering tradition (but don't be too harsh on someone who isn't there to defend him/herself). Be as creative as you wish to be in setting the scene and developing the characters, but please limit your conversation to two pages.

Note: The objective of this assignment is to give you practice at "getting behind" engineers you meet from other countries in order to understand the challenges that confront them. Think of it as a "thought experiment" in an Engineering Cultures laboratory. One way to avoid developing overly narrow characters is to remember that this course identifies only some of the dominant images that confront engineers on the job. Every engineer has to grapple with configurations of challenges from different dominant images. For example, many non-U.S. engineers you meet may already have significant experience with U.S. engineering life, and all engineers have non-engineering issues to cope with in a given day. Feel free to draw on other knowledge you may have about engineering workplaces and engineers' lives to make the dialogue feel real.

HW: *Japan—Dealing with Different Images*

In Module 5, we looked at certain images that people in the U.S. face working as engineers. Now we have shifted to a different country where people are impacted by another set of images. This assignment has two parts 1) two lists of images, and 2) two first person narratives.

Begin this assignment by writing the term "Japanese engineer" and putting below it a list of at least five images that an engineer in Japan may confront. Then write the term "U.S. engineer" with a list of at least five images that an engineer trained and working in the United States may face.

Now imagine that the two engineers switch jobs for a while. Write the titles "Japanese engineer working in the U.S." and "U.S. engineer working in Japan." Beneath each title, write two paragraphs from that person's perspective, first person narrative. In these paragraphs, describe the images that would be most difficult for you to face, and why (especially given the set of images you have become used to facing).

Be sure to draw from readings, classes, and personal reflections over the course of the semester.

Threaded Discussion Assignment. A threaded discussion contribution is an online, written response to the readings and other class activities during the previous week.

The main purpose of this assignment is to help you practice positioning yourself in a world of differing perspectives. Your challenge is to be disciplined in your reading and thoughtful in your reactions. When the assignment works well, it sharpens your ability both to listen to other perspectives and to develop and articulate your own. In addition, contributing to weekly threaded discussions will help you prepare for Friday lab/recitations and complete your Reflections assignments.

You are required to contribute one or more responses at least 8 of the 10 weeks for which online discussions will be held. Each response should be 1–2 paragraphs in length and is worth 10 points. You will receive credit and a grade per week rather than per response. If you contribute to 9 or 10 discussions, we will drop one or two of your lowest grades, as appropriate.

You post your contribution on a Discussion Board in your Blackboard site. Each response must demonstrate an understanding of the reading for that week. In particular, responses should quote directly from at least one assigned reading (cite the author's last name and page number of the quotation). Feel free to respond to other class material as well.

At least 4 of your 8 postings should respond to at least one other student's posting. Feel free either to contribute to one of the topics we identify or introduce a new topic. When you respond to other classmates' postings, you may constructively challenge another's assumptions, seek to describe one another's perspective, or otherwise account for similarities and differences in the positions you take.

The due date for all postings is noon Thursdays. Please review all online postings prior to coming to lab/recitation on Friday.

RUBRIC FOR EVALUATION OF CONTRIBUTIONS TO THREADED DISCUSSIONS

○ *For the grade of A (9, 9.5, or 10 pts):* In addition to meeting all the requirements for the B grade, asks generative questions that point readers in the direction of more sustained inquiry and discussion. Provides insightful analysis of readings and classroom discussions, and goes beyond issues raised in class.

○ *For the grade of B (8 or 8.5 pts):* Shows clear comprehension of the readings, and understanding of classroom discussions and assignment. Is thoughtful and reflective, written in a clear, comprehensible style without major spelling or grammatical errors.

○ *For the grade of C (7 or 7.5 pts):* Appropriately addresses the readings, classroom discussions, and assignment, but demonstrates more limited comprehension, thought, and reflection. Is not entirely clear and comprehensible. May have significant grammatical and/ or spelling errors.

○ *For the grade of D: (6 or 6.5 pts):* Significantly fails to comprehend the readings, classroom discussions, and assignment. Demonstrates very little thought and reflection. May be unclear to the point of being almost incomprehensible. May have major grammatical and spelling errors.

○ *For the grade of F: (5 pts or below):* Entirely fails to comprehend the readings, classroom discussions, and assignment. No thought or reflection. Entirely unclear or incomprehensible. Major grammatical and spelling errors.

SAMPLE THREADED DISCUSSION TOPICS

○ German module: reactions to reading Hitler; Feder, Todt and National Socialism; Jews and German geist; German critiques of capitalism?; implications of political neutrality for engineers; "stopping the design"; Daimler and Chrysler: what's going on?; the German autobahn: what's it like?

○ 19th century civil engineers in the U.S.; apprenticeship vs. school training in the U.S.; the American system of manufacturing; America becomes a nation after the War between the States?;

○ ME + science = new discipline?; battle over the copper-cooled engine; design vs. manufacturing; reform in engineering: increasing the number of engineers; interactions between images of engineers and images of gender and race; the issue of under-representation

SAMPLE ONLINE QUIZ QUESTIONS (USED IN ONLINE VERSION; STUDENTS COMPLETE QUIZZES AFTER VIEWING MULTIMEDIA PRESENTATIONS)

1. During the reign of Kaiser Wilhelm II, Higher Technical Institutes gained an official status

    a. **Equal to the universities**

    b. About like American community colleges

    c. Lower than in previous times

    d. Above the universities

2. The Dr.-Ing degree is a

    a. **Research degree**

    b. Basic trades degree

    c. Medical degree

    d. None of the above

3. In Germany, "anti-mathematicians"

    a. **opposed the new idea that technology is nothing but applied natural science and mathematics**

    b. welcomed the French approach to engineering

    c. argued for reducing the amount of mathematics taught in high schools

    d. none of the above

4. According to Hardensatt, an early 20th Century German engineer, the deeper cultural meaning of technology

    a. Was German, spiritual, cosmic, whole, permanent, formed and orderly

    b. In essence non-Capitalistic

    c. Like reason in the 19th century

    d. **All of the above**

Sample Exam Questions. Note: Engineering students frequently regard courses in humanities and social sciences as "opinion courses," in which the major task is to figure out the opinion of the instructor and react to it without reducing one's grade-point average. To avoid rejection as an opinion course, Engineering Cultures includes exams and insists student learn knowledge content. Exams always include writing.

○ (8 pts) British engineers have always struggled to be seen as "professionals." In 4–5 sentences, explain the significance of this concept in the British context by describing (a) the British system of engineering training and (b) the main strategy through which engineers sought higher social status.

○ (6 pts) In the module in Great Britain, we read Morice's "Britain and European Engineering Education," Buchanan's "Education or Training?: The Dilemma of British Engineering in the 19th Century," and selections from Smith's article on British engineers, including the sections "What is a British Engineer?," "British Industrialization," "The Politics of Representation," and "Engineering Institutes and the Division of Labor." In 3–4 –sentences, summarize the main argument of one of these three readings, offering two examples of evidence the author used to support the argument.

○ (7 pts) In 4–5 sentences, explain the development of the French concept of social progress and the role of engineers in pursuing it. Be sure to draw on the extensive class discussion of the Enlightenment and the role of the state in France.

○ (7 pts) During the 18th and 19th centuries, the ideal basis for one's acceptance into the elite engineering schools shifted one's social status to one's merit. Describe what "merit" means in the French context, in contrast with social status In 4–5 sentences, briefly explain how a student demonstrates his or her merit in order to be "promoted" into an engineering school.

○ (1 pt) France has no courses in engineering ethics because_____.

Reflection Assignment. The Reflection Assignment provides you an opportunity to chart your growth throughout Engineering Cultures. In part, this course attempts to broaden experiences and perspectives helping you to become more prepared for an international working environment.

The reflection is a two-part assignment in which you explore your personal experiences, relationship to others, and problem solving methods, with the second part providing a more in-depth follow-up to the first.

○ Reflection part 1 (week 2 or 3)

In approximately 1 page (~250 words), reflect on why you are taking the course, your goals with respect to engaging with the course concepts, any concepts that cause you to struggle and why, and what you hope to gain from the class and develop within yourself.

○ Reflection part 2 (week 14 or 15)

Go back and re-read your first reflections assignment. Also review your old homework assignments and notes. Then reflect on the entire semester of Engineering Cultures, the concepts and readings from class. Reflect on how you engaged this material, and any concepts with which you struggled. In 2.5–3 pages (~625–750 words), share your evaluation of how well you met your goals, engaged with course concepts and readings, changes or development in perspectives/problem solving, and your personal growth. Please share personal experiences of how you experienced course concepts in your own life.

"Advanced Legal Ethics: Finding Joy and Satisfaction in Legal Life" (Spring 2003)

Daisy Hurst Floyd
Mercer University School of Law, Macon, Georgia
Course last taught at Texas Tech University School of Law, Lubbock, Texas

This seminar examines the professional identities of American lawyers, which affect their relationships, career decisions, and a broad range of ethical and moral choices. The study of professional identity encompasses issues of personal satisfaction and professional success and must necessarily take into account individual personalities, experiences, and talents. Through the seminar, we will collectively develop some insights into the ways in which American lawyers develop their professional identities and the impact on the practice of law. Additionally, and more importantly, it is hoped that each student in the seminar will be helped in his or her own development of professional identity. We will draw on assigned readings, reflective exercises, class discussion, and conversations with lawyers and other professionals to meet those goals.

Text

Steven Keeva, *Transforming Practices: Finding Joy and Satisfaction in the Legal Life*

Assignments

All students will complete the following assignments:

○ Assigned readings;

○ Several short (3–4 pages) reflective essays on topics to be assigned; and

○ One major experiential or research project that results in a substantial written product, on a topic to be developed.

There will not be an exam. Grades will be based on students' performances on the above and participation in class discussion.

Topics

We will discuss the following topics:

I. Profession

   a. The meaning of profession

   b. Becoming a professional; forming a professional identity

   c. Being a professional

II. The role and nature of lawyers in society

III. The legal culture

   a. The representational aspect of lawyering: relationships with clients

   b. Adversarialism/winning/competition

   c. Expanding the possibilities: new visions of lawyering

IV. The lawyer as a member of the legal culture

   a. Who are lawyers?

   b. Development and exercise of moral and personal judgment

   c. Developing the inner life

   d. The practice of law as a calling

      1. Meeting a need: lawyers making a difference

      2. Being satisfied:

         a. the connection between satisfaction and competence

         b. definition of and expectations for success as a lawyer

         c. balancing the personal and professional

      3. Coping with fear

V. Summing up and looking ahead

Sample Reflective Writing Assignments

○ What qualities, apart from a solid work ethic and strong case-analysis skills, will you seek to cultivate in yourself that you think would make you a better lawyer? How do these qualities relate to your notion of profession and particular characteristics of the profession, either as it exists or as an ideal? At its best, what do you think being a lawyer can bring to your life?

○ Think about the times in your life when you have felt or you feel the most yourself—when you feel the most authentic and alive. Do these times occur when you are in a particular place, doing a particular thing, or with a particular person or people? What do these times tell you about who you are and what is important to you? Do you ever experience this feeling when you are doing something related to the law or to being a law student? Do you think you can experience this feeling through being a lawyer? Why or why not?

○ Recall a time in your life when you have sought the services or help of a professional (this covers a wide range of persons, including lawyers, doctors, accountants, dentists, teachers, ministers, and anyone else you think qualifies). Write a short description of the encounter and your assessment of whether it was a positive or negative experience and why. Be specific about the behavior of the professional and your reaction to it.

○ We will collectively design an ideal law school. We will have the luxury of designing it without regard to budget or accreditation concerns because we will pretend, at least initially, that neither will be obstacles. Please write a short description of your conception of an ideal law school, including answers to the following:

Who: Who should be admitted as students? Who should be hired as members of the faculty?

What: What should be included in the curriculum, including how much time should be spent in law school (defined in terms of the calendar, or credit hours, or any other appropriate measure)? What teaching methods should be employed? What method of evaluating student performance should be used?

When: At what point in a person's life should he or she be in law school, e.g., after certain educational or life experience requirements have been fulfilled?

Where: Should our law school be free-standing or part of an educational institution that includes other disciplines; should it be public or private?

Why: Be prepared to justify the choices you have made.

"Contracts" (Fall 2006)

Allen S. Hammond, IV
Santa Clara University School of Law, Santa Clara, California

All assignments are in *Contract and Related Obligation*, 4th Ed., by Summers and Hillman (hereinafter Summers and Hillman). Students are encouraged but not required to read *Concepts and Case Analysis in the Law of Contracts, 4th Ed.*, by Chirelstein (hereinafter Chirelstein). The assignments below include all cases, all references to the Restatements (Rest.) and the Uniform Commercial Code (UCC), all notes and all problems appearing on the assigned pages, unless otherwise indicated. Cases are specifically identified in bold. The references to Chirelstein are suggested readings.

The Professor's PowerPoint slides will be placed on Claranet at the end of the week following the classes in which the topic was covered in class.

The final Exam to be held on December 5th at 6pm will be 3.5 hours long and will consist of one essay question and 10–15 multiple choice questions.

ASSIGNMENTS	PAGES
CHAPTER ONE—INTRODUCTION	
Non-Commercial Agreements: **White**	
Summers and Hillman	2–29
Commercial Agreements: **Nim Plastics**	
(Attached Supplement)	
The Contract Curve And Expectation Damages	
Chirelstein	1–11
Theories of Obligation & Remedies: **Sullivan**	
Summers and Hillman	33–42
Expectation Damages	
Chirelstein, Expectation Damages	174–183
Reliance	
Chirelstein (Reliance Section Only)	199–204
CHAPTER TWO—GENERAL THEORIES OF OBLIGATION	
Consideration (Theory # 1)	
Hardesty, Dougherty, Maughs, Hamer, Baehr	
Summers and Hillman	43–61

Consideration and the Bargained-for Exchange,
and Section A., Promises to Make A Gift

    Chirelstein   12–22

Forbearance

    Springstead, Dyer

    Summers and Hillman   62–70

Illusory Contracts

    De Los Santos, Wood

    Summers and Hillman   70–74

Illusory Promises

    Chirelstein   25–28

Conditions of Satisfaction

    Weiner, Mattei

    Summers and Hillman   74–81

Justified Reliance (Promissory Estoppel)
(Theory # 2)

    **Kirksey, Ryerrs, Seavey, Siegel,
Restatement 1st§ 90**

    Summers and Hillman   81–93

Reliance and Promissory Estoppel (up to
Illusory Promises)

    Chirelstein   22–25

    **Wheeler, Hoffman, Local 1330,
Restatement 2nd§ 90**

    Summers and Hillman   93–111

Reliance and Restitution, Reliance Damages
Section

    Chirelstein   199–204

Unjust Enrichment (Theory # 3)

    **Bloomgarden, Sparks, Gay, Kearns,
Anderco**

    Summers and Hillman   112–130

Restitution Remedies

    Chirelstein   204–212

Unjust Enrichment

Posner, Kelley, Britton, Watts

Benefit Received (Moral Obligation) (Theory # 4)

Mills, Webb, Harrington, Edson

Moral Obligation and Past Consideration

Obligation Arising in Tort

Maudlin, Hargrove

Warranties (Statutory Obligations) (Theory # 5)

Keith, Webster

Sale of Goods and Perfect Tender

Statute of Frauds

Howard M. Schoor, Jonesboro, McIntosh

CHAPTER THREE—REMEDIES

Introduction to Expectancy Damages

Expectancy Damages for Breach of Agreement
with Consideration

Cost of Completion vs. Loss of Value

Groves, Peeveyhouse, Rock Island, Radford

Thorne, Warner, Handicapped Children

Market Based Damages

Cooper, UCC

Remedies for Detrimental Reliance

Goodman, D&G Stout, Walters, Grouse

Summers and Hillman   307–318

Restitution Damages

Susi Contract'g, Bausch & Lomb, Osteen

Summers and Hillman   318–336

Chirelstein   204–212

Specific Performance

Kitchen, Curtice, Pratt

Summers and Hillman   336–351

Warranties and Disclaimers

UCC 2–313, 2–314, 2–316

Summers and Hillman   601–604

Contracts Assignment Grid Fall 2006

Week	Date	Topic	Pages	Total	Ppt
1	8/21	Introduction (Non Commercial); Commercial Distinguished (Nim Plastics)	2–29	28	1
	8/23	Theories of Obligation & Remedies	33–42	10	1
2	8/28	Basics of Consideration	43–61	19	2a
	8/30	Forbearance	62–70	9	2a
3	9/4	LABOR DAY—No Class			
	9/6	Illusory Contracts & Conditions	70–81	12	2b
4	9/11	Promissory Estoppel	81–90	10	2c
	9/13	Promissory Estoppel	90–111	12	2c
5	9/18	Unjust Enrichment	112–130	19	2d
	9/20	Unjust Enrichment	130–144	15	2d
6	9/25	Moral Obligation	144–157	14	2e
	9/27	Obligation Arising in Tort	157–171	15	2e
7	10/2	Warranties	173–185	13	2f
	10/4	Statute of Frauds	185–204	20	2f

8	10/9	FALL BREAK–No Class			
	10/11	Expectancy Damages:Cost of Completion vs. Loss of Value	205–226	22	3a
9	10/16	Expectancy Damages: Cont'd.	226–237	12	3a
	10/18	Market Based Damages & Lost Profit for Volume Sellers	237–245	9	3b
10	10/23	Limits on Expectancy: Consequential Damages	245–252	8	3c
	10/25	Mitigation of Damages	252–266	15	3c
11	10/30	New Business Rule, Mental Distress, Personal Injury	266–279 & 35–43	22	3c
	11/1	Reliance Damages	279–292	14	3d
12	11/6	Liquidated Damages	293–307	15	3d
	11/8	Remedies for Detrimental Reliance	307–318	12	3e
13	11/13	Restitution Damages	318–336	19	3e
	11/15	Specific Performance	336–351	16	3e
14	11/20	Warranties	601–04	4	3e
	11/22	DAY BEFORE THANKSGIVING–No Class			
15	11/27	IN CLASS COURSE REVIEW			
	11/29	IN CLASS COURSE REVIEW			

HOW DOES HAMMOND INTRODUCE HIS STUDENTS TO THE PROCESS OF LEGAL REASONING? (SELECTIONS FROM HAMMOND'S PRESENTATIONS TO STUDENTS)

Goals of the Course

1. Legal Analysis
2. Knowledge of Contract Law

Managing 1st Semester Law School
What are the major skills to be developed during the 1st Semester?

- Case Reading [Briefing]
- Comparative Case Analysis
- Theory Building
- Comparative Theory Analysis
- Critical Legal Analysis & Reasoning
- Articulation of Legal Analysis & Reasoning

Managing the Work Load
The conclusion of each topic area in the syllabus is a critical time for students to review and strive to comprehend the theory or principle discussed.

- Comparative Case Analysis
- Theory/Rule Building
- Theory Comprehension
- Theory Comparison

From Skill Development to Outline

SKILL:

- Case Analysis
- Case Comparison
- Theory Building
- Theory Comparison
- Theoretical Framework

OUTLINING TASK:

- Case Briefing
- Rule Identification
- Rule Defined/Applied
- Rules Distinguished
- Rules, Elements, Applicability, Defenses & Remedies Organized in Coherent Framework

Course Theoretical Framework
The Grid—Contracts

	Theory & Elements	Defenses	Counter Defenses	Remedies	Qualifications on Remedies
Agreement w/ Consideration					
Promissory Estoppel					
Unjust Enrichment					
Moral Obligation					
Warranties					

About Those Skills: The Dilemma
When reading and studying the law using the case system, what should I be focusing on? There are four levels of analysis a 1st year student must master to be successful. They are:

- ○ Case analysis
- ○ Rule building & application
- ○ Comparative rule analysis
- ○ Application

Case Analysis: 1st Level
  Component parts:

- ○ Parties?
- ○ Reason for Appeal?
- ○ Issue(s) presented?
- ○ Rule(s) or Theory(ies) Identified?
- ○ Rule(s) or Theory(ies) Applied?
- ○ Court's Reasoning
- ○ Court's Conclusion
- ○ **Warning this is not as mechanical as it sounds.**

What is one of the most important aspects of case analysis? Identifying the rule and its application:

- What is the rule?
- Why is it applied? [i.e. what facts in the case compel its application?]
- How is it applied?
- Was it applied appropriately?

Rule Construction/Theory Building: 2nd Level

Comparative Case Analysis: What story are the cases telling? Cases are organized to explain a rule or rules via use of certain themes:

- Rule's elements
- Rule's exceptions
- Rule's evolution
- Rule's distinction from other Rules
- Rule's public policy rationale
- Rule's dysfunction

Comparative Rule/Theory Analysis: 3rd Level

Component Parts:

- Identify relationships and distinctions between the rules.
- Develop an inclusive theory incorporating the rules, defenses and exceptions.

Critical Legal Analysis & Reasoning:

- Using rules/theories and their respective elements to ascertain what rules/theory(ies) may apply based on the facts presented.
- Determining whether public policy supports the particular applications of law elicited by the fact pattern.

Managing the Classroom: Different Teaching Styles

- Emphasize case analysis more than statutory or rule interpretation or vice versa.
- Discuss a theory or rule by ascertaining what it is and then seeking to distinguish it from other theories or rules.
- Discuss a theory or rule by describing what it is not rather than what it is.

Query

What do the case materials require you to do in order extract the critical information contained in them? What am I looking for?

○ Controversy Between Parties

○ Issues Before the Court

○ Theories Addressed by the Court

○ Definition of the Theories' and Elements

○ Court's Conclusion

What am I supposed to understand after reading this case?

"Ethical Issues in Engineering" (Spring 2005)

Robert McGinn
Science, Technology and Society/School of Engineering
Stanford University, Stanford, California

Course Description and Purpose

E 131/STS 115 is a limited-enrollment class (see pp. 107 and 566 of the 2004–05 STANFORD BULLETIN and Axess) devoted to study of ethical issues in contemporary engineering work. The purpose of the course is threefold: to expose students to ethical issues of the sorts that engineers often face in professional workplaces, to help students think more clearly and deeply about such issues, and to explore intellectual and other kinds of resources for grappling with such conflicts. Topics covered will include: moral responsibilities and rights of engineers in relation to society, employers, colleagues, and clients; cost-benefit-risk analysis, safety, and informed consent; the ethics of whistle-blowing; ethical conflicts of engineers as managers, consultants, and expert witnesses; ethical issues in engineering design, manufacturing, and operations; ethical issues arising from engineering work in foreign countries; ethical issues in high-tech workplaces; and ethical implications of the social and environmental contexts of contemporary engineering. The course will make extensive use of real-life case studies of ethical issues drawn from different fields of engineering.

The size of the class will be limited to 25 students to maintain its intended seminar character. The reason for doing so is that students derive more intellectual value by actively analyzing and exchanging views about these course materials in a seminar setting than by taking notes on a lecture delivered to a larger-than-seminar-sized group.

Note Well: E 131/STS 115 satisfies the Humanities component (Area 3a) of the Stanford General Education Requirements (GERs) and the School of Engineering's "Technology in Society Requirement."

Course Requirements

1. Completion of and reflection on assigned readings;
2. Thoughtful participation in class discussion;
3. Identification of and research into an original case study of real-life ethical issue in engineering, presentation of one's case in class, and write-up of that case. The case searches, presentations, and write-ups will be done by student duos.

Grading

1. Class discussion: 50%
2. Original Case Study: 50%

     A. 40% for the in-class presentation;

     B. 10% for the written report.

REQUIRED READING

1. R. McGinn, ed., **STS 115/E 131 Course Reader, 2005** (Stanford Bookstore, 2005).

Calendar of Topics and Reading Assignments

FOUNDATIONAL MATERIALS

1. TU 3/29, INTRODUCTION TO THE COURSE

Why study ethical issues in engineering?

A survey regarding ethical issues in engineering

What makes an issue in engineering work an "ethical issue?"

What's important about the history of the engineering profession in the U.S.?

What is a "profession?" Why is that an important question for this class?

1. R. McGinn, "'Mind the Gaps': A Survey of Engineering Students and Practicing Engineers"
2. T. Reynolds, "The Engineer in Nineteenth-Century America"

3. T. Reynolds, "The Engineer in Twentieth-Century America"

4. E. Greenwood, "Attributes of a Profession"

Note: obviously you will not have read these articles before today's class. However, they must be read as soon as possible after the first meeting and will be revisited at the beginning of second session.

2. TU 4/05, CODES OF ENGINEERING ETHICS AND MORAL RESPONSIBILITIES OF ENGINEERS, PART A

1. National Society of Professional Engineers (NSPE), Code of Ethics for Engineers (1990)

2. American Society of Civil Engineers (ASCE), Code of Ethics (1993)

3. Institute of Electrical and Electronics Engineers (IEEE), Code of Ethics (1990)

4. Association for Computing Machinery (ACM), Code of Ethics (1992)

PART B

1. R. DeGeorge, "Ethical Responsibilities of Engineers in Large Corporations: The Pinto Case"

2. D. L. Parnas, "SDI: A Violation of Professional Responsibility"

3. M. Martin and R. Schinzinger, "Engineering as Social Experimentation"

4. T. Broome, "Engineering Responsibility for Hazardous Technologies"

5. J. Anderson, "Ethics and the Expert Witness"

CASE STUDIES

3. TU 4/12, CASE STUDIES I

1. F. Sawyier, "The Case of the DC-10"

2. K. Vandivier, "'Why Should My Conscience Bother Me?'"

3. W. Broad, "Missile Contractor Doctored Tests, Ex-Employee Charges"

4. W. Broad, "Antimissile Testing Is Rigged To Hide a Flaw, Critics Say"

4. TU 4/19, CASE STUDIES II

1. J. Morgenstern, "The Fifty-Nine Story Crisis"
2. W. Wilson, "The Case of the Composite Material Bicycle"

5. TH 4/28, CASE STUDIES III: CHALLENGER, GM PICKUP, AND FORD PINTO

1. T. Bell and K. Esch, "The Fatal Flaw in Flight 51L"
2. R. Boisjoly, "Ethical Decisions: Morton Thiokol and the Space Shuttle Challenger Disaster"
3. B. Meier, "Courtroom Drama Pits G.M. Against a Former Engineer"
4. P. Applegate, "G.M. Is Held Liable Over Fuel Tanks In Pickup Trucks"
5. W. Shaw, "Ford's Pinto"
6. M. Hoffman, "The Ford Pinto"

6. TU 5/03, CASE STUDIES IV: BHOPAL AND HYATT REGENCY HOTEL

1. G. Stix, "Bhopal: A Tragedy in Waiting"
2. S. Diamond, "The Bhopal Disaster: How It Happened"
3. S. Diamond, "The Disaster In Bhopal: The Workers Recall Horror"
4. Robert Reinhold, "Disaster in Bhopal: Where Does the Blame Lie?"
5. S. Diamond, "The Disaster in Bhopal: Lessons for the Future"
6. Ibrahim, Youssef, "Successors Ready, U.S. Oilmen Bow Out of the Saudi Empire"
7. H. Petroski, "Accidents Waiting To Happen"
8. H. Petroski, "The Kansas City Tragedy: There Is Not Always Strength in Numbers"
9. R. Rubin, L. Banick, and C. Thornton, "The Hyatt Decision: Two Opinions"

7. TU 5/10, CASE STUDIES V: HAZARDOUS WASTE SITES AND HI-TECH ENGINEERING ETHICS

1. S. Beder and M. Shortland, "Siting A Hazardous Waste Facility: the Tangled Web of Risk Communication"
2. K. Noble, "Ecology War Brews in California Desert"

3. S. Decatur, "Who's Being Consulted? Science, Authority, and Politics in the Siting of a Waste Facility at Ward Valley"

4. R. Ho, "Ethics and High-Tech Engineering: Unique Ethical Issues of the Silicon Valley Workplace"

5. J. Markoff, "Marketer's Dream, Engineer's Nightmare"

8. TU 5/17, ETHICS, NANOSCIENCE, AND NANOTECHNOLOGY

1. R. McGinn, "Ethical Issues in Nanoscience and Nanotechnology: Reflections and Suggestions"

2. R. McGinn, "Ethics, Nanoscience, and Nanotechnology: Views of NNIN Users and Students" (revised version to be distributed in class)

3. G. Khushf, "The Ethics of Nanotechnology: Vision and Values for a New Generation of Science and Technology"

4. Members of the seminar will be given a small research task to complete for this session.

5. There is the possibility of a guest this week.

STUDENT PRESENTATIONS

9. TU 5/24, STUDENT REPORTS I
10. TH 5/26, STUDENT REPORTS II

RETROSPECTION AND SYNTHESIS

11. T 5/31, REFLECTIONS AND CONCLUSIONS

1. R. McGinn, "Ethical Issues in Engineering: Some Overarching Themes, Theses, Ideas, Concerns and Quotes"

2. L. Winner, "Engineering Ethics and Political Imagination"

3. Ferguson, Eugene, "The Gap Between Promise and Performance"

4. S. Beder, "Making Engineering Design Sustainable"

THE IN-CLASS PRESENTATIONS. On Tuesday, May 24, and Thursday, May 26, seminar members, having organized and worked in pairs or (if necessary or desired) in trios, will make joint in-class presentations. While not required, you are encouraged to link up with a class member who is majoring in your field, so that the two of you will then be able to choose a case that relates to your major field.

Each presentation, lasting 15 minutes (if a duo) or 23 minutes (if a trio), must take the form of an **original case study** of an incident or episode involving an interesting, non-obvious ethical issue or conflict in contemporary engineering work. The case study may be based on one or more kinds of research, e.g., location and analysis of courtroom records, in-person or telephonic interviews with engineer participants and others involved in the situation under scrutiny, etc. To secure the cooperation of reluctant participants, you may wish to assure potential interviewees that you will maintain confidentiality, and/or not cite them by name or other identifying particulars on paper. I have found that it sometimes helps to tell potential participants (truthfully) that you are doing a research project for a class at Stanford University, that you want to get all relevant sides of the story, and, if true, that you've already spoken with other parties or received useful documents reflecting their perspectives and would find it useful to obtain theirs for the sake of doing justice to the case.

Regardless of the kind of study undertaken, each presentation must include the following:

1. appropriate general background information about the case;

2. description of the socio-technical situation in the case in sufficient detail to enable the listener/reader to appreciate the situation that faced the engineer(s) in question;

3. explicit identification and characterization of the ethical issue or conflict in question;

4. elaboration and probing analysis of the issue or conflict (e.g., of its genesis, trajectory and outcome; evaluation of the strengths and weaknesses of the arguments made on both sides; etc.); and

5. delineation of noteworthy morals or lessons about ethical issues in engineering extracted from the case presented.

Each duo/trio must also submit a carefully written report of about 1250 words describing the case studied and specifying the resources used in putting together the presentation. The paper should be more than simply a repetition of what you did in the presentation. Feel free to pursue an issue you didn't get into in the presentation or one that you did but now will explore in greater depth. Please attach any tapes, articles, transcripts, or other documents that you have gathered or generated in your research. A word count *must* be included at the end of your report. A word of advice: *do not wait until shortly before your presentation date to identify or research your case*; that is a recipe for a mediocre presentation and will be graded accordingly.

Selected Cases from "Ethics and Law" (1993)

Timothy Murphy and Michele Oberman
University of Illinois College of Medicine, Chicago, Illinois

Legal and Ethical Conflicts in the Care of the Elderly or Terminally Ill: Insistence on Futile Treatment

An 86-year-old woman was hospitalized and successfully treated for a broken hip. But shortly thereafter, she went into respiratory failure and has been on a respirator for five months. During an attempt to wean her from the respirator, she went into cardiopulmonary arrest. She has been diagnosed with severe and irreversible brain damage. Her physicians advise limiting any further life-sustaining treatment. Her family insists that all forms of treatment be continued. Some physicians ask the hospital legal staff to intervene, since in their view continued support of this kind was futile and not in the patient's best interests. They asked for a court order to clarify that family members were not entitled to demand treatment. Thus, at one level, the case is about a conflict between health professional and family about continuing or discontinuing treatment near the end of life. At another level, it is about the judgments involved in determining whether the patient's condition is indeed irreversible, but the medical students are not expected to be able to make their own judgments about this. At still a third level, the case is about the allocation of scarce medical resources, since the money spent by the public (hospital, government) treating this patient is not available for other patients.

Refusal of Medical Treatment

A woman is four months pregnant with her fifth child, and both she and her husband want this baby. In three previous pregnancies, a "purse string" operation has been needed to suture the cervix to permit her to carry the pregnancy to term. Since then, the woman has become a "born-again" Christian and based on her religious convictions, refuses the operation. Her husband does not share her religious views, and begs her physician to find some legal way to force his wife to submit to the operation. He threatens to sue the physician and the hospital for negligence if the pregnancy miscarries.

Question: How should the physician involved (and the medical profession generally) respond to this type of conflict? What ethical considerations should guide your response to this dilemma? What are the limits on patient autonomy when a third-party's interest is involved?

Cultural Variations in the Treatment of Children

A Laotian woman living in the USA brings her youngest child to a community clinic for routine immunizations. The baby has five red, blistered quarter-inch round markings on the abdomen that appear to be burns. The mother explains that she has used a traditional cure for a suspected case of a rare illness among the Mien, characterized by restlessness, crying, agitation, and loss of appetite. The mother explains that the cure had been successful: the child has stopped crying, calmed down, and has regained her appetite.

Questions: To what extent is it ethical to accept treatment of this baby as part of another culture's folk medicine, particularly when the dominant American culture would regard the action as child abuse? What ethical principles ought to govern decisions in this area? Are ethical principles universal, transcending all cultures? Or are they grounded within a specific cultural context?

Impaired Physicians

Through conversations with his roommate and observations of his behavior, a medical student learns that his roommate uses injections of a mild amphetamine to stay awake for long hours and then uses intravenous valium to calm down.

Question: How should you react to your friend's drug use? Is there an ethical obligation to act on the information you have? At what point, if any, would you consider telling medical school officials about this situation? Who should be advised and why?

Access and Equity: Problems in Organ Transplantation

A university medical center wants to undertake an organ transplant program designed to "harvest" the organs of anencephalic babies so that they can be used as medically appropriate for other children around the country. Death is inevitable in this condition. The protocol entails obtaining parents' permission to place the newborn on life support for up to seven days to maintain the other organs while an appropriate recipient is located. The baby will be checked for brain function every 12 hours, and if none is present, would be declared brain dead and the organs could be donated. If brain function was detected, the respirator would be removed and the child allowed to die. To preclude conflicts of interest, the physicians making the final diagnosis of death were unaffiliated with the transplant team.

Parents of these children frequently request organ donation so that "some good may come of this tragedy." Yet this program generated considerable conflict in the medical community. It is difficult to diagnose brain death in infants, and traditional criteria of brain death are not readily applicable to anencephalic newborns because they lack higher brain functions. Some opponents fear that human life is cheapened by treating these newborns as "organ containers." Others fear that the policy risks exacerbating public fears about being declared dead "prematurely" and will inhibit willingness to donate organs. Still others see these newborns as severely disabled, not brain dead, and object to using a vulnerable class of persons in this way.

Questions: Is harvesting of organs of anencephalic newborns morally justifiable, if the parents consent? Why or why not? Is widespread social concern about this policy a sufficient reason to suspend the practice? Is this practice ethically problematical in any other way that should control whether or not it is implemented?

"Scripture and the Moral Life" (Spring 2003)

William C. Spohn
Department of Religious Studies
Santa Clara University, Santa Clara, California

This course will investigate the role that Scripture plays in the moral life of Christians with special attention given to the figure of Jesus Christ. Is it possible to draw theological ethics from the experience of discipleship? How did the early Christian communities adapt the teachings and example of Jesus to their contexts? How should Christians today apply that story to a vastly different world? We will address these issues through examining the relation between Scripture, character ethics, and spiritual practices. We will pay special attention to the way that reflecting and acting on Scripture changes moral perspective, dispositions and identity.

This course is a third course in Religious Studies which is described by the department as: "APPLICATIONS: Critical engagement of current, open-ended issues in religion.

As the last required course, the third course should model on-going intellectual engagement with difficult questions and issues involving religion. In terms of cognitive development, this course should be organized around problems, issues, or controversies that require students to explore and assess multiple positions and then make intellectually defensible, integrative, and nuanced decisions.

As the last substantive core curriculum course for most undergraduates, the third course should serve as a "capstone," giving students the opportunity to bring together their core and disciplinary knowledge, their acquired analytic skills, the intellectual challenge of current issues, and the larger questions that will invoke ethical and ontological concerns."

This course is structured to help the students reach these aims.

Requirements

Scripture calls for a special way of reading because it is claimed to be divine revelation. For believers, it is not simply a historical text or a source of moral guidance, but a text that is read for meaning, that is, for truth we can live by. This kind of reading requires us to engage imagination, memory, emotions and personal reflection.

1. In order to read this challenging set of texts in an engaged way, students will commit ten minutes a day over the ten weeks of the quarter to meditate on specific biblical texts that will be listed for each day in the syllabus. Each passage is coordinated with the material being considered at that time in class. This regular practice is instructive whether you read the text as literary inspiration or as spiritual revelation.

2. Students will keep a daily journal on what they experience during these reflective periods. Every two weeks each student will submit a typed version of the daily journal for feedback from the instructor (usually about three to four double-spaced pages). Early in the course, each student will schedule a brief meeting with the instructor to discuss this "spiritual practice."

3. At every class session one student will offer brief reflections on the biblical text assigned for that day.

4. This class will be participatory: its success depends upon careful reading of the texts, regular reflection and journaling, informed and active engagement in the conversation. Every seminar member is expected to bring a Bible to every class, preferably the New Revised Standard Version or the New American Bible.

5. Three brief in-class examinations will occur on the assigned readings. A final take-home examination will pull together the themes of the course and the results of the student's participation in the practice of meditation.

Grading will be based equally on participation, the journals, the three quizzes, and the final exam. Unexcused absences will affect the student's final grade. Do not take this evening class unless you can give it the highest priority.

Texts

The Bible, preferably New American or New Revised Standard Version

John C. Endres and Elizabeth Liebert, *A Retreat with the Psalms* (Paulist, 2001)

William Reiser, *Jesus in Solidarity with His People: A Theologian Looks at Mark* (Liturgical, 1997)

William C. Spohn, *Go and Do Likewise: Jesus and Ethics* (Continuum, 1999)

Syllabus

M 3/31 INTRODUCTION: SCRIPTURE AND ETHICS TODAY
Daily readings: 4/1: Psalm 6; 4/2: Ps13

W 4/2 PSALMS OF LAMENT
Endres and Liebert, *Retreat with the Psalms,* pp. 1–65
Daily Readings: 4/3: Ps 42 and 43; 4/4: Ps 22; 4/5: Ps 69
4/6: Ps 137; 4/7: Ps 9

   **Bring Bible to every class

M 4/7 PSALMS OF TRUST, THANKSGIVING AND PRAISE
Endres and Liebert: pp. 66–137
Daily Readings: 4/8: Ps 32; 4/9: Ps 30

   *Schedule appointment with instructor

W 4/9 FILM: JESUS OF MONTREAL
Daily Readings: 4/10 Ps 29; 4/11: Ps 103; 4/12: Ps 46
4/13: Ps 139; 4/14: Ps 23

   *First Installment of Journal due

M 4/14 PSALMS OF FORGIVENESS AND WONDER

Endres and Liebert: pp. 138–228

Daily Readings: 4/15: Matt 5:21–32

4/16: Matt 5:33–48

*Quiz on Endres and Liebert and psalms

W 4/16 SERMON ON THE MOUNT AND MARK

Reiser, *Jesus in Solidarity,* pp. ix-29

Daily Readings: 4/17 John 13; 4/18 Ps 22

4/19 John 18; 4/20 John 20:1–9

4/21 Mark 1:1–15

M 4/21 SON OF MAN AND CALLING

Reiser, Jesus in Solidarity, pp. 31–71

Daily Readings: 4/22 Mk:1:16–20; 4/23 Mk:2:13–14

*Second Installment of Journal due

W 4/23 FORGIVENESS AND SOLIDARITY WITH THE SUFFERING

Reiser, Jesus in Solidarity, pp. 73–105

Daily Readings: 4/24 Mk 2:1–12; 4/25 Mk:9:14–29

4:26 Mark 10:46–52; 4/27 Mk 5:21–43; 4/28 Mk 8:1–10

M 4/28 MIRACLES AND PARABLES

Reiser, *Jesus in Solidarity,* pp. 107–147

Daily Readings: 4/29 Mk 5:1–20; 4/30 Mk 4:1–20

W 4/30 THE COST OF DISCIPLESHIP

Reiser, *Jesus in Solidarity*, pp. 149–185

Daily Readings: 5/1 Mk 8:27–38; 5/2 Mk 9:30–37

5/3 Mk 10:17–27; 5/4 Mk 9:1–7; 5/5 Mk 14:1–15:39

M 5/5 RESURRECTION OF JESUS

Reiser, *Jesus in Solidarity,* pp. 187–215

Daily Readings: 5/6 Mk 5:35–41; 5/7 Matt 7:15–20

*Quiz on Reiser

W 5/7 NEW TESTAMENT AS WAY OF LIFE

Spohn, *Go and Do Likewise*, pp. ix-26

Case Study: "A Question of Inheritance"

Daily Readings: 5/8 Lk 1:26–38; 5/9 Lk 4:14–30;

5/10 Lk 5:1–11; 5/11 Galatians 5:13–26; 5/12 John 13

*Third Installment of Journal due

M 5/12 CHARACTER ETHICS, SPIRITUALITY AND THE
IMAGINATION

Spohn, *Go and Do Likewise*, pp. 27–71

Daily Readings: 5/13 Luke 15:1–32; 5/14 Lk 10:25–37

W 5/14 PERCEIVING THE WORLD ACCORDING TO GOD

Spohn, *Go and Do Likewise*, pp. 73–99

Case Study: "Sabbath-Keeping: Balancing Work and Life"

Daily Readings: 5/15 Matt 6:24–33; 5/16 Ps 104;

5/17 Ps 103; 5/18 Matt 13:31–33; 5/19 Matt 20:1–16

M 5/19 BLINDNESS AND CONVERSION

Spohn, *Go and Do Likewise*, pp. 100–119

Daily Readings: 5/20 John 3:19–21; 5/21 Romans 7

*Quiz on Spohn, pp. 1–119

W 5/21 REDIRECTING EMOTIONS AND DISPOSITIONS

Spohn, *Go and Do Likewise*, pp. 121–140

Case Study: "The Practice of Fidelity in Marriage"

Daily Readings: 5/22 Ps 84; 5/23 Matt 6:9–13; 5/24 Matt 8:18–22;
5/25 Luke 7:36–50; 5/26: Rom 8:12–17, 26–27

*Fourth Installment of Journal due

M 5/26 MEMORIAL DAY: NO CLASS

Daily Readings: 5/27 Acts of Apostles 9:1–22;

5/28 Romans 12:1–8

W 5/28 THE RE3ASONING HEART

Spohn, *Go and Do Likewise*, pp. 142–162

Case Study: "Job, Career and Calling"

Daily Readings: 5/29 Phil 2:1–11; 5/30 Phil 3:1–21; 5/31 1
Corinthians 12:12–31; 6/1 1 Cor 8; 6/2 Matt 18:21–35

M 6/2 FORGIVENESS AND SOLIDARITY

Spohn, pp. 163–187

Case Study: "Terrorism and the Duty to Forgive"

Daily Readings: 6/3: 2 Cor 8:8–24; 6/4 Matt 5:23–24

W 6/4 FINAL LECTURE: GO AND DO LIKEWISE

Case Study: Biblical Morality and Preventive War

   *Final Installment of Journal due

W 6/11 FINAL EXAMINATION DUE AT SOBRATO 34 BY 4PM

If you wish the examination returned, please include a stamped,
self-addressed envelope.

"Foundations of Modern Education" (2007)

Barbara S. Stengel
Educational Foundations
Millersville University, Millersville, Pennsylvania

> *"Education, in one perspective, is a process of initiating young
> people into the ways of thinking and behaving characteristic of
> the culture into which they were born. In another perspective, it
> is the development of a person from innocence to experience,
> from the confines of childish immediacies to the open plains of
> conceptual thought. In still another, it is the effort of a commu-
> nity to recreate itself with the rise of each new generation and to
> perpetuate itself in historic time."*

—Maxine Greene, *Teacher as Stranger*

We begin the semester with a set of "essential questions" to guide our
learning together:

1. How are teaching and learning, schooling and education related?
   What is the responsibility of the teacher? The purpose of schooling
   in 21st century America?

2. What is the structure of our educational system? How does it work? How is power generated? How does it flow in that system? Can/should that structure be changed? (the political question)

3. Who pays the bill? Who benefits? Is there equal educational opportunity? Is it fair? (the economic question)

4. Is there one "American culture?" Whose knowledge, culture and way of life are privileged and preserved in contemporary schooling? Is it better to be white than black? Male than female? Christian than any other religious persuasion? Can schools construct an American culture while respecting the cultural background kids bring to schools? (the socio-cultural question)

5. How did we get the educational system that we have? Which individuals, events, social forces and common values shaped our educational system? (the historical question)

6. What is the purpose of schooling in a democracy and how should it be carried out? How has this question been answered in America and how would YOU answer it? (the philosophical question)

Our ultimate goal can be characterized as "pedagogical responsibility," the ability to respond in a fitting and defensible way to your students and their instructional circumstances. In the foundations bloc, we help you to recognize and interpret the factors that frame responsive and responsible pedagogical action. In Foundations of Modern Education, we will look at teaching and learning from the *outside in*, examining the historical, socio-cultural, economic and political contexts that shape contemporary schooling. In this process of recognition and interpretation, you will acquire a critical, moral perspective regarding the profession of teaching and the domain of schooling in 21st century American democracy.

"Pedagogical responsibility" plays a role in each of the three lenses that serve to ground and orient the Millersville University teacher education program: 1) professionalism, 2) a focus on student learning, and 3) learning communities of inquiry and action. "Professionalism" captures the sense in which teachers make use of specialized knowledge in the service of others. "A focus on student learning" requires that we craft instruction based on the experience of learners who wrestle with concepts and skills that we have already mastered. "Communities of inquiry and action" suggests both goal and process; knowledge is community property constructed through shared inquiry and reflection on action.

These three lenses yield seven program proficiencies which articulate the standards against which you will be measured prior to graduation

and certification: demonstrating content knowledge, developing pedagogical content knowledge, applying theory to practice, understanding
students, assessing student learning, developing professional dispositions,
and understanding context and facilitating community. *These outcomes
will serve as a framework for your foundations bloc portfolio and end-
of-semester comprehensive assessment.* I encourage you to spend some
time reading the full text of each outcome now and as the semester pro-
gresses. We will reach our goals by reading, responding to and exploring
in depth several classic and contemporary educational texts and by critically reflecting on your experience in the schools in light of these texts.
The essential questions noted above will frame our deliberations. Additional readings and supplemental activities will be assigned as appropriate. At the end of our time together, you will be knowledgeable about
schooling in America and your knowledge—enlivened by the critical,
moral perspective noted above—will guide your perceptions and actions
as a teacher.

Schedule

Date	Topic	Reading	Assignment Due
8/30	**Unit 1: Introduction to 211**	Postman; NCLB packet	
9/1	in class		
9/6	in class		
9/8	**Unit 2: Diversity and fairness**	Tatum; Lazerson; Kozol; Spring; MacIntosh	Unit 1 tasks completed. Work submitted
9/13	in class		
9/15	in class		
9/20	in class		Prep EEO lesson.
9/22	in class		
9/27	in class		
9/29	**Unit 3: Power and responsibility**	Benham; Tye; Follett; Taking Sides debate	Unit 2 tasks completed. Work submitted

(Continued)

Date	Topic	Reading	Assignment Due
10/4	in class		
10/6	**Penn Manor Scholar in Residence Program**		
10/11	in class		
10/13	in class		
10/18	in class		
10/20	in class **Field Experience Assignment Meeting**		
10/25	Field Experience		Unit 3 tasks completed. Work submitted
10/27	Field Experience		Blackboard: Student demographics
11/1	Field Experience		
11/3	Field Experience		Blackboard: Classroom management? Instructional management?
11/8	Field Experience		
11/10	Field Experience		Blackboard: Assessment practices
11/15	Field Experience		
11/17	Field Experience		Blackboard: EEO redux
11/22	Field experience review in class		Visual record
11/29	**Unit 4: Continuity and change**	Dewey; Lazerson	
12/1	in class		

Date	Topic	Reading	Assignment Due
12/6	in class		Philosophies Lesson prep / standardized assessment
12/8	in class		
12/12			Portfolio due (Unit 4 work completed, integrated into portfolio)
12/13–14	Cumulative bloc assessment: Case study		211 Self-assessment due

All students will automatically be enrolled in a Foundations Bloc Blackboard site and will be able to communicate with the entire class, including both course instructors. It is important that you enter the Blackboard site and correct your own personal information as soon as possible to ensure that you are part of all course communications.

Texts

Neil Postman, *The End of Education*

Barbara Benham Tye, *Hard Truths: Uncovering the Deep Structure of Schooling*

Marvin Lazerson (ed.), *American Education in the Twentieth Century: A Documentary History*

John Dewey, *The School and Society/The Child and the Curriculum* (available on-line at School and Society)

Beverly Tatum, *Why are all the Black Kids Sitting Together in the Cafeteria?*

211 Self-created BlocBook

Assignments

1. At least one visit to "office hours." I will offer a sign-up sheet to ensure that everybody doesn't come at once. This visit need not have a specific purpose. Just show up. I'll take it from there. The visit must be completed by 2/18. (Additional office hour visits are encouraged!!)

2. A "flow chart" of our educational system and its decision-making structure, to be done using Inspiration software. (For assignment specifications, click here.)

3. Attendance at one School Board meeting (Penn Manor or School District of Lancaster recommended, but any board meeting—including your own home school district—will be fine). Based on your observation (and additional research as needed), you will prepare a lesson plan and teach a 5–7 minute mini-lesson about A SINGLE ASPECT of school board function to a small group of peers. Notes from the observation should be placed in your BlocBook. (For board meeting schedules and assignment specifications, click where highlighted.)

4. A "web quest"/electronic search that insures that you are acquainted with the academic standards that are relevant to your future as a teacher and that you understand the political and educational issues surroundings standards, testing and accountability. Click here for browser copy of assignment sheet.

5. Completion of a profile of your home school district, showing enrollment, finance information, and test achievement figures. Click here for the profile form.

6. Participation in a field placement.
   - Completion of a visual record of your experiences (15–20 pictures) with written reflection.
   - Complete an Observer's Guide (based on the Jackson et al., The Moral Life of Schools). This guide will focus your attention on the moral contours of teaching and learning. (For data collection form, click here.)
   - Complete a student assessment chart for at least six students, "label" those students, and discuss the ramifications of that labeling.
   - Observe and work with a student with special needs. For reflection form, click here.)
   - Reflections on field experience (AT LEAST 4) posted on the Bloc Blackboard site. You MUST address student demographics and diversity, classroom management/power, motivation (04) or cognition and learning (03), and equal educational opportunity. (All messages should use readings and class concepts as the scaffolding for your observations.) You may address any other topics, experiences you wish. Feel free to ask for advice or respond to other students' experiences.

- Contact me by e-mail to discuss ANY field experience problems or to set up an appointment for group or individual conference as needed.

7. Reading related assignments

   - Three mini-lessons based on 1) Lazerson readings, 2) school board meeting and readings, and 3) alternate philosophies of education. Click here for lesson plan form.

   - Dewey questions

   - Benham Tye questions

8. A completed PA Teacher Application to be brought to the final regular class. (You should download the application from the PA Department of Education website, complete it on your computer and then print it out.)

9. Self-created portfolio ("Blocbook") incorporating course materials (assignments, handouts, exercises, notes, study guides, etc.), organized according to the seven Program Proficiencies. This book/binder should be accompanied by a 1000–1500 word self-assessment essay, exploring what you have learned/how you have changed through this course, and assigning a grade for the semester based on the evidence amassed in the portfolio. (For portfolio specifications, click here.)

10. A cumulative bloc assessment (scheduled during finals week). You will be given a case study and asked to interpret the case, demonstrating your ability to recognize those psychological, sociological, cultural, political, economic, and personal factors that require teachers to plan instruction to meet each student's needs. You may use your blocbook (including all course materials) to assist you in completing this task.

11. Completion of all reading assignments in preparation for class discussions.

12. Intelligent and critical participation in class discussion and activities.

13. Written work submitted in a timely fashion. Extensions will be granted if necessary. If you need an extension, you must hand in a written (or e-mail) request before the due date, indicating the reason for the extension and the date you will hand in the assignment. No second extensions will be given. Written work will not be accepted after the due date/extension date.

Self-assessment is a key theme in this course and will play the central role in the determination of your grade at the end of the semester. We will share responsibility for your learning, for establishing high standards of performance, and for the honest and candid assessment of what you know and can do when our time together is complete.

Field Experience Agenda

1) Visual Record. This is basically a picture journal of your experience. Complete directions are in the packet. The purpose of this assignment is to train you to "see" the important elements of a school context. If you can see them, then you can interpret what's going on. Only then can you respond professionally and pedagogically in the best way possible. You'll need a camera for this. A disposable camera with 24 shots on it will do nicely if you don't have a camera of your own. Please ASK PERMISSION before taking any pictures and show your co-op the assignment sheet if he/she has any questions. Make it clear that these pictures will only be used for a class assignment and seen by you and I.

(Students have a clear right to privacy and any public use of any pictures requires their parents' explicit permission.) All of our students do this, so most teachers are familiar with it, but to be sure there are no misunderstandings, ask first.

2) Moral Life of Schools Observer's Guide. This is a very simple form that simply asks you to record features of the school (teacher action, school or classroom set-up or procedures) that contribute to students' being and becoming "good" as well as "smart." This includes teacher talk, posters, dedicated lessons or anything else that you think encourages moral values, good behavior, responsibility or citizenship. At the end of each day in the school, take a look at the form and make note of anything that struck you during the day.

3) Student assessment charts for six students. You should pick up SIX charts (white) and ONE key (Gold). Select any six students that you expect to see at least four times while you are in the school. (Select them randomly on any basis you wish). Record some identifying information about them (names are not important and privacy should be respected) and then make a special point to pay attention to those students while you are in the classroom. At the end of the day, take a look at each student's chart and record any behaviors (using the code numbers from the key) you observed during that day. Note that the behaviors on the key are all stated positively. Thus, a student who is faring well will have a full chart. Students who are struggling will have relatively empty charts.

The emptiness will alert you to the need to pay additional attention so you can "read" this student and figure out how to respond to him or her appropriately. You do NOT need to consult the co-op or the student for this assignment. Record only the information that you can pick up in your interaction with the student. (You may be surprised how much they offer if you are open.) At the end of your experience, make note of how you would approach and work with this student to ensure success. Note that it could be something as simple as asking him about his favorite sports team or as complex as recommending a behavior plan/contract that will guide prosocial behaviors without being punitive. (This assignment should tap 241 knowledge . . .)

4) Special Needs Student Essay. Directions are available on a handout. This is a brief essay that asks you to assess one student with identifiable "special needs." That is, one student with an Individualized Education Plan (IEP) or an Act 504 plan (usually ADHD). Please ask your co-op to identify one student to whom you can attend.

5) Reflections on field experience (AT LEAST 4) done in response to prompts on Blackboard. You MUST address student demographics and diversity, bureaucracy vs. learning, racism and prejudice, and equal educational opportunity. (All messages should use readings and class concepts as the scaffolding for your observations. E.g., you should use concepts from Tatum to ground your discussion of racism and prejudice.) You may address any other topics, experiences you wish. Feel free to ask for advice or respond to other students' experiences. I will remind you each week about your message being due. I hope you can tell that all these assignments are intended to enrich your experience by getting you to see more clearly who and what is around you. The actual experience is more important than the assignments so, when in doubt, do whatever your teacher asks. Don't forget to let your co-op know that you want to do everything you can, including teaching a lesson or two.

Foundations Bloc Portfolio Guidelines

The culminating project for the foundation bloc will be a portfolio that showcases your work and development throughout the semester. In addition to serving as evidence of your learning this semester, the portfolio will also be useful once you enter your Advanced Professional Studies Courses (Junior Bloc) and Student Teaching experiences.

Your portfolio should be organized around the seven proficiencies for the School of Education's Conceptual Framework (see syllabus). Each proficiency should have a notebook divider that is labeled with a keyword from the proficiency. You will need to include a table of contents that shows the organization of materials in the book. Each proficiency needs to have supporting documents (i.e., the artifacts) and a reflection essay that show your developing competence at meeting the proficiency.

Each reflection essay should document *how* the artifacts included provide evidence of your learning. That is,

1. What are the artifacts associated with each proficiency?
2. Identify the most important artifacts in each section and explain how they are linked thematically to each other and the Proficiency.
3. What do these artifacts say about your growing competence as an educator?

Remember, each proficiency must have a reflection essay. Even those proficiencies that don't have artifacts should have a reflection essay explaining why there are no artifacts under that proficiency.

In the event that an artifact provides evidence of more than one proficiency, you may include it under either proficiency but in the table of contents list it under both proficiencies. Please include a note behind the listing that it is also filed under a second proficiency.

The portfolio is a joint assignment for EDFN 211/241, and will be factored into your final grade for both courses. You are required to also include outside materials (from other courses or from outside of school) that may fit into the portfolio. Here is a list of suggested materials for your portfolio:

o All class assignments and activities
o All class notes and handouts
o Appropriate materials from the field placement
o Artifacts from outside EDFN211/241 that support your learning (can be independent readings, assignments from other courses such as EDUC 220 or content courses, web sites, comics, pictures, etc.)

Please have your name and section number prominently displayed on the spine, and make sure to have your portfolio reviewed by a peer prior to handing it in for final evaluation. You should use the portfolio rubric when conducting this peer review.

NOTE. This portfolio is a working portfolio, not a performance portfolio. As you progress through your education program, you will develop this portfolio into a performance portfolio.

Self-evaluation Guidelines

You must write a 700–800 word essay (approximately 3–4 typed pages) analyzing what you have learned/how you have change this semester and, based on that analysis, you must assign yourself a letter grade (with + or − as appropriate) for EDFN 211. Your essay should have as its theme the concept of pedagogical responsibility (or response-ability as we have discussed it) and integrate your knowledge with your concept of yourself as an intelligent, moral educator.

The word limit IS critical, because it suggests the extent of the kind of evaluation I expect. It would be impossible to provide as much detail as you need to justify a grade in less than three pages, but more than three would just be "filler."

Begin with the assumption that you will get a "C" in this course. That represents average work. It is up to you to make a strong case if you claim a "B", representing very good work, or an "A" representing excellent work. The burden of proof is on you!!!! (Please consult the following "rubric" for guidance.)

All essays are to be typed and PROOFREAD CAREFULLY, as if you were being scrutinized by someone who would consider hiring you. The grade assignment will not be taken seriously if you do not take the time to present your case with care.

I suggest that you begin by considering each course objective in turn, jotting down notes about any reading/activities/assignments we did around those objectives and making note of what you now know that you did not know before. (Your BlocBook should help you in this.) Then SELECT several of the more significant items (probably 4–5) and develop those in a full paragraph each linked to the theme of pedagogical responsibility. Follow those up with a "catch-all" paragraph which lists, but does not develop, other things you did or learned in the course of the semester. Complete your essay with a summary paragraph describing how all this adds up to the grade you have assigned yourself, and how that will translate into effective, intelligent, moral teaching practice in the future.

Self-assessment rubric

As you consider the quality of your work and knowledge gained throughout the semester (using your self-assessment log and your completed BlocBook as data), please use the following rubric to determine your appropriate grade. Please complete this form and enclose with your self-evaluation essay.

Keep in mind that we all begin with the presumption that we have done "Acceptable" work and learned enough to precede toward the teaching profession. (If your work was not at least acceptable, I would have been "in your face" from the beginning.) If you determine that your work and knowledge gained warrants "Very Good" or "Superior," the burden of proof is on YOU to provide justification for that decision.

USEFUL KNOWLEDGE GAINED. Mark each item listed below 5 (YES!), 4 (Yes), 3 (Sorta), 2 (Sometimes), 1 (No). Average score indicates "grade" for knowledge gained.

_____I can use power and perspective as concepts for analyzing and understanding educational practice and institutions.

_____I can identify the "players" in the American educational system, describe their functions, and analyze their interaction in terms of "power over" and "power with."

_____I can tell a detailed, accurate story about how public schools developed into their present form, and use that story to show how history helps us to understand the educational present.

_____I understand the learning theory and philosophy of John Dewey and can describe how this view is like or different from those typically found among today's educators (including my own!) as well as those prescribed by other educational philosophies.

_____I can discuss socio-economic and socio-cultural conflicts in modern American schools and offer an evaluation (with examples and statistical evidence) of whether equal education opportunity should and does exist.

_____My self-assessment essay demonstrates my understanding that the various readings and course activities are interrelated. I make specific reference to links between and among different authors' / educators' views as well as with my own experiences as both student and (to be) teacher.

WORK QUALITY. Check all that describe the quality of your work during the semester.

SUPERIOR/PROFESSIONAL GRADE = A

_____All assigned work complete and "in time."

_____All required readings completed.

_____Quality of thinking/inquiry demonstrated in assignments is outstanding (always on target, sometimes enlightening!).

_____Both written work and class participation demonstrates insightful analysis with logical, well supported explanations and conclusions.

_____Portfolio is professionally and carefully completed, with neat dividers/markers and thorough, insightful introductory paragraphs.

_____Placement of items within objective sections demonstrates accurate understanding of course content.

VERY GOOD GRADE = B

_____ALL assigned work complete and usually "in time."

_____85% of required readings complete.

_____Quality of thinking demonstrated in assignments is above average.

_____Both written work and class participation demonstrates substantial analysis, with logically developed explanations and conclusions.

_____Portfolio is neatly and carefully completed, with neat dividers/markers and introductory paragraphs.

_____Placement of items within objective sections demonstrates generally strong understanding of course content.

ACCEPTABLE GRADE = C

_____All assigned work complete but often not "in time."

_____75% of required readings complete.

_____Quality of thinking demonstrated in assignments is average.

_____Both written work and class participation demonstrates adequate analysis, with underdeveloped explanations and conclusions.

_____Information is basically accurate in broad scope, but includes significant errors in detail and/or understanding. Quotes/cites incompletely or inaccurately noted and/or misunderstood.

_____Portfolio is complete, organized, but lacking careful presentation, dividers/markers and/or introductory paragraphs.

_____Placement of items within objective sections demonstrates acceptable understanding of course content.

Be prepared! If you claim an "A" and I am unconvinced, I will first ask you to document the completion of all assignments "in time." I will then ask you to provide me with additional data in person or in writing that supports and or all of the stated objectives. For example, I might ask you to draw on the spot a chart outlining the functioning of American public schools. Or I might ask you to make a generalization about development of education in the 20th century and cite at least four events/documents that support your generalization. Or I might ask you to describe what you saw during field experience that was an example of Deweyan philosophy at work. Or I might ask you to reconstruct both the schooling and the education of one student from your field experience class. Or I might ask you to explain how you understand the concept of "equal education opportunity" and what data you can cite to make a case that it does or does not exist in our time.

If you claim a "B" and I am unconvinced, I will first ask you to document the completion of all assignments. Then I will go on to pursue the same kind of questions above.

If you claim a "C" or a "B" and I wonder if it should be higher, I will ask you to walk me through your self-assessment log and BlocBook, highlighting the perceived weaknesses in your work. I will ask you to provide additional information about the kinds of questions noted above and then ask you why your answers are weak.

In all cases, be prepared!

Appendix 2

SEMINAR ASSIGNMENTS

Assignment for Session One, September 2002

In your packet is a copy of the case that will be the basis for the first discussion session on the morning of Thursday, September 19th. It is entitled: "Case 2: Moments of Truth: Teaching Pygmalion." On pp. 21–22 of the paper by Sullivan, you will find a more extended discussion of the use of this case.

For this session, please jot down some short reflections on the following questions.

1. How would you describe this case? That is, what is this a case of?
2. What seem to be the teacher's options? How is the teacher thinking about what she should do?
3. How would you think about this situation?
4. What should the teacher do—what counsel would you offer to a person confronting this situation?
5. In reflecting on your answer to #4, what intellectual resources do you find yourself using to give an answer?

Assignment for Session Two, January 2003

We hope the new year is starting out well for all of you. In order to get the next meeting of our seminar off on a good footing, we are presenting the following "assignment" to stimulate our collective thinking. (Be assured that we will be doing it along with you.)

To stimulate our collective thinking about pedagogies of practical reasoning, we would like to suggest that we all engage in some mutual learning and self-reflection about our own or a colleague's teaching practice. We have taken the liberty to organize our group—including Lee, Bill, Al, and Gary—into pairs. (The list of partners, together with telephone numbers and email addresses, is given below.)

The exercise is as follows. First, swap syllabi. That is, each partner should provide the other with a copy of a course syllabus of his or her own that is at least in part concerned with developing practical reasoning and judgment skills. (If you prefer, provide your partner with the syllabus of a colleague that you think fits the bill.) Second, ask the author to describe and explain the course by "walking through" the syllabus. That is, each partner is to interrogate the other's syllabus by asking the partner to discuss the syllabus submitted around the following four questions. We ask that each partner keep notes of the responses, if by phone, or copies of the answers, if you do this by email.

1. To what situation requiring practical judgment might this course contribute?
2. What are the key topics or organizing principles implicit in your syllabus?
3. What is the narrative or argument of this course as represented by the syllabus? What are the key surprises or critical transitions in this narrative? How are these connected to practical judgments?
4. If you had substantially less time for the course (⅔ or ½ the time), how would you change the syllabus? What might this reveal about the key organizing principles or practical issues at stake in the course?

When we convene on the morning of Thursday, February 6th, our first order of business will be for the partners to connect in person to recapitulate their previous conversation about their respective syllabi and courses. We will then ask each pair of partners to consider any new insights or possibilities their conversation may have generated for reshaping these courses, allowing time for consideration and reflection by the seminar as a whole.

Syllabus Narrative Writing Assignment, Summer 2003

At our previous gathering of the Carnegie Cross-Professional Seminar in February 2003, we occasionally described syllabi and courses in narrative terms. This writing assignment, in anticipation of our next meeting in

December 2003, pursues this narrative idea further, exploring its full implications for syllabus construction, practical reasoning, and the techniques and underlying purposes of disciplines and professions. To begin, we will here briefly explore several examples with which we are already familiar from our previous meeting: the syllabi presented by Daisy Floyd, Barbara Stengel, Robert McGinn, and Sam Wineburg. The present interpretations of these syllabi are not intended to be exhaustive; rather, they endeavor to provide brief and suggestive examples of how syllabi might be read for their narrative drama and how the notion of "topics" comes into play.

Courses are like stories. Stories proceed according to widely shared cultural structures for their telling and sharing that shape our anticipations of what to expect. Narratives depend upon the anticipation of a particular part-whole structure: beginning, middle, and end. Stories portray journeys; we expect them to "go somewhere" and "have a point." The obstacles or conflicts that manifest themselves over time during this journey—which provide the drama of the middle part of the narrative and enable an intelligible beginning and ending—provide a challenge to the protagonist's activity, requiring effort and a transformative struggle in order to hopefully achieve some new resolution or state of balance. The story's purpose or moral serves as the destination of the journey and secures the meaning (or "point") of the story's telling, whether or not a full resolution of the problematic situation is actually possible.

We can also consider a syllabus as a narrative document that systematically provides for such problematic episodes. These narratives are constructed with special sensitivity to their audience (i.e., the specific student population), the anticipated future task environments in which those students will live their own professional lives, and the key techniques and values that organize the profession and ought to motivate the students' future professional identities. The problematic situations that are provided by the syllabus are precisely the moments that require and educate practical reasoning. These acts of learning induct students into the methods, values, and dispositions of a discipline or profession through practical problem solving.

Professional reasoning is thus the practical marriage of technical competence and normative purposes. A genuine understanding of the normative purposes of a profession is practically meaningless apart from technique, for without technical accomplishment one is a public menace to those same professional values; likewise, technical competence without an understanding of the normative purposes of one's profession is merely purposeless activity that is easily turned toward other, less noble ends.

It is with the techniques and normative commitments of the discipline in mind that the events of learning offered by a syllabus are sequentially organized so that they "go somewhere." The syllabus' underlying understanding of the key issues that organize a discipline, when practiced at its best, provides the "moral" or "point" of the narrative. These normative ideals are thus central to the course's pedagogical attempts to form responsible professional identities.

For example, consider the narrative drama and normative importance of several cases from our February 2003 meeting:

1. Daisy Floyd's syllabus, "Advanced Legal Ethics: Finding Joy and Satisfaction in Legal Life," explores an underappreciated yet pervasive problem of professional education. This is the existential problem of integrating one's nobler professional ideals with the professional culture and competing demands that come to organize one's life in law school and beyond. Beginning from a sense of crisis within the legal profession, whereby legal education itself tends to denude the noble purposes with which students enter law school, students navigate a series of exercises—questioning practicing professionals, writing assignments, etc.—that help the students to consider and cope with the continuities and discontinuities between their own life purposes and the practice of law. Students reflect upon the qualities that foster good lawyering and their relation to the qualities that they cherish about themselves. The goal of the course is thus to enable students to live responsible, purposive professional lives that also enable them to be able to live with *themselves*. The course presupposes that this profound difficulty of meaning and purpose, which produces the crisis of a pathologically divided professional identity and self, is already becoming manifest within the students' own experience over the course of their legal education—that is, that law school pedagogy tends to precipitate this crisis of identity and thus ought to also take responsibility for the re-integration, or continuing resolution, of their students' life purposes. The transformative acts of learning provided by the syllabus enable students to better consider and cope with the moral imperatives that properly ought to distinguish the legal profession, so that they might construct worthy narratives of their own professional identities.

2. Barbara Stengel's syllabus on the foundations of modern education presupposes a different starting point. Stengel's students, who are aspiring but inexperienced prospective teachers, enter the class with many naïve cultural conceptions of their eventual roles as teachers. These need dramatic critique and reconstruction, lest the students become mere instruments of cultural reproduction in their chosen careers. Students develop

portfolios throughout the course that lead them through inquiries into educational standards and decision-making structures, inquiries into the students' own home school districts, and the compilation of a repertoire of critical concepts. These portfolios grow into rich and complex portrayals of the key considerations and difficulties of educational practice, the possibilities for transformative action within professional situations, and the students' own positioning within this network of relationships. Students are brought to recognize that their highest educational ideals are in constant jeopardy both from within and without, and that the demonizing of contrary agents and viewpoints does no justice to the complexity of educational decision-making. Professional reasoning and identity are imagined as a process of constantly positioning oneself to resolve the competing tensions of everyday practice, so that the commitments and concerns that ought to organize the teaching profession can be adequately realized within particular situations through risk taking.

3. To paraphrase his own comments at our meeting in February 2003, Robert McGinn's course constitutes an effort to critically eradicate the "weeds" that prevent moral action within an engineering profession that too often divorces moral deliberation and social negotiation from its efforts to educate technical competence. As McGinn notes in his account of the flooding of Venice, for example, no technical knowledge is alone capable of solving the problem of which course of action to pursue. A social and ethical risk is required. Engineering pedagogy therefore ought to be better conceived as a matter of educating socio-technical competence. McGinn's engineering ethics syllabus proceeds from this insight, first providing students with a repertoire of analytical concepts and methods for engaging the social and ethical complexity of practical situations. Students are then challenged to apply these tools to cases of engineering decision making and to reckon fully with the presuppositions and implications of their own positions, while also granting serious attention to the strengths and reasonableness of the positions of others. Students are brought to recognize the proper and central place—and the complexity—of ethical and social deliberation within engineering practice, particularly where equity in public policy and the consideration of the consequences of engineering practice are concerned. McGinn's syllabus endeavors to form professionals capable of sensitively and charitably analyzing the motivating presuppositions and ethical principles that guide actual decision-making. The course strives to help future engineers develop tools for diagnosing the dynamics of particular professional situations—and does so according to an enriched conception of the engineering profession's normative social and moral structure and commitments.

4. William Breitenbach's "Doing History" course at the University of Puget Sound, which was provided by Sam Wineburg, is intended as an undergraduate introduction to the practice of history, inviting students to diligently take on the role of apprentice historians. Students first consider the meaning of professional history and the nature of historical knowledge, exploring the relevance of multiple perspectives and the challenge of making the past accessible to study without sacrificing its unfamiliarity and strangeness. Students then reckon directly with primary sources, learning how to form significant research questions and construct historical evidence, how to draw defensible inferences from this evidence, and how to organize those inferences into coherent historical interpretations. This education of historical judgment, whose standards and commitment to the difference of the past from the present exceed the norms of everyday discussion, culminates in the writing of a major research paper. Each student develops a topic that can be defended as meaningful within the professional historical community, researches the topic, engages in drafting that is mindful of professional standards of citation and plagiarism, and critically revises the document through discussion. The research project thus serves as an embodiment of the students' competent performance of historical technique and mindfulness of professional standards of practice, as well as an opportunity for further dialogue and participation that will serve the students well in more advanced classes. The normative expectations of the profession are thus inextricable from the practical techniques of historical judgment.

○

Each of these four syllabi reveals important dimensions of the richness of practical reasoning and professional identity as they are lived out within professional lives. Each syllabus takes seriously the pedagogical challenge of interrogating this richness in the construction of a course. Practical reasoning figures prominently as the navigation of social relationships and public commitments in order to chart professionally responsible courses of action capable of resolving particular, unique problematic situations. Professional identity emerges as the ever-unfinished process of integrating one's professional ideals and commitments with the competing demands of the specific instances of practical reasoning that comprise the narrative of one's professional life. The process of "finding joy" (to borrow Daisy Floyd's phrase) within one's discipline is a lifelong challenge to responsible and meaningful practice. Moreover, it is precisely in terms of the normative concerns and values of one's discipline that the unique situations that constitute professional practice must be responsibly negotiated. This normative content is always purposively directed toward judgment and the charting of unique courses of action.

The syllabus provided by Sam Wineburg further reminds us, however, that all such purposive acts are dependent upon technical accomplishment for professional judgment to responsibly proceed. All professional practical reasoning presupposes both technical competence and an underlying conception of the normative purposes that ought to properly structure a profession at its best—and thus ought to structure the pedagogical formation of new professionals as well. Professional practice, pedagogical or otherwise, is ever poised between the technical challenges of each unique situation (such as the problematic situations provided by the narrative of a syllabus) and the normative, public commitments of one's community (e.g., the "moral" or "purpose" of the syllabus' narrative).

Taking these all-too-brief sketches as spurs to writing and reflection, *consider the following questions regarding your syllabus:*

o What is the moral, or purpose, of your course when viewed as a narrative? What are the ideal professional values and key concerns that you wish to instill in your students? How do the events of practical reasoning and learning that your syllabus provides relate these ideals to specific situations and techniques—i.e., how are the parts related to the whole? Is there a particular conception of agency that is implied by this dual negotiation of both normative professional commitments and the technical demands of unique circumstances?

o How does practical reasoning appear in your syllabus? How is the syllabus a case or embodiment of practical reasoning in some field, offering acts of learning that develop the capacity to practically reason within that field? What are the problematic situations that your syllabus provides for your students, and what technical skills are developed thereby? How does the narrative of the syllabus sequentially organize these learning events, and how does this organization relate technical competence to the normative purposes of the profession (i.e., the "moral" of the syllabus)?

o What sort of audience—i.e., the students that will serve as the narrative's primary protagonists—does your syllabus imagine? What sort of future task environment does the syllabus anticipate for these students? What sorts of roles will they perform and what will they be expected to do?

o What is the relation of your course to larger curricular structures? If we imagine an entire curriculum as another form of narrative,

does your course cut against the grain of a dominant narrative? If
so, how do the organizing morals or purposes of your course help
us to better understand what professional and pedagogical concerns
ought to properly organize the curriculum?

○ Could the narrative of your course also provide a learning situation for students in other fields, including a relation between the
professional and liberal arts? How would such a relation take
place and be made meaningful?

With these reflections in hand, also consider further the "purpose" or
"moral" of your syllabus' narrative journey. Might we also describe these
motivating concerns of the syllabus, which derive from your understanding of the structure and value of your discipline, more systematically in
terms of "topics?" Indeed, the concepts of "topics" and "narrative" are
closely related through the concept of a "journey" or "course of action."
As Al Jonsen observes—see Jonsen's short essay included in this packet—
the concept of "topics" is itself a geographical metaphor based upon the
experiencing of the placement and location of objects in space, according
to which a course of action is charted and a journey is navigated. Topics
(or *topoi*) denote the "topography" of a discipline or area of inquiry, or
the "places" according to which arguments and courses of action are
socially negotiated. Topics are thus always purposive in character, constituting the professional values and concerns according to which meaningful professional narratives—such as course syllabi—are constructed and
acted upon. They constitute that which the practitioner must ideally take
care for and value in order to reason and act responsibly—i.e., that *about*
which one must argue and consider in forming a plan of action.

Topics are thus not intended to mirror subjective processes within individual situations, but rather are reconstructions of that which is most
valuable and central about an activity. While every situation is indeed
unique and requires a unique act of practical reasoning and positioning,
these circumstances must still be placed within a larger appreciation of
what the activity (e.g., a profession) is *about*—i.e., the very same normative commitments and features of disciplines, practiced at their best, that
are detailed in our earlier discussion of the worthy "morals" or "purposes" that inform syllabi when considered as narratives. Topics are the
substantive places of interest within such professional narratives, and
constitute the ideal concerns that ought to properly motivate the imaginative and responsible development and navigation of reasoned *courses* of
action within particular, situated circumstances.

As a second analytic consideration, therefore, is it possible to *re-code*
or *catalogue* the key organizing considerations and imperatives that

inform your syllabus in terms of "topics," in order to make this normative content more explicit and available for public discussion and responsible pedagogy? What does your syllabus take your discipline to be *about*,
and how does this normative understanding shape the instances of practical reasoning that the syllabus provides for, which serve in the formation
of your students' professional identities? What values and concerns should
your students internalize over time throughout the course, and how do
they learn to act out the imperatives of this cultural role within specific,
unique situations that demand practical reasoning?

Assignment for Session Three, November 2003

Our "A Life of the Mind for Practice" seminar will be holding its third
meeting in about a month, on Monday and Tuesday, December 1 and 2.
We are pursuing an important set of questions. The most salient among
these questions are two: Why teach practical reasoning? And how can
practical reasoning be best taught?

Neither the traditions nor the institutional logic of the academy give a
great deal of support to these concerns. The academy valorizes and
rewards knowledge rather than competence in practice, save the practices
of research and scholarship. Professional academics are typically scrutinized for their ability to discover and transmit ideas rather than for their
capacity for design, problem-solving, or intervening in an effective yet
humane way in the lives of clients, let alone for making decisions with the
public welfare in mind. Higher education gives much less attention to
competence in action than to understanding and even less to the effective
integration of the two in practical judgment.

Yet that integration of understanding and competence is the essence of
professional judgment. It forms the basis for professional identity. It is the
raison d'etre for the distinctive forms in which professional work
is organized, as in the institutions of mentorship and peer review.
The lengthening shadow of academic norms has tended to eclipse the
unique importance of the teaching and learning of practical reasoning in
the varied domains of professional preparation.

Professionals must be able to assess situations effectively, make judgments reliably, and act responsibly. They must develop the habits of making good decisions. These are the traits of practical reasoning. It is indeed
to ensure the reliability of these capacities that professional communities
have been instituted. For this reason too, professional schools have long
used "cases," "problems," "simulations," "design," and "clinical" teaching
formats in crucial parts of their curricula. But these aims—and these pedagogies—are not peculiar to professional practice. The ability to assess

situations, bring to bear theoretical understanding as well as savvy acquired through experience, is also essential to living well in a complex modern society.

In this key sense, practical judgment ought to also be, as it often implicitly is, the aim of liberal learning. The liberal arts have been assumed, by many, to be of value to professional students because liberal education has been believed to expand the range of intellect and imagination. However, there has been comparatively little analysis of how this process might contribute to and inform practical deliberation—either in professional work or in the demands of making life-choices or acting as a citizen.

Still, it would be a mistake to imagine the liberal arts as purely detached forms of knowledge, with no bearing upon the way in which professionals or citizens must think and act. Historically, it has only been when academic intellectuals have effectively controlled their own institutions—in the European Middle Ages and again with the rise of the modern research university—that liberal learning has been understood as exclusively or primarily detached from questions of social and personal import, such as how particular types of specialized knowledge and skill shape a common mind among their practitioners, and how these diverse sets of perception and skills can and ought to be pursued and related one to another, both in the life of the society and the individual.

The seminar has been intended to explore the possibility of an intervention into the academic world of both professional and liberal education to redress the relative neglect of practical reasoning in both areas. However, it is also our hope that a focus on practical reasoning can serve like a newly discovered channel to foster renewed commerce between educators in professional schools and those who teach the liberal arts.

Our attention to the pedagogy actually employed by the members of the seminar is, we believe, a useful first step toward identifying and exploring how the teaching of practical reasoning can become an intentional act. The spread of the academic disciplines and professional domains represented in the seminar is a source of hope, even a kind of demonstration, that this is a project that can appeal broadly in today's academy. We are excited and pleased that we will have another opportunity to work together toward our goals in December.

Assignment

Prior to our previous meeting in February 2003, we teamed up in pairs to interrogate one another's syllabi with an eye toward the ways in which these courses educate practical reasoning, within the moral and technical framework of some particular discipline or profession—or, in some cases, toward critical citizenship writ large. In preparation for our upcoming meeting in December, we would like to revisit this activity in a new form, in order to re-orient ourselves to the concerns of the seminar and to one another.

We have organized our group—including Bill, Al, and Gary, with Lee as our floating kibitzer—into five trios. The list of partners, together with telephone numbers and email addresses, is included in this packet. We hope each member of each trio who has been designated to initiate email discussion can do so *by November 10th (or thereabouts)*. This designated member will also be relied upon to present a *short* summary of his or her trio's discussion at the December meeting.

The new "assignment" is as follows. First, we ask you to once again swap draft copies of your work—in this case the essays that you wrote in preparation for our meeting. (If your essay is not yet complete, please share key excerpts from the essay with your trio that will enable a searching discussion.) In most cases, these essays will be based upon the same syllabi that were presented at our last meeting in February.

Second, have each member of your trio "walk through" his or her essay. As before, each participant should interrogate the others' essays by asking them to discuss their work with respect to the following four questions. We again ask that each member keep notes of the others' responses, if by phone, or copies of the answers, if you do this by email.

1. Prior to our previous meeting in February, we asked you to consider your syllabus as a way of structuring your students' action within your class, in order to begin to shape each student's narrative of his or her own professional identity. What practical situations and forms of decision-making does your course imagine for your students in their future work?

2. What are the key topics or organizing principles that have motivated your consideration of your syllabus and your students' practical reasoning, as articulated or implicit in your essay? What ought your students come to care about, and what qualities of character should be cultivated in the formation of their professional identities?

3. Please now turn your inquiry upon yourself as a teacher whose task is to structure the activities and emerging identities—professional or otherwise—of your students. How has the reflective work referred to in Questions One and Two affected your conception of your own practice as a teacher? Are there any changes that you

would now make in your syllabus and practice as a result of this critical reflection, in order to make your course more responsive to your emerging conception of your identity as a teacher of practical reasoning? How would you articulate this challenge and its importance to colleagues in your discipline who are interested in engendering similar changes in their own pedagogy?

4. How has your engagement in the Cross-Professions Seminar informed your thinking about the relation of professional education to the liberal arts?

   a) If your teaching takes place in a professional context, how has your engagement with the participants representing the liberal arts in particular influenced the way you think about your teaching and your students' professional lives? What might the liberal arts contribute toward students' abilities to solve problems, reason effectively, decide and judge issues in your professional domain?

   b) If your teaching takes place within a liberal arts context, how has your engagement with the professions influenced your conception of your teaching? Specifically, in what ways might your teaching influence your students' understanding and competence as future professionals in areas such as problem solving, reasoning, judgment and decision?

When we convene on the morning of Monday, December 1, our first order of business will be for the trios to connect in person to revisit their conversations about their respective essays. Each trio will consider any new insights or possibilities that their initial conversation may have generated in the meantime. We will again allow time for consideration and reflection by the seminar as a whole, with the work of each trio presented in summary form by its designated member.

Follow-Up Reflection Questions, January 2004

Question 1: Do you find that your thinking about or approach to your teaching has changed as a result of your participation in the seminar? If so, could you describe these changes? If not, please help us understand your thinking.

Question 2: How might you describe the relationship between what you have learned about your own teaching practice and the learning that you wish to develop in your students about practical reasoning? Have you found any new insights in relation to what you hope to be able to accomplish for your students?

Question 3: Is there something about the idea of teaching practical reasoning that has made or continues to make you uneasy as a teacher? Has the seminar addressed that? Do you think it could be addressed?

Question 4: Did you find the cross-professional and professional-liberal arts conversations in and around the seminar enlightening or useful for your own teaching practice? Would you say that your experience in the seminar has affected in any significant way your view of liberal and professional education in relation to each other?

Question 5: Finally, please help us understand the implications of this work for the scholarship of teaching. Do you think you were acting as a "scholar" with respect to your teaching and that of other participants? Was this a productive learning experience for you? Could a version of what we did have impact and value on your own campus?

REFERENCES

Anonymous, Ladson-Billings, G., and Desser, K. (1993). Moments of Truth: Teaching *Pygmalion* and Commentaries. In J. H. Shulman and A. Mesa-Bains (Eds.), *Diversity in the Classroom: A Casebook for Teachers and Teacher Educators*. Hillsdale, NJ: Research for Better Schools and Lawrence Erlbaum Associates.

Ball, D. L. (1993). With an Eye on the Mathematical Horizon: Dilemmas of Teaching Elementary School Mathematics. *The Elementary School Journal, 93*(4), 373–397.

Booth, W. C. (1988). *The Company We Keep: An Ethics of Fiction*. Berkeley, CA: The University of California Press.

Bouma, H. (2001). Small-Group Discussions of Contemporary Issues in Bioethics to Promote Intellectual and Moral Development Through a Non-Majors Course in Human Biology. Final Report to the Carnegie Academy for the Scholarship of Teaching and Learning. Menlo Park, CA: The Carnegie Foundation for the Advancement of Teaching.

Bouma, H. (2005a). Christian Perspectives on Moral Issues in Human Biology. Course Reader for "Human Biology." Grand Rapids, MI: Calvin College.

Bouma, H. (2005b). Course Syllabus for "Human Biology." Grand Rapids, MI: Calvin College.

Bruner, J. (1986). *Actual Minds, Possible Worlds*. Cambridge, MA: Harvard University Press.

Bruner, J. (1990). *Acts of Meaning*. Cambridge, MA: Harvard University Press.

Cambridge, B. L. (Ed.). (2004). *Campus Progress: Supporting the Scholarship of Teaching and Learning*. Washington, DC: American Association for Higher Education.

Colby, A., Ehrlich, T., Beaumont, E., and Stephens, J. (2003). *Educating Citizens: Preparing America's Undergraduates for Lives of Moral and Civic Responsibility*. San Francisco, CA: Jossey-Bass.

Collins, R. (1998). *The Sociology of Philosophies: A Global Theory of Intellectual Change*. The Belknap Press of Harvard University Press.

Cook, C. E. (2004). Introduction to Section One: Developing Infrastructure. In B. L. Cambridge (Ed.), *Campus Progress: Supporting the Scholarship of*

Teaching and Learning. Washington, DC: American Association for Higher Education.

Dewey, J. (1902). *The Child and the Curriculum.* In J. A. Boydston (Ed.), *The Middle Works, 1899–1924, Vol. 2: 1902–1903.* Carbondale, IL: Southern Illinois University Press.

Dewey, J. (1916a). *Democracy and Education.* New York: Macmillan.

Dewey, J. (1916b). *Democracy and Education.* In J. A. Boydston (Ed.), *The Middle Works, 1899–1924, Vol. 9: 1916.* Carbondale, IL: Southern Illinois University Press.

Dewey, J. (1920). *Reconstruction in Philosophy.* In J. A. Boydston (Ed.), *The Middle Works, 1899–1924, Vol. 12: 1920.* Carbondale, IL: Southern Illinois University Press.

Dewey, J. (1929). *The Quest for Certainty.* In J. A. Boydston (Ed.), *The Later Works, 1925–1953, Vol. 4: 1929.* Carbondale, IL: Southern Illinois University Press.

Dewey, J. (1938). *Logic: The Theory of Inquiry.* In J. A. Boydston (Ed.), *The Later Works, 1925–1953, Vol. 12: 1938.* Carbondale, IL: Southern Illinois University Press.

Dinovitzer, R., and others. (2004). *After the JD: First Results of a National Study of Legal Careers.* Overland Park, KS, and Chicago, IL: The NALP Foundation for Law Career Research and Education and the American Bar Foundation.

Dorff, E. N. (1998). *Matters of Life and Death: A Jewish Approach to Modern Medical Ethics.* Philadelphia, PA: The Jewish Publication Society.

Dorff, E. N. (2002). *To Do the Right and the Good: A Jewish Approach to Modern Social Ethics.* Philadelphia, PA: The Jewish Publication Society.

Dorff, E. N. (2003a). Course Syllabus for "Issues in Jewish Ethics." Bel-Air, CA: American Jewish University.

Dorff, E. N. (2003b). *Love Your Neighbor and Yourself: A Jewish Approach to Modern Personal Ethics.* Philadelphia, PA: The Jewish Publication Society.

Dorff, E. N. (2003c). Syllabus Narrative for the Carnegie "A Life of the Mind for Practice" Seminar. Stanford, CA: The Carnegie Foundation for the Advancement of Teaching.

Dorff, E. N. (2006). E-mail communication to M. S. Rosin. September 5, 2006.

Downey, G. L. (2003). Location, Knowledge, and Desire: Cultural Competence and the Engineering Method. Syllabus Narrative for the Carnegie "A Life of the Mind for Practice" Seminar. Stanford, CA: The Carnegie Foundation for the Advancement of Teaching.

Downey, G. L., and Lucena, J. C. (2005). Course Syllabus for "Engineering Cultures." Blacksburg, VA: Virginia Polytechnic Institute and State University and Golden, CO: Colorado School of Mines. [http://www.engcultures.sts.vt.edu/].

Downey, G. L., and others. (2006). The Globally Competent Engineer: Working Effectively with People Who Define Problems Differently. *Journal of Engineering Education, 95*(2), 107–122.

Edgerton, R. (1997). *Higher Education.* Unpublished white paper. Philadelphia, PA: The Pew Charitable Trusts Education Program.

Elstein, A. S. (2003). Medical Ethics: Arts of the Practical for Medical Practice. Syllabus Narrative for the Carnegie "A Life of the Mind for Practice" Seminar. Stanford, CA: The Carnegie Foundation for the Advancement of Teaching.

Elstein, A. S., Shulman, L. S., and Sprafka, S. A. (1978). *Medical Problem Solving: An Analysis of Clinical Reasoning.* Cambridge, MA: Harvard University Press.

Epictetus. (1988). *The Discourses and Enchiridion.* Cambridge, MA: Loeb Classical Library, Harvard University Press.

Floyd, D. H. (2002). The Development of Professional Identity in Law Students. Final Report to the Carnegie Academy for the Scholarship of Teaching and Learning. Menlo Park, CA: The Carnegie Foundation for the Advancement of Teaching.

Floyd, D. H. (2003). Syllabus Narrative for the "A Life of the Mind for Practice" Seminar. Stanford, CA: The Carnegie Foundation for the Advancement of Teaching.

Floyd, D. H. (2003). Course Syllabus for "Advanced Legal Ethics: Finding Joy and Satisfaction in Legal Life." Lubbock, TX: Texas Tech University School of Law.

Frank, D. J., and Gabler, J. (2006). *Reconstructing the University: Worldwide Shifts in Academia in the 20th Century.* Stanford, CA: Stanford University Press.

Garvin, D. A. (2003). Making the Case: Professional Education for the World of Practice. *Harvard Magazine 106*(1), 56–65, 107.

Geertz, C. (2000). *Available Light: Anthropological Reflections on Philosophical Topics.* Princeton, NJ: Princeton University Press.

Golde, C., and Walker, G. (Eds.). (2006). *Envisioning the Future of Doctoral Education: Preparing Stewards of the Discipline—Carnegie Essays on the Doctorate.* San Francisco, CA: Jossey-Bass.

Hammond, A. S. (2006). Certainty, Ambiguity, and Dissent in the Rule of Law. Santa Clara, CA: Santa Clara University School of Law.

Huber, M. T., and Hutchings, P. (2004). *Integrative Learning: Mapping the Terrain.* Washington, DC: Association of American Colleges and Universities and The Carnegie Foundation for the Advancement of Teaching.

Huber, M. T., and Hutchings, P. (2005). *The Advancement of Learning: Building the Teaching Commons.* San Francisco, CA: Jossey-Bass.

Iiyoshi, T., Richardson, C., and McGrath, O. (2006). Harnessing Open Technologies to Promote Open Educational Knowledge Sharing. *Innovate: Journal of Online Education* (Vol. 3).

Jonsen, A. R., and Toulmin, S. (1988). *The Abuse of Casuistry: A History of Moral Reasoning.* Berkeley, CA: University of California Press.

Katz, S. N. (2006). What Has Happened to the Professoriate? *The Chronicle of Higher Education, 53*(7), B8.

Kelsey, D. H. (1993). *Between Athens and Berlin: The Theological Education Debate.* Grand Rapids, MI: Eerdmans.

Kimball, B. A. (1986). *Orators and Philosophers: A History of the Idea of Liberal Education.* New York, NY: Teachers College Press.

King, P. M., and Kitchener, K. S. (1994). *Developing Reflective Judgment: Understanding and Promoting Intellectual Growth and Critical Thinking in Adolescents and Adults.* San Francisco, CA: Jossey-Bass.

Kuhn, D. (2003). Understanding and Valuing Knowing as Developmental Goals. *Liberal Education, 89*(3), 16–21.

Kurfiss, J. G. (1988). *Critical Thinking: Theory, Research, Practice, and Possibilities.* Washington, DC: Association for the Study of Higher Education.

Lasch, C. (1995). *The Revolt of the Elites.* New York, NY: W. W. Norton.

Lauer, J. M. (2003). Writing as Practical Reasoning: A Rhetorical Perspective. Syllabus Narrative for the Carnegie "A Life of the Mind for Practice" Seminar. Stanford, CA: The Carnegie Foundation for the Advancement of Teaching.

Lauer, J. M. (2004). *Invention in Rhetoric and Composition.* West Lafayette, IN: Parlor Press and The WAC Clearinghouse.

Lauer, J. M., and others. (2000). *Four Worlds of Writing: Inquiry and Action in Context.* New York, NY: Longman and Pearson Custom Publishing.

Marsden, G. (1994). *The Soul of the American University: From Protestant Establishment to Established Nonbelief.* New York, NY: Oxford University Press.

McDermott, R. P. (1974). Achieving School Failure: An Anthropological Approach to Illiteracy and Social Stratification. In G. Spindler (Ed.), *Education and Cultural Process: Toward an Anthropology of Education.* New York, NY: Holt, Rinehart and Winston.

McGinn, R. E. (2001). Course Syllabus for "Ethical Issues in Engineering." Stanford, CA: Stanford University.

McGinn, R. E. (2002). Moral Responsibilities of Professional Engineers: Empirical and Theoretical Approaches. Paper presented at the Engineering Ethics Forum, University of Nagoya, Nagoya, Japan, December 8, 2002.

McGinn, R. E. (2003). Course Syllabus for "Ethics and Public Policy." Stanford, CA: Stanford University.

McGrath, D., and Spear, M. B. (1991). *The Academic Crisis of the Community College.* Albany, NY: State University of New York Press.

McKinsey, E. (2003). Syllabus Narrative for the Carnegie "A Life of the Mind for Practice" Seminar. Stanford, CA: The Carnegie Foundation for the Advancement of Teaching.

McPeck, J. E. (1981). *Critical Thinking and Education.* New York, NY: St. Martin's Press.

Mertz, E. (2007). *The Language of Law School: Learning to "Think Like a Lawyer."* New York, NY: Oxford University Press.

Meyer, J. W. (2006). Foreword. In D. J. Frank and J. Gabler (Eds.), *Reconstructing the University: Worldwide Shifts in Academia in the 20th Century.* Stanford, CA: Stanford University Press.

Millgram, E. (Ed.). (2001). *Varieties of Practical Reasoning.* Cambridge, MA: The MIT Press.

Montgomery, K. (2005). *How Doctors Think: Clinical Judgment and the Practice of Medicine.* New York, NY: Oxford University Press.

Murphy, T., and Oberman, M. (1993). Sample Cases from "Ethics and Law." Chicago, IL: University of Illinois College of Medicine.

Niebuhr, H. R. (1963). *The Responsible Self: An Essay in Christian Moral Philosophy.* New York, NY: Harper & Row.

Nussbaum, M. C. (1995). *Poetic Justice: The Literary Imagination and Public Life.* Boston, MA: Beacon Press.

Nussbaum, M. C. (1997). *Cultivating Humanity: A Classical Defense of Reform in Liberal Education.* Cambridge, MA: Harvard University Press.

Pascarella, E. T., and Terenzini, P. T. (2005). *How College Affects Students: A Third Decade of Research, Volume 2.* San Francisco, CA: Jossey-Bass.

Plato. (1974). *Republic.* Trans. G.M.A. Grube. Indianapolis, IN: Hackett Publishing.

Readings, B. (1996). *The University in Ruins.* Cambridge, MA: Harvard University Press.

Reich, R. B. (1991). *The Work of Nations: Preparing Ourselves for Twenty-First Century Capitalism.* New York, NY: Alfred P. Knopf Publishers.

Reuben, J. A. (1996). *The Making of the Modern University: Intellectual Transformation and the Marginalization of Morality.* Chicago, IL: University of Chicago Press.

Rhode, D. L. (2000). *In the Interests of Justice: Reforming the Legal Profession.* New York, NY: Oxford University Press.

Roberts, J. H., and Turner, J. (2000). *The Sacred and the Secular University.* Princeton, NJ: Princeton University Press.

Royce, J. (1995). *The Philosophy of Loyalty.* Nashville, TN: Vanderbilt University Press. (Original publication in 1908)

Schofer, E., and Meyer, J. W. (2005). The Worldwide Expansion of Higher Education in the Twentieth Century. *American Sociological Review, 70*(6), 898–920.

Shore, B. (1996). *Culture in Mind: Cognition, Culture, and the Problem of Meaning.* New York, NY: Oxford University Press.

Shulman, L. S. (2004a). Making Differences: A Table of Learning. In *Teaching as Community Property: Essays on Higher Education.* San Francisco, CA: Jossey-Bass. (Original publication in 2002)

Shulman, L. S. (2004b). Professing the Liberal Arts. In *Teaching as Community Property: Essays on Higher Education.* San Francisco, CA: Jossey-Bass. (Original publication in 1997)

Sloan, D. (1980). The Teaching of Ethics in the American Undergraduate Curriculum: 1876–1976. In D. Callahan and S. Bok (Eds.), *Teaching Ethics in Higher Education.* New York, NY: Plenum Press.

Spohn, W. C. (1999). *Go and Do Likewise: Jesus and Ethics.* New York, NY: Continuum.

Spohn, W. C. (2001). Intellectual Autobiography. Delivered to the Pacific Coast Theological Society. November 2, 2001.

Spohn, W. C. (2003a). Course Syllabus for "Scripture and the Moral Life." Santa Clara, CA: Santa Clara University.

Spohn, W. C. (2003b). Reasoning from Practice. Syllabus Narrative for the Carnegie "A Life of the Mind for Practice" Seminar. Stanford, CA: The Carnegie Foundation for the Advancement of Teaching.

Stengel, B. S. (1999a). Pedagogical Response-ability: Dewey and Buber Lay the Groundwork. Paper presented at the Annual Meeting of the Ohio Valley Philosophy of Education Society. October 1999, Dayton, OH.

Stengel, B. S. (1999b). Responsibility as Root Metaphor: A Moral Structure for Teacher Education. Paper presented at the Annual Meeting of the American Educational Research Association. Montreal, Canada.

Stengel, B. S. (2000). Pedagogical Response-ability. Paper presented at the Annual Meeting of the American Association of Colleges of Teacher Education. Chicago, IL, February 2000.]

Stengel, B. S. (2001). Teaching in Response. In *Philosophy of Education 2001.* [http://www.ed.uiuc.edu/EPS/PES-Yearbook/2001/stengel%2001.pdf].

Stengel, B. S. (2003a). "As If We Were Called": Responding to (Pedagogical) Responsibility. In *Philosophy of Education 2003.* [http://www.ed.uiuc.edu/EPS/PES-Yearbook/2003/stengel.pdf].

Stengel, B. S. (2003b). Teaching Responsibility: Practical Reasoning in a Pedagogical "Wonderland." Syllabus Narrative for the Carnegie "A Life of the Mind for Practice" Seminar. Stanford, CA: The Carnegie Foundation for the Advancement of Teaching.

Stengel, B. S. (2005). Course Syllabus for "Foundations of Modern Education." [http://marauder.millersville.edu/~bstengel/courses/211index.htm]. Millersville, PA: Millersville University.

Sullivan, W. M. (2002). A Life of the Mind for Practice: Professional Education and the Liberal Arts. Introductory Essay for the Carnegie "A Life of the Mind for Practice" Seminar. Menlo Park, CA: The Carnegie Foundation for the Advancement of Teaching.

Sullivan, W. M. (2005). *Work and Integrity: The Crisis and Promise of Professionalism in America*. San Francisco, CA: Jossey-Bass.

Sullivan, W. M., and others. (2007). *Educating Lawyers: Preparation for the Profession of Law*. San Francisco, CA: Jossey-Bass.

Toulmin, S. (1958). *The Uses of Argument*. Cambridge, UK: Cambridge University Press.

Toulmin, S. (2001). *Return to Reason*. Cambridge, MA: Harvard University Press.

Veysey, L. (1965). *The Emergence of the American University*. Chicago, IL: University of Chicago Press.

Weber, M. (1977). Science as a Vocation. In H. H. Gerth and C. W. Mills (Trans. and Eds.), *From Max Weber: Essays in Sociology*. New York: Oxford University Press. (Original publication in 1919)

INDEX